MW00643358

WACO-McLENNAN C
1717 AUSTIN AVE
WACO TX 76701

BRINGING TH
MONSTER
TO ITS KNEES

BRINGING THE MONSTER TO ITS KNEES

BEN HOGAN, OAKLAND HILLS, AND THE 1951 U.S. OPEN

Ed Gruver

LYONS
PRESS

Guilford, Connecticut

An imprint of Globe Pequot, the trade division of
The Rowman & Littlefield Publishing Group, Inc.
4501 Forbes Blvd., Ste. 200
Lanham, MD 20706
LyonsPress.com

Distributed by NATIONAL BOOK NETWORK

British Library Cataloguing in Publication Information available

Library of Congress Cataloging-in-Publication Data available

ISBN 978-1-4930-5673-6 (cloth : alk. paper)
ISBN 978-1-4930-6296-6 (electronic)

♾️™ The paper used in this publication meets the minimum requirements of American National Standard for Information Sciences—Permanence of Paper for Printed Library Materials, ANSI/NISO Z39.48-1992.

For Prudence, Hudson, and Henry:
May you always bring monsters to their knees

CONTENTS

CONTENTS

ACKNOWLEDGMENTS

This book could not have been completed without the aid and input of numerous people. First, I would like to thank my wife, Michelle, my daughters, Patty and Katie, and my family for their continued love and support. I am blessed to have them in my life.

I want to thank Niels Aaboe at the Lyons Press for his belief in this project and his help in bringing to fruition the compelling story of Ben Hogan and The Monster of Oakland Hills. Alden Perkins did great work in helping to edit the manuscript.

I also thank Bruce Devlin for graciously providing the foreword to this book and for an interview that was both interesting and informative. A PGA Tour professional and champion, Bruce was a playing partner and friend of Mr. Hogan and was one of those whom I spoke with who provided personal and previously unpublished insight into Mr. Hogan and Oakland Hills.

Such insight is invaluable, particularly when dealing with a subject who has been written about as extensively as Ben Hogan. The Hogan family and friends I interviewed gave great insight into the man behind the mystique. Their respect for the man is such that Mr. Hogan's niece, Jacque, told me she now goes by Jacque Hogan rather than her married name Jacque Hogan Towery because, as she says, "I was born a Hogan and I want to die a Hogan."

Mr. Hogan's grandniece, Lisa Scott, likewise lent her personal recollections of her great uncle, whom she knew more as a lion in winter than as a champion golfer.

Fred Hawkins, now passed, was one of the last surviving golfers from the 1951 U.S. Open when I interviewed him. He furnished tremendous recollections of Ben Hogan and The Monster that only a competitor could.

Jack Fowler, a caddie at the 1951 U.S. Open, has extremely valuable firsthand memories that take the reader inside the ropes at one of the most famous majors in golf history. His recollections of following Mr. Hogan on Open Saturday were an incredible resource.

Robert Trent Jones Jr., the son of the celebrated "Open Doctor" and an accomplished golf course architect, spoke at length of his famous father, his controversial redesign of Oakland Hills, course architecture from the days of Donald Ross to the present, Ben Hogan, and golf's Golden Age.

Ben Wright is another whose personal memories of Mr. Hogan and Oakland Hills's majestic South Course proved vitally important.

Donna Bonk of Oakland Hills Country Club was very gracious with her time in preparing lists of people to contact and access to photos of Oakland Hills. Donna's help was invaluable. Glenn Diegel, chairperson of the Oakland Hills Heritage Committee, shared historical knowledge of Oakland Hills, the South Course, and the 1951 U.S. Open.

Robert Stennett, executive director of the Ben Hogan Foundation, was exceptionally gracious in sharing his time and personal memories of Mr. Hogan. It is through the recollections of personal friends and family members that a full picture of Mr. Hogan and the 1951 U.S. Open emerges.

Dick Howting is an expert on the 1951 U.S. Open, and I thank him for sharing his thoughts on Ben Hogan and the Oakland Hills Monster.

To all of the above, and to many more, my sincerest thanks and gratitude.

FOREWORD

The Greatest Player Ever, Beating the Hardest Test of Golf Ever

Bruce Devlin

On June 16, 1951, the day of Mr. Hogan's winning of the U.S. Open at Oakland Hills Country Club, I was a 13-year-old high school student living in Goulburn, NSW Australia. I loved to play Rugby League Football and especially field hockey. Little did I know what great changes would soon happen in my life.

Just after my 14th birthday, my father lost his right arm in a horrible automobile accident. He loved the game of golf, and I thought that would be the end of his playing days. I was completely wrong. After returning home from the hospital and undergoing many days of rehabilitation, he wanted to start playing golf again with one arm and suggested to me that I should play with him. That was when rugby football and field hockey were replaced by my learning how to play golf.

I never imagined that in 11 short years I would be shaking hands with the greatest player who ever played the game of golf. It was April 1962, and I was in the locker room at Augusta National Golf Club when my dear friend and golf coach Norman Von Nida introduced me to Mr. Hogan. To say I was nervous would be a gross understatement.

After the introduction, Norman asked Mr. Hogan if he would play a practice round with me, the thought of which made me really nervous. That first practice round was the start of many rounds Mr. Hogan and I would play together over the next nine years. Our playing days together continued until his last competitive round at the Champions Golf Club in

Houston. The par-3 fourth hole was the last competitive shot Mr. Hogan would hit.

My greatest and most memorable time spent with Mr. Hogan and his wife, Valerie, was when my wife, Gloria, and I traveled to San Francisco with them to play in the 1966 U.S. Open at the Olympic Club. We stayed with them at the Top of the Mark Hotel, traveled to and from the course together, played each practice round together, and joined them for dinner each evening. During two dinners, Mr. Hogan gave us the most detailed account of the automobile accident, his rehabilitation, and what most people regard as the "Miracle at Merion," his grueling physical victory in the 1950 U.S. Open Championship.

During one of our many rounds of playing golf together, I asked him how many days he took off from hitting practice balls. He looked me straight in the eyes and said, "Bruce, do you realize that if you don't hit golf balls for a day, it takes two days to get back to where you were?" While I was not able to live by that statement, everyone knows how difficult this game can be when you don't practice or play.

After his retirement from golf, Mr. Hogan concentrated on his Ben Hogan Golf Club Company, which became quite a force in the golf club and golf ball industry as well as helping the younger players who were on his staff playing his clubs and golf balls.

I have treasured my time spent with Mr. Hogan both on and off the golf course and feel fortunate to have called him a friend.

Mr. Hogan was not only the greatest player, but also a caring and wonderful human being.

I hope that you will enjoy this book about the greatest player who ever lived, beating the hardest test of golf ever created and winning the 1951 U.S. Open Championship.

PROLOGUE

Best Test of Championship Golf

June 14, 1951.

The reigning Masters and U.S. Open men's champion awoke early in his room in Detroit's Sheraton Hotel, then began what had become a daily necessity since his body had been broken two years earlier in a horrific head-on collision with a Greyhound bus.

His left shoulder, so critical to a swing he had labored years to perfect, throbbed; he sought to subdue the pain by taking aspirin and rubbing liniment into his shoulders. His collarbone, fractured in the accident that left him near death, would require three surgeries through the years. Huge calcium deposits were building on his shoulders at the top of his collarbone; in time they would grow to the size of the top half of a golf ball.

The champion's left eye, crucial to his putting, was damaged. His blurred vision would worsen to the point that it was likened to placing transparent tape over one's eye. His legs, which had carried him around countless golf courses over the previous 20 years, now swelled and ached when he walked for even a short time. In an effort to aid his circulation and ease the excruciating cramps he felt in every step, he wrapped himself in Ace bandages, which extended from his waist to his ankles.

Only when his ritual was complete was Ben Hogan prepared to head to Oakland Hills Country Club in Bloomfield Township, a leafy suburb located 12 miles north of downtown Detroit. Arriving 90 minutes prior to his tee time, Mr. Hogan—he was addressed as such out of respect for a comeback considered the greatest in sports history—would make his way to the men's locker room, limping on his left side and feeling searing pain in his legs, back, and shoulders. He filled his locker with medications and balms; he was hurting but refused to use his condition to excuse performances below his high standard.

Not far from where Mr. Hogan sat in the locker room sipping ginger ale, the great green cathedral of Oakland Hills stood in sun-soaked silence that served as a prelude to the heightened excitement and emotion that would mark this 51st U.S. Open. For thrills and theater, no tournament can match the Open. Its drama is pure, its stakes the highest since it is the championship coveted most by those who match their nerves and skill against golf's most rugged courses.

Mr. Hogan knew he was up against it at Oakland Hills. Over the next three torturous days, the greatest golfer of his era would hobble around the huge, rolling South Course; not a fast player, Hogan's rounds could take up to 4½ hours on a layout as lengthy as Oakland Hills's emerald expanse.

"A typical 18-hole walk on the South Course is nearly seven miles," says Glenn Diegel, chairperson of the Oakland Hills Heritage Committee. Wracked in pain, Mr. Hogan chain-smoked Chesterfield cigarettes for comfort. Since his accident, there had been some terrible moments; he would tire physically, and the phlebitis that his niece Jacque Hogan says he suffered from forced him to use his golfing irons as canes, leaning on them for support. Yet his fans knew he would soldier on; as Lisa Scott, Mr. Hogan's grandniece and founder of the Ben Hogan Foundation, established in 2006, says now, "To not finish something, his will would not allow that."

When each long day was done, Mr. Hogan would return to his hotel, standing straight but at times leaning his sore back against a wall or pillar for support. Once in his room, he would peel off the elastic stockings— "this horrible hose," his wife, Valerie, called them—and lower his legs into a tub filled with warm water and Epsom salt. He would soak for 1–2 hours to bring down the swelling.

"Quite a Herculean effort," says former PGA pro and Hogan friend Bruce Devlin, "for him to do what he did."

Hogan.

The very name carries an undeniable magic and stirs vivid images of a champion golfer who majored in grit and guts. Hogan in June 1951 was two months shy of his 39th birthday, but his battered body felt decades older.

Ravaged by life-threatening injuries and soul-crushing loss, held together by bandages and indomitable determination, Hogan pulled his club from the bag held by his caddie, 13-year-old Dave Press, and stepped to the first tee at Oakland Hills. As was his custom, the terse Texan's communication to his caddie was limited to brief commands—1.) Do not use steel wool on the face of his clubs, as it had taken him three years to build up the rust on his irons; 2.) He would use three golf balls every six holes (Dick Collis, who caddied for Hogan later that summer at the World Championship of Golf in Chicago, rotated the golf balls from pocket to pocket to ensure that Mr. Hogan was getting a fresh one on every hole; 3.) If he hit into a trap, the ball was to be taken out of play immediately.

Jack Fowler was a young teen caddie for 1936 U.S. Open titlist Tony Manero when he saw Hogan in person for the first time at Oakland Hills. "All the assigned caddies had their bags next to the locker room outside the clubhouse," he recalls. "Ben Hogan came around; he was short and was wearing a cardigan sweater. Dave was scrubbing Hogan's irons with Brillo pads. Hogan said 'Whoa. Use water only to clean the clubs.' Hogan was protective of his clubs. He didn't want the grooves messed with because it could affect the flight and accuracy of his shots."

Hogan was a perfectionist, a trait Jacque says he and his brother Royal inherited from his mother, Clara. "Their mother, my grandmother, had a saying, 'If you're going to accomplish something, do it right or don't do it,'" Jacque says.

No detail was too small for Hogan. He used a magnifying glass to inspect his golf balls for excess paint in the dimples and soaked them in salt water to ascertain which ones were perfectly round. To anchor himself to the ground throughout his powerful swing, Hogan had his Peal golf cleats customized to include a 13th spike in each sole of his size 8½ C shoes. He drank ginger ale to make his hands feel thin—he believed ginger ale had a diuretic property that drains excess fluid and made his hands wiry—and soaked them in pickle brine to toughen the skin.

Hogan approached his Spalding ball—a potential controversy since he was paid to endorse MacGregor equipment—and applied a slightly modified Vardon grip to his club. Countless hours of abrasion from Hogan's ungloved hands had worn the rough-textured rubber cord-line grips to slickness. Wrapping his large calloused hands around the club, golf's greatest striker of the ball took aim on golf's toughest test—The Monster of Oakland Hills.

Before Brooks Koepka battled Shinnecock Hills to win the 2018 U.S. Open, before Tiger Woods withstood a torn ligament and double stress fracture in his left knee in the 2008 Open, and before Ken Venturi valiantly endured heat exhaustion in the 1964 Open at Congressional, Hogan hand-fought The Monster of Oakland Hills. For four rounds, Hogan would struggle to overcome his own pain and doubt, a competitive field filled with all-time greats—"Slammin'" Sammy Snead, Gene Sarazen, and Jimmy Demaret among them—and a controversial redesign by architect Robert Trent Jones that made an already menacing course monstrous with dense rough, deep bunkers, and fairways thin as a reed.

A year earlier, Hogan's courage helped him highlight a spectacular comeback with his famous "Miracle at Merion." His steely determination and steel-shafted 1-iron—perfectly captured by photographer Hy Peskin—combined to whistle an approach shot to the green on Merion's fearsome 18th. It remains the most iconic shot—and photo—in golf history.

Now, Hogan stood on the South Course of Oakland Hills, his cold stare surveying a sight more intimidating than Merion—The Monster. The course confused him; along with being a stylish shot maker, Hogan was a shrewd strategist, but he proclaimed Trent Jones's layout "the toughest 18 holes I've ever seen."

Herbert Warren Wind, golf's famous essayist, said of Oakland Hills in 1951 that it "very possibly was the most difficult assignment the country's top golfers had ever encountered in the Open and very possibly it was also the best overall test of championship golf we had in this country in a long, long time."

When the world's greatest golfers arrived in Michigan and saw Trent Jones's creation, they turned a whiter shade of pale and renamed Oakland Hills "Oakland *Hells*." It seemed more curse than course. Even the hard-edged Hogan was taken aback; in his rough Southwestern speech, he called the redesign "ridiculous." The brutality of it affronted him, and a blood feud ensued that would cause Hogan to step completely out of character. Normally as cold and silent as snowfall, a fired-up Hogan vowed to "burn up" the beast.

The sheer size and length of Trent Jones's leviathan presented a formidable challenge for a man who stood a shade over 5-8, weighed 150 pounds, and was nicknamed "Bantam Ben." Yet, when the tournament teed off on Thursday morning, there stood a defiant Hogan, the swirling smoke of his cigarettes adding to the mystique of an athlete already considered otherworldly by fellow golfers, the gallery, and the sporting press.

The Hogan who shuffled on shattered legs to the first tee at Oakland Hills was larger than life, a legend whose story seemed mythical. He was known for his talent and tenacity; beyond that, his enigmatic personality made him a mystery. For the gallery, peering through periscopes to get a glimpse of him, Hogan cut a distinctive figure in his elegant attire. His trademark white linen ivy cap, tilted at a 15-degree angle, came from one of the most expensive hatters in the country. He wore an Allen Solly shirt and dark cardigan sweater made of cashmere. His cream-colored pleated pants, custom made by a Fort Worth tailor, were cuffed and touched the tops of his white buck golf shoes.

Hogan's haberdashery was as much an ornament of golf in the 1950s as the patterned shirts and pants paraded by the "Peacock of the Fairways," Doug Sanders, in the psychedelic 1960s; the loud and proud polyester sported by Jack Nicklaus and Lee Trevino in the disco-dominated 1970s; and Tiger Woods's red shirts in the 2000s.

Henry Ward Beecher, the famed American clergyman, disputed the claims of Shakespeare and Mark Twain that "clothes make the man," stating instead, "Clothes . . . do not make the man, but when he is made, they greatly improve his performance."

From Snead's straw Stetson, to Sarazen's splendid plus fours, to Demaret's Technicolor clothes, which led sportswriter Grantland Rice to call him "a human rainbow in action," the flashy field at Oakland Hills would need every aid in dealing with a diabolical design. Glenn Diegel calls the 1951 Open "probably the seminal championship in club history";

it was also a seminal moment in golf history in that it was the first time the United States Golf Association deliberately toughened a course in advance of the National Open.

Trent Jones's makeover of the renowned Donald Ross's layout was a response to the dramatic alterations golf was undergoing. Power-built clubs and lively golf balls were changing the sport. Players were markedly improved as well, evidenced by the fact that 11 eventual Hall of Famers would tee off at Oakland Hills.

To modernize Ross's venerated venue and frustrate the field, Trent Jones added fairway bunkers and placed them where their effect on play proved most dramatic. Where Ross's bunkers were scattered, Jones's were strategic. There was method to what some saw as Trent Jones's madness. He wanted the first bunker to catch a drive from light hitters like "Little" Jerry Barber, the second to catch longer hitters like Hogan, and the third to catch Snead and the sport's siege guns. Since golfers drove the ball different distances, Jones felt it only fair that every man shared the same difficulty on his next shot.

The rough was grown to 6–8 inches and reached as high as 12–14 inches in some areas. It prompted a disgusted Snead to drawl, "I thought I was going to a golf tournament, not on a safari." Turning his attention to Oakland Hills's greens, Trent Jones made them incomparable to any other course, their rising and falling representing the very beating heart of his beast.

The fast, undulating greens and firm fairways and bunkers made the course as tough as any in the country. Snead noted the narrow fairways—No. 6 was the narrowest, stepping off in just 22 paces—and was only half-joking when he said, "you had to walk sideways to keep from snagging your pants."

Trent Jones's plotting was more than just challenging; the contoured fairways, bunkers deep in landing areas, and complex greens and putting surfaces made The Monster a frightening thing to behold. It was a snarling, Spalding-starved creature whose traps caused bogeys to become doubles and triples.

The approach taken by Trent Jones was innovative; by designing two "target areas" on each hole, the architect made Oakland Hills the original site of "target golf." He built one target area in each fairway for tee shots and another into each green for approach shots. In so doing, he created a course that demanded double accuracy on the majority of holes.

"Oakland Hills was unique," Trent Jones wrote. "No mistake could be made without a just penalty."

Hogan spent five days meditating on The Monster and emerged convinced this was the greatest test of golf he had ever faced. The radical redesign of the hallowed South Course, one of the crown jewels of American golf, set the stage for an epic confrontation between the cruelest course in U.S. Open history and the champion believed to be golf's greatest shot maker.

Like his contemporary, baseball star Joe DiMaggio, Hogan was known for his aloofness and ability to perform under pressure. He was nicknamed "The Hawk" because of his piercing gray-blue eyes and attacking style of play. Hogan was a hard case; Grantland Rice thought him "soft as a fire hydrant." His smoky countenance, stony stare, and sphinxlike silence unnerved opponents.

"Hogan was tough on everybody," recalled Fred Hawkins, a member of the field at Oakland Hills. More than anything, Hogan was tough on himself. He was a superstar so dedicated to his craft that he distanced himself from nearly everyone.

"There are no shortcuts," the solitary Hogan stated, "in the quest for perfection."

Hogan was a grinder; for him, golf was like life—a war of attrition. He grew up poor and was not a natural golfer, like Snead and Byron Nelson, who combined with Hogan to form golf's great triumvirate of the 1940s. Hogan friend and writer Dan Jenkins said it took Ben years to build his swing. Demaret credited his playing partner with inventing modern practice; a typical day for Hogan was to arise early and work his way through his golf bag, all 14 clubs. He would start with wedges, go to short irons, break for lunch, and resume practice. Jenkins estimated Hogan hit 600 shots a day.

Hogan's hard work created a swing admired by generations of golfers. Even Jack Nicklaus stopped to watch Hogan practice; he marveled at the man's unmatched control of his shots. Lee Trevino watched Hogan maneuver the ball—high, low, draw, fade—and make every shot imaginable.

"Hogan's swing was machinelike," says former golfer and commentator Ben Wright. "It was like you switched on a machine at the start of the round and switched it off on 18."

Making his swing more famous was his celebrated "Secret," a modification that enabled him to play a controlled fade. The true secret remains a mystery. Jacque says Hogan told her his secret was more spiritual than physical. "He was a very spiritual person," she remembers. Ben's wife, Valerie, believed the Secret was hitting golf balls until his hands bled. Hogan would point to the callouses that golfer Chi Chi Rodriguez described as rough as sandpaper and state, "The secret's in the dirt."

"He would say 'The secret's in the dirt' and he certainly believed that," says Robert Stennett, executive director of the Ben Hogan Foundation. "He didn't have the natural abilities of others, so he had to outwork everybody. When everyone else went back to the bar for a drink, he went back out and practiced."

Opposing Hogan at Oakland Hills was a colorful PGA Tour. This was the Golden Age of golf, and rarely has the sport seen a group like the one that boasted such showbiz flair in the fairways. There was Snead, "The Slammer"; Sarazen, also known as "The Squire"; Demaret, called "The Wardrobe" and a jet-setter before there was a jet age; "Terrible" Tommy Bolt; Bad Boy Bobby Locke, whose moniker was "Old Muffin Face"; fiery Clayton Heafner; and Ed "Porky" Oliver, aka "Pork Chops" or "Chops," who packed 260–280 pounds on his 5-11 frame.

The flamboyant field also counted among its members Julius "Moose" Boros; Paul "Little Poison" Runyan; Craig Wood, the "Blond Bomber"; Cary "Doc" Middlecoff; Al "Red" Brosch; Robert "Skee" Riegel; E. J. "Dutch" Harrison, the "Arkansas Traveler"; Lyman "Smiley" Quick; Lew "The Chin" Worsham; Lloyd "Mr. Ice" Mangrum; "Little" Johnny Palmer; Denny Shute, "The Human Icicle"; Roberto De Vicenzo, the "Gay Gaucher"; Johnny Revolta, the "Iron Master"; Chandler Harper, called "Old Bones"; Jim Ferrier, aka "The Undertaker" and "The Wolf"; and Al "Bessie" Besselink, aka the "Dapper Adonis" and "Prince of Merchantville."

Yet, even among this colorful clan, Hogan stood out. Ed Sullivan was so enamored with him that the television host restricted his guest list of golfers one season to the man he called "the most fabulous golfer of our generation—Ben Hogan." Sullivan wasn't the only celebrity fascinated by Hogan; singers Frank Sinatra and Bing Crosby, entertainer Bob Hope, boxing legend Joe Louis, and famed restaurateur Toots Shor were fans as well.

What helped endear Hogan to others were his hardships; people related to his personal and professional struggles. As a boy, he was in the family home in Texas when his father, Chester, committed suicide by placing a .38 caliber revolver to his heart and pulling the trigger. For years, many believed nine-year-old Ben had witnessed the tragedy on that dark February day, but Jacque reveals that it was her father, Royal, Ben's older brother, who was in the room. "My father said in front of Uncle Ben that he was in the room when their father killed himself."

Suddenly fatherless, the Hogan family struggled to survive. A decade of failure followed and Ben was so poverty-stricken that he was forced to scale fences to snag oranges from orchards in order to eat. Hogan turned pro at age 17 but didn't win his first PGA event until eight years later; it took him 16 years to win his first major. He played through poverty and pain, but his total immersion in his sport, combined with his Secret, led to a startling turnaround that saw him win nine majors in eight years and the coveted career Grand Slam.

Hogan's stunning success invited comparisons to sports immortals of the then-recent past—Bobby Jones, Babe Ruth, Red Grange, Jack Dempsey, and Bill Tilden. Through sheer determination he ushered in the Age of Hogan. He transcended from sports star to hero when he saved the life of his wife and nearly lost his own in a violent collision with a Greyhound bus on a fog-filled morning in Texas.

Hogan's bones were broken, his muscles torn, his legs permanently damaged; Jacque remembers his doctors doubting he would ever again play competitive golf. Not play golf? Hell, Hogan *was* golf. A year after the accident, he was winning the U.S. Open at Merion, his courageous comeback creating front-page news across the country and capturing the public's imagination. Writing for the *New York Times*, Lincoln Werden called Hogan's return to golf "one of the greatest of all sports comebacks."

The *Times* esteemed sports columnist Red Smith opined that there had never been another achievement in competitive sports comparable to Hogan's comeback from near death. "We shall not live to see anything like it again," he wrote.

Hogan's story inspired Hollywood to bring it to the silver screen as a full-length feature film. His stirring triumph of the human spirit remains revered. In April 2018, one year before his own remarkable comeback at Augusta, Tiger Woods paid homage to Hogan.

"One of the greatest comebacks in all of sports is Mr. Hogan," he said. "He got hit by a bus and came back and won major championships. The pain he had to endure, the things he had to do just to play, the wrapping of the leg, all the hot tubs, and just how hard it was for him to walk."

Those who saw Hogan at Oakland Hills marveled at his mastery of himself and his sport. Writer Marshall Smith, covering the U.S. Open for *Life* magazine, captured the essence of watching Hogan in person. Off the tee, Smith wrote, Hogan swung with "all the businesslike authority of a machine stamping out bottle caps."

More than 50 years later, Hawkins recalled Hogan's heralded swing. "His swing was quick," Hawkins remembered. "But he used to tell me, 'It doesn't matter how quick your swing is, as long as it's smooth.'"

"Hit it like Hogan" has become the mantra for generations of golfers. Hogan's swing was so quick and forceful that it controlled clubs that were like the man himself—forged from steel. Devlin recalls Hogan's clubs being "as stiff as telephone poles."

In 2017, Hogan's hefty sticks were placed in the hands of PGA pros; they couldn't hit them. Even Tiger struggled to control his shots with Hogan's clubs.

Compared to the big modern drivers, the clubs used by Hogan had a small face and less forgiveness. "Hitting it on the dime-sized sweet spot" was extremely important to golfers of the 1950s and precisely what Hogan and his competitors would have to do to tame Jones's toughie. "With the equipment they had," says Fowler, "I didn't know how they were going to handle that course."

The Monster's teeth were bared from the beginning. From the elevated tee, Hogan could see the entire first hole. Lying just off the narrow fairway was very thick fescue. The Monster's bunkers were more than ready to catch errant shots in sandy maws surrounding both sides of the green. Just beyond the bunkers stood leafy green trees.

The first hole had bite, and with The Monster threatening to sink its teeth into the pros from the start, Hogan knew his initial tee shot had to be threaded; there was little margin for error. Hogan believed the drive off the tee to be the most important shot in golf. "It governs the nature of the entire hole," he stated. "It tells you whether you have problems or don't."

The Hawk narrowed his gunmetal gaze, took a final pull on his Chesterfield—Jacque believes he could burn up half a cigarette with his deep drag—and threw down the smoldering butt. The heavy-smoking Hogan would leave a trail of Chesterfields across Oakland Hills. "A lot of players smoked; it was a comfort thing," Fowler recalls. "Hogan was a chimney. When he wanted to get rid of his cigarette, he threw them in the grass."

With the dramatic toss of his cigarette, the man Gary Player calls the "king of U.S. Open golf" was ready for battle. A great king seeking to slay a nightmarish monster is the stuff of legend. Hogan at Oakland Hills was Saint George dueling the dragon in Cappadocia, Beowulf in grim battle with Grendel. Because of his private obsession with the savage course, some saw Hogan as a modern-day Ahab, his cursed prey not a white whale but a green monster.

"It was like a personal vendetta for Hogan," says Oakland Hills's historian Dick Howting. "He thought the course was a son of a bitch."

Something mythic, almost fabled, would emerge from Hogan's ferocious fight with The Monster; the storied showdown between a man and a course dripped with drama. Famed British essayist Henry Longhurst noted that every sport other than golf is played on the same kind of pitch the world over. Each football field is 100 yards long; every major league mound 60 feet, 6 inches from home plate. "Yet not only is every golfing pitch different from all others," Longhurst wrote, "but it consists of 18 little pitches within itself. Thus, an almost inexhaustible supply of golfing problems presents itself."

The problems presented by The Monster were indeed inexhaustible; they were also unprecedented. Snead stated that, if this weren't the U.S. Open, "there wouldn't be many players sticking around *this* course." One player, 1950 PGA champion Chandler Harper, chose not to stay, fleeing the hellish battlefield before the first round was even complete.

"The Monster," Hawkins remembered, "was very difficult. Pars were tough. You had to drive the ball between the bunkers to get to the green."

Hawkins and others saw the course as difficult; Hogan saw it as golf's Armageddon. Valerie believed her husband's triumph at Merion was important but that he got "even more satisfaction" battling The Monster. Hogan relished crushing opponents and courses, and record crowds crammed the South Course to watch him wage war with The Monster. The gallery swelled to 17,500 fans for Saturday's sun-drenched final round, the largest crowd, an Oakland Hills historian stated, to ever follow a golfer. The enormous throng recognized this tournament for what it was—a historic confluence of legends in Hogan, Trent Jones, and The Monster.

"The 1951 U.S. Open was a defining moment in golf," says Howting. "Hogan became recognized as one of the greatest golfers who'd ever lived—if not the greatest. Robert Trent Jones became the best-known golf architect in history and the first 'Open Doctor.' And Oakland Hills became the first modern championship golf course and the template for championship venues for the next four decades."

It would all begin on the first tee of the opening round. It was a Coppertone kind of day, a bright blue sky and the sort of summer wind Sinatra would sing of. "The weather was perfect," Fowler remembers. "Warm, in the high 70s." The skies contained few clouds, but the surrounding air was filled with excitement. Dave Press thought the atmosphere electric, the promise of an exercise in golfing brinksmanship proving irresistible to fans.

Hogan dug his white bucks into the sunbaked ground and issued a wristy address and the waggle he adopted from Revolta, the 1935 PGA winner. A pregnant pause ensued as Hogan positioned his clubhead behind the ball; a slight breeze brought a scent of summer to the historic grounds. Amid the lush surroundings, there was a hush, the moment eagerly awaited by so many finally at hand.

Hogan's wrists arched high, his hips turned, and with his left wrist cupped follow through on a swing that sent his Spalding spinning skyward on the first of its many flights into The Monster.

What would take place at Oakland Hills would be nothing less than combat at a country club, a bruising back-and-forth battle having all the elements of a Homeric epic.

"The setting at Oakland Hills in 1951 was unique . . . in those days a first," said Marshall Dann, at the time a sportswriter for the *Detroit Free Press* and later executive director of the Western Golf Association. "By the turn of events it came down to a man attacking a golf course."

News of the events unfolding at this U.S. Open gripped fans and grabbed headlines across the country and around the world; *Golf World* magazine proclaimed, "Golf's greatest tournament reached a new peak in public interest."

"The Open was the big event, it was *the* event," says Robert Trent Jones Jr. "My father's redesign was a radical change from before, and with all of the controversy in the press, fans wanted the tension, the drama. They got it."

Indeed, Robert Trent Jones Sr.'s biographer, James R. Hansen, calls the 1951 U.S. Open "one of the most difficult, most controversial, most memorable, and most fundamentally transformational championships in the history of golf."

The indomitable Hogan combating a force of nature, The Monster being both majestic and malevolent, was *the* sports story in the summer of 1951. As the great drama rushed toward its climax, Hogan, battered but unbowed, would mount a furious final push to overcome a star-studded field of competitors, his own fatigue and frustration, and bring this beast—The Monster—to its knees.

HOGAN

The Man and His Mystique

Fred Hawkins could still clearly recall decades later the air of mystery surrounding Ben Hogan.

"He didn't have a lot to say," remembered Hawkins, who competed against Hogan in the 1950s, and said this silence added to the man's mystique. Hogan's countenance was as cold and stoic as the stone faces on Mt. Rushmore. If Hogan emoted, it wasn't with words. It was through the sheer force of his personality.

"He would fix those eyes on you," Hawkins said, recalling Hogan's icy stare through the swirling smoke of his cigarettes. It was said that Hogan's glare, which earned him the nickname "The Hawk," reduced brave men to quivering masses. Hogan looked at you, one of his contemporaries stated, like a landlord demanding last month's rent.

"Hogan," said Hawkins, "was a tough guy."

Hogan had to be tough to survive the many tragedies of his life. According to the Ben Hogan Family Papers housed in the University of Texas at Austin, he was born on August 13, 1912, in Stephenville, Texas, though some sources list his birthplace as Dublin, Texas. Byron Nelson and Sam Snead, the other two members of America's great golf triumvirate of the 1940s, were also born in 1912, and the fact that three of the greatest golfers in history were born within months of each other is one of the more amazing coincidences in sports history.

Ben was the youngest of Chester and Clara Hogan's three children. Daughter Princess was born in 1907, brother Royal in 1909. Chester

Hogan, a blacksmith, and Clara, a seamstress, moved their family from Dublin, some 70 miles northeast, to Fort Worth in 1921. Not long after the move, Chester, in poor health and suffering financial reverses, engaged in an argument with Clara. He turned on his heels, and, striding into another room, pulled a .38 revolver from his carpetbag, pointed it at his chest, and pulled the trigger. At least one account placed nine-year-old Ben in the room, but his niece Jacque Hogan states that it was her father, Royal, who witnessed the gruesome scene.

It was February 13, 1922, the night before Valentine's Day, the holiday of hearts, when Chester aimed his revolver at his own chest. His family's collective heart was likewise shattered and left in pieces that night.

Ben and Chester were close, the younger son idolizing his father. A sepia-toned family photo shows Ben as a baby being held closely by his father as the two sit atop a horse; another picture shows father and family in an advertisement for Chester's blacksmith business. Chester is holding the reins of a horse pulling a wagon holding Clara and their children. The signage on the side of the horse and wagon reads: "Pappa Is a Blacksmith. Let Hogan Shoe Your Horse."

Ben's future wife, Valerie, told *New York Times* sportswriter Dave Anderson in 1999 that Chester's suicide "hurt Ben so much." At Chester's funeral, the family was not able to get Ben to enter the church; the boy was inconsolable and unable to bear seeing his father's casket. The family didn't speak of the incident for years.

"I was in high school," Jacque says, "before I was told that their father had killed himself."

Hogan spoke of his father's death only a spare few times. He told Valerie he remembered being held by his father, adoring him. "Ben's father was his idol," she told Anderson.

For young Ben, his brother Royal, and sister Princess, Fort Worth must have seemed like the largest and loneliest city in the world in the wake of their father's suicide. Husbandless, fatherless, and strangers in a big city, Clara and her children struggled to survive. "We were poor," Hogan said. Royal quit school at age 13 to sell *Fort Worth Star Telegram* newspapers on Seventh Street. Outfitted in an old aviator cap, Ben helped Royal, whom he affectionately called "Bubba," sell papers in downtown Fort Worth. They sold them at hotels and at the "T&P"—

Texas & Pacific railroad station—and met for dinner as late as 11:30 p.m., dinner often being an orange soda and nickel hamburger.

When the *Fort Worth Star Telegram* put out an extra addition, Ben and Royal remained on the job after their late-night meal. Many nights found Ben out all night, sleeping on a waiting-room bench, his head resting on a stack of papers and his cap pulled over his eyes. No longer having a father as the breadwinner, Ben took additional jobs to help his family survive. When a friend told him caddies were getting paid 65 cents a day at the Glen Garden Country Club, Ben became enthusiastic about golf, though he knew little about the sport. He also knew little of carrying a golf bag around a course, but what he did know was that he wasn't making 65 cents a day selling newspapers.

Hogan headed to Glen Garden—a seven-mile hike from his home—to see, in his words, "what (golf) was all about." He stuffed his small pockets full of red haw berries, brightly colored but rather tasteless treats that served as his lunch. Hogan made a habit of also carrying two editions of the *Fort Worth Star Telegram* to Glen Garden. He would spread the pages of one newspaper in the bottom of a bunker on the 18th green to serve as a makeshift bed. He then covered himself with the pages of the second newspaper to keep warm. He slept in the bunker on Saturday nights to be first in line Sunday morning to caddie; his hope was to get two loops in one day in order to earn extra money.

Physically small in comparison to other boys who gravitated toward golf and hustled to make a buck, Ben would be shoved to the back of the line by the larger members of the caddie yard. Bullying the new kid was standard practice for caddies determined to protect their turf and eliminate competition. Byron Nelson, like Hogan a member of the Glen Garden caddie yards, recalled the rough treatment of newcomers as similar to a fraternity initiation. "They did try to run the new boys off," Nelson wrote in his memoir *How I Played the Game.*

Ben endured numerous hazings in the hardscrabble yards. He was stuffed in a barrel made of curved wooden staves and rolled down a hill; Jacque Hogan described it as a 40-yard roll and 20-foot drop. He was forced to run through a gauntlet of bigger boys in which he was hit repeatedly on the backside with belts. The established caddies held a kangaroo court, and for new kids to break in they had to win a fight against one of the older boys. Just as he had to fight to protect his newsboy beats, Hogan had to ball up his small fists and fight larger boys to earn acceptance at Glen Garden.

"Thanks to my experience at the depot, I was handy with my fists and gave my opponent a pretty good working over," Hogan once said. "So I was accepted."

Golfer Ben Crenshaw believes that growing up in the caddie yards in Hogan's era was a sobering experience for Ben. It was an experience that would toughen any young man. Older boys made life rough on newcomers, but Hogan gained acceptance by becoming pretty fair with his fists.

Failure was not an option for Hogan, a character trait that can be traced to his mother. A tough woman made tougher by tragic circumstances, Clara excelled as a seamstress and demanded that her children likewise do quality work in their endeavors. Tasks had to be done correctly, and the Hogan children held themselves to a high standard lest they disappoint their mother.

"She was a beautiful seamstress," Jacque Hogan remembers. "She could *sew*. When she was teaching me, if there were even a little pucker in the seam, she would make me take it out. I would tell her, 'No one can see it.' She would say, 'I don't care. Take it out.'

"Everything had to be done right, and that carried over to Ben in his golf life. I think my uncle and my dad wanted everything they did to be the best they could do. Their strength and their mother's guidance guided them in the right direction."

Hogan said once that he was driven to succeed by three things. One, he didn't want to be a burden to his mother. Two, he needed to help put food on the table. Three, he needed a place to sleep.

The golf bug bit Ben hard. He struck up a friendship—and golfing rivalry—with Nelson. That two legends grew up in the same caddie yard at the same time is a startling happenstance. In December 1927, Hogan and Nelson dueled for first place in the Christmas caddie tournament. Hogan led until Nelson sank a 30-foot putt on the final hole to force a tie. When Hogan appeared to have won the sudden-death playoff, he was suddenly told it was a nine-hole playoff. Club members clearly favored Nelson, thought to be more refined than the hard-edged Hogan. "Byron," the club captain said, "is the only caddie who doesn't drink, smoke, or curse." Minus a club membership, young Ben was refused permission to enter club tournaments or practice on the course.

In an interview with *Golf* magazine's editor George Peper in September 1987, Hogan revealed that the first club he owned was an old left-handed, wooden-shafted, rib-faced mashie given to him by an acquaintance. In the early-morning hours before club members arrived, caddies would bang the ball up and down the practice range. Despite being right handed, Hogan said he did his formative practice with his left-handed mashie. "That's the club I was weaned on," Hogan told Peper.

Hogan was also weaned on the golf game of Glen Garden club member Ed Stewart. Stewart was in his early 20s at the time, and while he wasn't the best tipper in the club, he was the best player. Recognizing this, Hogan would wait around to caddie for Stewart even though there were days that Ed didn't have enough money to pay him. Despite the hard times, Ben believed he was getting something far more valuable than money from Stewart; he was learning the elements of the game he was becoming enamored with.

Hogan would mimic Stewart, a practice that continued for years as he watched the top players and emulated them. Hogan's fascination with golf led him to drop out of Central High School his senior year to join the pro tour. Clara tried to steer her son away from golf, telling him he had no future in the sport. When she finished speaking, she recalled Ben's eyes ablaze. "Momma, someday I'm gonna be the greatest golfer in the world."

Hogan tied for 38th in his first tournament and pocketed $8.50. Two years later, he made the audacious decision to head west for the Los Angeles Open despite having less than $100 to his name. His first PGA Tour event was the 1932 Los Angeles Open. He finished tied for 13th and earned a paycheck of $50. He had hoped to win enough prize money to continue playing tournaments, but when success did not follow, Hogan headed home.

"My father was more of a natural golfer than my Uncle Ben," Jacque says. Royal won four Colonial Country Club championships and four City of Fort Worth tournaments. Ben was besieged by his tendency to snap hook his drives in pressure situations. "I would win $25, $50 if I got in the money at all," Hogan once recalled. "I was a terrible player."

It was only after he had retooled his swing to overcome his wicked hook, Jacque states, that her Uncle Ben would become the Hogan of legend.

In 1933, with the nation on its knees financially, Hogan made another run at staying on tour. His flawed swing caused him to fail again, and he was forced to return home. He supported himself with odd jobs while re-tooling his golf game. He worked in a bank, a garage, a hotel, in oil fields, and dealt cards in a gambling house. Sam Snead surmises that it was in dealing cards that Hogan "learned that stone face." Writer Henry Longhurst agreed, stating he could see Hogan sitting at a poker table, his face and voice expressionless as he stared at his opponent and upped the ante.

"He might have four aces," Longhurst said of Hogan, "or a pair of twos."

The man who would dominate his sport by the end of the 1940s struggled mightily for the better part of the 1930s. World economies were in the death grip of the Great Depression, and Hogan was making little more than pocket change pursing his passion. He practiced endlessly, but his perseverance paid few dividends. Hogan and his new wife, Valerie, were down to their last $86 when he arrived at the Oakland Open.

"He had that little black book in which he wrote his winnings down," Lisa Scott says. "He told Jacque, 'If I don't win I'm going to quit. We can't keep living on oranges.'"

The morning of the final round, Snead saw Hogan outside the Claremont Country Club, beating his fists against a brick wall. When Snead asked what had happened, a distraught Hogan told him, "I can't go another inch. I'm finished. Some son of a bitch stole the tires off my car."

His maroon Buick jacked up, his two rear wheels sitting on rocks, and he and Valerie staying in the cheapest hotels they could find, Hogan bummed a ride and played harder that day, he later told Ken Venturi, "than I ever played before or ever will again."

Playing the final round with what one observer described as "a set jaw, lips locked into a tight smile that was not a smile, and eyes of steely intensity," Hogan finished second and won $385. "The biggest check I've ever seen in my life," he told Venturi, "and I'm quite sure it will be the biggest check I've ever seen."

Hogan credited former champion Henry Picard with his development as a golfer, referring to the man who preceded him as club pro at the Hershey (Pennsylvania) Country Club as "the greatest teacher I ever knew." It was high praise from Hogan, who handed out compliments as if they were precious diamonds. In 1953 Hogan dedicated his first book, *Ben Hogan's Power Golf*, to his former instructor:

"Picard by his offers of financial assistance, his recommendation, words of encouragement, and golfing hints has helped me more than I can ever repay."

Hogan had gone to Picard in 1940 for help with his duck hook. Picard instructed Hogan to rotate his left hand slightly to the left in his grip. By turning his hand to the left, Ben would weaken his left-hand grip and beat the hook that was hampering his game and holding him back from achieving the success he sought. Picard's instruction and Hogan's willingness to work hard and "dig [success] out of the dirt," as he said, created a left-to-right power fade. The trajectory of what became known as the "Hogan Fade" would come to influence how golf is played.

Picard's teaching philosophy focused on fundamentals—posture, balance, and the plane of the swing. He mentored Jack Grout, who earned renown as the only golf instructor Jack Nicklaus ever had and was gracious with numerous other golfers. Picard offered his assistance in other ways as well. When Ben and Valerie were struggling financially in the mid-1930s, the couple got into a heated argument because he didn't have enough money to take her with him to tournaments on the West Coast. Picard, who was in a Fort Worth hotel when he overheard the argument, offered to lend Ben money. Hogan, while appreciative, did not accept Picard's offer.

"He never used a penny of my money," Picard told *Sports Illustrated* in 1995. "It was the safety of knowing [the money] was there that kept [Ben and Valerie] going together."

Hailing from Hershey, Picard was called the "Chocolate Soldier" and "Hershey Hurricane." Grantland Rice gave him the latter nickname, the sportswriter stating Picard swept into town and stormed to victories. Like Jimmy Demaret, aka "The Wardrobe," Picard had a fondness for elegant clothes. The well-to-do Massachusetts native also owned a gentlemanly deference for authority that attracted chocolate mogul Milton Hershey. Hershey hired Picard as the club pro for the Hershey Country Club, and it's accepted by historians that Picard put HCC on the golf map by bringing the 1940 PGA Championship to Hershey's West Course.

It was in Picard's backyard that Hogan finally earned his first PGA Tour win, the victory coming in 1938 when he teamed with Vic Ghezzi in the Hershey Four-Ball. In 1939 Hogan qualified for the U.S. Open and made the cut but finished tied for 62nd. He needed another year to gain his first solo victory, winning the prized North and South Open at Pinehurst Resort. It was the first of four wins Hogan claimed in 1940—he earned the Greater Greensboro Open one week later—and followed with five victories in 1941. He added six more victories the following year to give him a total of 15 wins from 1940–1942.

Hogan emerged as the most consistent low scorer and was the Tour's leading money winner in 1940, 1941, and 1942. He seemed poised to break out in a big way but spent the next three years in the Army Air Corps during World War II, rising to the rank of captain. His responsibilities included training pilots, playing golf exhibitions to raise money for the war effort, and playing golf with army brass.

The 3½ years Hogan spent in the service affected his career totals for tournament titles and victories in majors, but he was not alone in that regard. Hogan returned to the Tour in 1945 and earned five victories. The first of these affirmed that he was picking up where he had left off, winning the Portland Open with a record 261 that was 27 under par. Major championships continued to elude him, however, and Hogan became known as the perennial second-placer, the golfer who couldn't win the big one. In the 1940 U.S. Open, he finished three shots behind Gene Sarazen and Lawson Little at Canterbury in Ohio. In the following year's Open, held in his hometown of Fort Worth, Hogan finished five shots behind champion Craig Wood in sweltering Texas heat at Colonial. In 1942, he lost a three-stroke lead in an 18-hole playoff to lose the Masters to Nelson. Hogan won 30 tournaments before claiming his first major—the 1946 PGA Championship.

Before his breakthrough title, Hogan recalled referencing himself by his alter ego, Henny Bogan, and thinking, "Henny Bogan, you have got to go home and correct this. Otherwise, you're never gonna make a living."

Hogan later told fellow pro Gardner Dickinson he was looking for a way to eliminate his troublesome hook and was leafing through an old golf book when he saw photos of a player favoring a fade. Hogan noticed that the player's left wrist was wrinkled at the top of his swing. The image stuck with Hogan; he would weaken the extension of his left-hand grip and shorten his left thumb's extension on the shaft. He would also allow his arms to rotate the clubface so it was open on the backswing. The cupped wrist position caused Hogan to utilize a flatter backswing plane, thus providing him the feeling that he could release the club as hard as he wanted without worrying that the clubface would close and produce the dreaded hook.

The lateral movement of his hips at the start of his downswing allowed Hogan to delay the release of his club until the last moment. Golfer Claude Harmon, a friend of Hogan, called it the most dramatic move by any great player ever. Dickinson said Hogan's changes had taken his biggest enemy—the huge, forward slide—and turned it into his biggest asset.

Hogan headed to the practice tee the next morning to try his new theory. His idea—it would famously become known as the Secret—worked, and Hogan told Peper the time on the practice tee following the previous night's inspiration was the moment everything about his golf swing began to click. When Peper pressed for more information on his "inspiration," Ben backed off.

"I'm not telling," he said smiling. Fellow golfer Chuck Kocsis believed Hogan wouldn't explain his secret because there was nothing to explain and nothing that could help aspiring golfers. "[I]nner strength, desire, and attention to detail cannot be transferred," Kocsis wrote. Still, Kocsis believed Hogan's secret added to his persona. There was, he said, "a mystique to the man, an imaginary halo created by his avowed personal secret."

Lisa Scott agrees that her great-uncle had a mystique about him. "He was very serious and had a reputation for being unapproachable, and that made him a mystery," she says. "People respected him because of what he accomplished, what he had overcome. That, and the thing floating around about his 'secret.' My grandmother, Valerie's sister, lived with them for a while in his competitive years, and he never talked about his secret; I don't think he had a secret. I think he just worked and worked. He wasn't afraid of hard work, and no one was going to outwork him."

Golf writer Herbert Warren Wind believed that guessing Hogan's secret became something of a national pastime. Wind wrote that, if the Secret meant that Hogan had introduced a movement or movements in his swing to impart a controlled fade to his shots, then no one would ever really know the Secret. If it meant Hogan was doing everything he could to protect against the hook and still maintain his power, wrote Wind, then the Secret was not really a secret at all.

Wind wrote that the swing Hogan arrived at and learned so thoroughly that he could execute it perfectly while under pressure featured the champion's right hand high on the shaft, a stance that was slightly open, the right forearm thrust at the start of the downswing, and an open clubface. The result was that Hogan lost some roll to his slight fade, but on those occasions when he failed to hit the ball just right, his shots did not hook dangerously into hazards but merely veered a few yards to the right.

Prior to developing his swing, Hogan struggled with the hook whenever he felt fatigued by an arduous tour and unceasing competition. "When he was tired," Wind said, "he hooked."

Gene Sarazen noted the same. Ben began his career, in the words of The Squire, "as a natural hooker." The full swing Hogan eventually developed contained several elements that served as braces against a hook. Sarazen knew that as long as Hogan was physically strong, as he was at the start of the winter circuit, he did not hook. Being a small man, Bantam Ben wore down as the tournament season wore on. The month of June would find Hogan tiring noticeably, and his braces against the hook would begin to break down.

When Hogan hooked, he invited punishing lies and penalty strokes. Developing his swing allowed room for error. Knowing there was no set schedule for enhancing his skills and that success wouldn't come overnight, Hogan realized he could be on the Tour for years before he broke through. Yet he was willing to work hard and experiment, lest he live what he called "a life of frustration." Hogan said he needed to practice all the time because, as he would tell Venturi, "My swing wasn't the best in the world, and I knew it wasn't."

Robert Trent Jones Jr. observed Hogan up close on the course and drew a comparison to Sam Snead's swing. "Snead was more fluid," he says, "Hogan more mechanical." Hogan compensated with grinding, relentless work. "I always outworked everybody," he said. "Work never bothered me like it bothers some people." If Bobby Jones was golf's king of the Roaring Twenties, Hogan was the tight-lipped, tireless titan of post–World War II America. "Nobody had to work as hard to play golf as Ben," said Nelson. "Nobody."

"He was a hard worker, no doubt," Bruce Devlin remembers. "When I asked him how many days he'd taken off in his career, he looked at me like I handed him a snake. 'Take a day off,' he told me, 'and it takes two days to get back to where you were.'"

Hogan's competitiveness drove him to play and practice up to 12 hours a day; he would hit golf shots long after his tournament round had ended. He ended his days with simulated swings and practice putts in his room. When he went to bed, he visualized the course he was playing for another hour, often playing a full 18 holes in his mind before sleep. Champions are never born, Hogan said; they're built from hard work, and the truth is, Hogan loved putting in the work, loved his solitary pursuit of perfection. Jimmy Demaret, a Hogan golfing companion, said, "Nobody gets close to Hogan." Jack Nicklaus thought that because no one seemed to know Hogan well that made him "more feared as a competitor."

Says Jacque, "He didn't talk to people when he got on the golf course. His attitude was, 'This is my job. This is where I work.' He could tune out everything. It was part of his mystique."

Hogan's single-mindedness led to what some fellow golfers felt was a lack of personality and social graces. Friends, acquaintances, the press, and some competitors forgave Hogan his shortcomings because of their admiration for his determination and drive. "He accepted the adulation and compliments from the press," Kocsis said, "and maybe they overdid it by putting him on a pedestal. He didn't know quite how to handle that, and he could never find a happy medium."

Kocsis saw Hogan as someone who was reluctant to join the crowd, who avoided small talk and conversation. Kocsis felt that was one reason Hogan was so friendly with Demaret. In his colorful conversation, personality, and clothing, Demaret emoted where Hogan couldn't. Demaret thrived in a world of bright Technicolor; Hogan confined himself to conservative colors—white, black, gray, and brown. Jenkins said once that if Hogan had ever worn a red shirt or green slacks, he would be so off his game that "he couldn't have broken 80." Hogan said he wished he could be more like the fun-loving Demaret. "If I had my game and Demaret's personality," he would say, "I'd really be something."

A golf historian seeking a comparison to Hogan can look to Walter J. Travis, a turn-of-the-century champion from Australia. Like Hogan, Travis was a late bloomer when it came to golf; in Travis's case it was due more to his taking up the game at age 35. Once Travis started playing, he was determined to become, in Herbert Warren Wind's words, "more than a dub." Travis studied the game as Hogan would years later. Travis was slight in physique, the same as Bantam Ben in his early years.

Just as Hawkins and other opponents considered Hogan a tough customer, those who competed against Travis likewise found him difficult to deal with. Like Hogan, Travis had little to say on the links, favoring the company of his cigar just as Hogan preferred the company of his cigarettes. Competitors found it difficult to read Travis's emotions, as did those who opposed Hogan. In both cases, opponents knew that Hogan and Travis were determined to win and did not want to disturb their concentration with small talk.

Like Hogan, Travis's accuracy negated the more substantial distance of his bigger rivals. Wind's description of Travis on the golf course could have been written about Hogan: "Then, with just the slightest flicker of pleasure in his menacing dark eyes, he was off to the next tee, taking a careful practice swing, stroking his drive down the middle and walking slowly after the ball . . . the smoke curling over the rim of his hat."

For too long, life had been the hammer and Hogan the anvil. Now, he was holding the hammer. He pounded golf balls with cold fury. Onlookers noted that his drives off the tee sounded different than those hit by his competitors, Hogan's shots resounding like gunfire. "It was like a rifle shot," remembers Ben Wright. "Wham!"

Watching Hogan hit golf balls was to view athleticism as an art form. Golfer Tommy Bolt noted that other golfers went out of their way to watch Hogan practice. Nicklaus was so impressed he said if he could pick any player in history to be his golfing partner, it would be Hogan. Asked if Tiger Woods in his prime was the best striker of the ball he had ever seen, Nicklaus shook his head. "No, no," he said. "Ben Hogan, easily."

Robert Trent Jones Jr. says Hogan has long been considered the master of controlling his shots, a skill honed by long days of practice at the Colonial Country Club. Because Colonial's fairways are dominated by rows of trees, the advantage goes to golfers who can control the shape and trajectory of their shots.

"I put him better than anyone for controlling his shots," says Devlin. "I was always enthralled with how he hit his shots."

Fellow pros were shocked when they saw Hogan practice for up to three hours just moments after shooting a tournament-leading score. That was the best time to practice, he explained, because he remembered what he had just shot. It was then that he could see where he hadn't practiced hard enough.

"He practiced all the time," Jacque says. "In hotel rooms, everywhere. It was his life, his passion. People sometimes have a passion for something but they don't go after it as wholeheartedly as my Uncle Ben or my father did."

Hogan sought perfection on the golf course; in 1987 he told *Golf Digest*'s Nick Seitz that he always felt as if he was in a slump. Snead said Hogan hated making mistakes and thought the manner in which Hogan spoke of his performance when it was less than his standard was so unforgiving that Snead actually felt sorry for him.

Devlin says Hogan's standard was so high he once told him that, of the hundreds of practice shots he hit every day, "If I hit six the way I want to, I'm happy with that."

Stories circulated that the Bantam was beating his brains out practicing. Gene Sarazen recalled a Four-Ball tournament in which Hogan, despite leading by a comfortable margin, seemed particularly edgy. "I want to get this match over as soon as possible," Hogan told Sarazen. "I want to get back to my room and practice my putting."

Sarazen was among those who believed Hogan sometimes left his finest shots on the practice ground. Bolt saw it differently. Golfers have long referred to the practice range as "Misery Hill." Bolt said when it came to Hogan, there wasn't any shot he had to make in a tournament that he hadn't already hit a thousand times on Misery Hill. "Nothing was a surprise to Ben Hogan in a golf tournament," Bolt once said. "That's the first thing that set him apart."

The Hawk's reputation as a shot maker is such that fans today think of him as a tee-to-green machine whose swing was flawless and never failed to produce perfect shots. The fact is Hogan was human and would sometimes spray shots as every golfer does. He addressed fan's misperception in 1953 when he was at the height of his career.

"You know, a great many people have built up in their minds a mythical Hogan who wins whenever he wants to win," he told Greg Gregston in a *Saturday Evening Post* article. "Well, it does not work out that way."

Hogan, however, gave himself more margin for error by maneuvering his shots. The famous "Hogan Fade" was an example of his strategy. On average, he could make the ball move a few yards; it wasn't a big drift, but control was the main thing. To have a good chance of placing the ball close to the pin, players have to hit the fairway from the tee. Hogan knew that a person could be the best iron player in the world, but if the shot off the tee was in the rough—the "boondocks," Hogan called it—the iron game wouldn't do any good.

For Hogan, the physical practice of hitting the ball day after day wasn't enough. He had to excel in the mental aspect of the game as well. He practiced visualizing his shots, making the ball move in different ways on the driving range. Hogan thought that, without visualization, hitting hundreds of golf balls was nothing but calisthenics. And if the shot he visualized didn't come off, he might hit 20 more before he got it right.

Once Hogan learned to hit those shots, golf became about course management. He knew if he couldn't manage his game he couldn't play championship golf. In competition, he would continually ask himself what club to play, where to aim it, whether to accept a safe par or go for birdie. Golf is a game of constant management; every hole can't be played the same way. In 1950, when he had 20 years of tournament play serving as experience, Hogan would state that golf was "80 percent management, 20 percent physical."

Demaret thought Hogan's "inside game"—his will to win, intense concentration, and quiet determination—set him apart and drove him to great heights. Writer Dan Jenkins said Hogan invented course management just as he invented practice. The Hawk would survey each hole, and his analytical mind would compute a variety of factors—the lie and the wind, the slope of the terrain, the presence of hazards, and pin position.

Hogan's extensive physical and mental preparation eventually paid off. At the close of World War II, he resumed his playing career, and in 1946 produced an amazing 13 victories and his first major, the PGA Championship. His stellar season ranks second only to Nelson's 18 wins the year before.

Hogan won seven tournaments in 1947, and in 1948 earned 10 additional titles, including six straight from June to August, along with two more majors—his second PGA Championship and first U.S. Open. Herbert Warren Wind noted that, when it came to tournaments on U.S. soil in 1948, the story lines were "Hogan, Hogan, Hogan." Ben claimed the demanding PGA Championship for the second time in three years. To recover from the strain, Hogan headed home to Texas, telling reporters that he was worn "to a frazzle" and was considering retiring from the nerve-wracking career of pro golf.

Hogan reconsidered retirement and teamed with Demaret to win the Inverness Four-Ball. He followed by fighting off fatigue and winning the Motor City Open. Physical practice, mental preparation, and the Secret combined to help Hogan produce one of the exceptional stretches of sustained excellence ever seen in sports. From 1946–1949, he finished first in 32 of the 85 official events he competed in, a pace exceeded only by Nelson.

When Hogan won the U.S. Open at Riviera in 1948, his performance captured the imagination of amateur Bob Rosburg. Rosburg had missed the cut but stayed to watch Hogan in the last two rounds. Decades later, the images he had of Hogan remain Rosburg's vision of the ultimate golfer. Fellow golfer Bill Flynn said Ben seemed bemused whenever Flynn mentioned the years from 1946–1949. "It wouldn't matter what shot I tried," Hogan said. "I hardly missed one."

Weighing a wiry 135 pounds but outfitted with broad shoulders, Hogan was built like a sturdy welterweight. The press called him "Bantam Ben," a nickname he disliked because Hogan never thought of himself as small. He inherited the big hands and strong body of his blacksmith father. Hogan was powerful enough to average 265 yards off the tee, a sizable distance in that era, but short of the more than 270 yards of Slammin' Sam and Jimmy Thomson, long hitters whose drives resembled the Guns of Navarone. "Hogan was a reasonably long hitter," remembers Devlin, "but he wasn't known as a long hitter like Snead." Golfer Bob Toski, a small man like Hogan but even smaller at 120 pounds, believed Hogan had to be an ultra-super athlete to hit as far as he did.

Golfers who are undersized have to have exceptional eye–hand coordination and use their body efficiently, and Toski considered Hogan the epitome of both traits. Sinewy and strong—in his prime he was said to be "135 pounds of whipcord"—Hogan was also double jointed; he could touch his thumb to his wrist. Gary Player thought Hogan as supple as a gymnast. Player tried to copy Hogan but gave up; imitating Hogan was wrecking his game. Tiger Woods's former swing coach Butch Harmon thinks many emulators were ruined because they couldn't match the athleticism that allowed Hogan to generate the power and accuracy in his swing.

Believing he had mastered his golf swing, Hogan began 1949 at the peak of his powers. "I was better in 1948 and '49 than I've ever been," he said. In those years the mere mention of his name could intimidate. Hardened men who had endured the Great Depression and fought on two fronts to preserve democracy, double-bogeyed at the sound of one man's name—Hogan.

The Hawk became feared for his fierce stare and attacking style. To look at Hogan on the golf course, one writer said, was to "shiver in the bones." Tournament golfer Al Geiberger, asked to describe a round of golf with Hogan, shivered. "It was spooky."

Snead said there were only two things he feared on a golf course—lightning and Hogan. *Los Angeles Times* columnist Jim Murray wrote that, throughout the history of civilization, there have been syllables of terror handed down from generation to generation:

"'Geronimo,' for example, could be counted on to empty one fort after another in the old West. 'Attila' would strike as much naked fear as the plague. In the littler world of golf, 'Hogan' elicited much the same effect. Nothing could paralyze a field of golfers as much as this whispered collection of syllables."

Hogan began the 1949 season by claiming the Bing Crosby Pro-Am and then the Long Beach Open in a playoff. He followed by nearly winning again, losing a playoff to Demaret in the Phoenix Open. Believing they needed time off from the tour, Ben and Valerie decided to head for the home they had recently purchased on Valley Forge Drive in Fort Worth. On Tuesday, February 1, they climbed into their black Cadillac sedan and drove 500 miles east from Phoenix. The following day dawned damp and foggy with a chill in the air. Hogan arose before the sun and visited the El Capitan Motel coffee shop for a quick breakfast. Valerie did not join him; road trips made her queasy, and they still had to drive another 500 miles east to reach Fort Worth.

Life on the Tour in the 1940s wasn't filled with private jets and chauffeur-driven cars. By February, Hogan had already driven 3,000 miles, and the golf season had only just begun. As he packed his Cadillac with luggage and golf clubs, Hogan was on top of the sports world. He had won two of the first four tournaments he played in 1949 and was the PGA Tour's leading money winner. He was featured on the cover of *Time* magazine, his face pictured above a quote reading, "If you can't outplay them, outwork them."

Hogan proved prophetic when he told *Time* that traveling was the toughest part of the tour. "I want to die an old man," he said, "not a young one."

Around 8:00 a.m., Hogan steered the Cadillac out of the El Capitan parking lot. He had purchased the fateful car from the Cadillac dealership owned by the father of his 14-year-old caddie, Ray Ramsey. The Hogans headed east on Highway 80. It was a two-lane road, and Ben and Valerie hadn't traveled 10 miles before they ran into a dense fog that blanketed the west Texas highway. The road was slick. Ben told Valerie, "There's a thin coat of ice on the highway this morning. . . . I'll drive slower."

Hogan dropped his speed to 25 miles per hour as he crossed a cement-lined bridge. In the fog outside Van Horn, Texas, Ben suddenly saw what he later described as "four lights winking at me."

A Greyhound bus, seeking to pass a truck on the narrow road, was in Hogan's lane and barreling toward his car. Instinctively, he looked to avoid the collision by driving off the road but saw a culvert to his right.

"I knew we were going to get hit," Hogan said. Valerie knew it too. "Honey," she screamed, "he's going to hit us!"

Hogan pulled on the steering wheel, jerking the car as far right as possible, and threw himself in front of his wife to protect her. "I just put my head down," he once recalled, "and dived across Valerie's lap like I was diving into a pool of water."

Hogan's heroism saved Valerie from a violent death; she likely would have been thrown through the windshield when the 20,000-pound bus slammed Hogan's car head-on. Instead, she suffered minor injuries. Her husband, however, was another story. Hogan's last-second jerk of the steering wheel meant the Greyhound plowed into the driver's side. The collision rammed the steering wheel through the seat Hogan had occupied a fraction of a second sooner; the car's engine was jammed into the front seat. Hogan's legs, still occupying the car's left side, were crushed as the engine was shoved through the cushion on his seat. Had Hogan not thrown himself sideways to save his wife, he likely would have been crushed to death.

The violence and force of the collision caused Hogan's head to be smashed into the dashboard, forever damaging his left eye. Ben and Valerie blacked out on impact. She regained consciousness first and could see only the gray sky. She didn't know where she was and didn't realize that the bus had pushed the Cadillac off the highway and into a gully. Ben and Valerie were pinned against the dashboard. Valerie managed to roll down the passenger side window and cried for help as her husband lay moaning amid the twisted, smoking metal. Slipping in and out of consciousness but aware that their car could explode in a fireball, Ben yelled for Valerie to "Get out!"

Suffering bruised ribs, bruised legs, and a black eye, Valerie freed herself from the wreck. She saw cars arriving and two men skidding on foot down to the crumpled Cadillac. "Please help me get my husband out of the car," she told them. "He's hurt badly."

The men pulled Hogan from the car. Ben's face was bruised—a rainbow of colors—and his left eye was nearly swollen shut. He had a double fracture of his pelvis, a fractured left collarbone, a broken bone in his left ankle, and a chipped rib. He would remain in this excruciatingly painful condition some 90 minutes before the ambulance arrived and drove him to the Hotel Dieu Hospital in El Paso, an interminable 120 miles away.

Hogan was 36 years old, and the man who moments before had stood astride the sports world like a colossus could now not even stand. News of the accident spread like sunrise. The initial word was that Hogan had been killed in the crash. His colleagues on the Tour, playing a pro-am in Arizona, strode solemnly off the course believing Ben was dead.

Doctors set his bones and then set his recovery time at two months, due largely to what they called Hogan's "fighting heart." They expected him to be released in a few weeks, but complications arose. Blood clots formed in his legs, and he had severe chest pains from a clot in his lungs. His blood count was dangerously low. Hogan was given several transfusions, and doctors feared he might not live. Valerie was told there was only one vascular surgeon who could do the needed operation—Dr. Alton S. Ochsner in New Orleans.

Dr. Ochsner was contacted but couldn't get a plane out of New Orleans because of Mardi Gras. Valerie remembered an offer from Brigadier General David Hutchinson, the commander of El Paso's Air Corps base, who had visited Ben a few days earlier. Because of Hogan's time served in the Air Corps in World War II, the general called him "one of our boys" and told Valerie if there was anything he could do to help, she was to call him.

Valerie contacted the general, and a special flight was arranged to get Dr. Ochsner to the hospital by noon the next day. He cut into Hogan's abdomen to tie off the large vein—an inch-thick tube known as the inferior vena cava—that carries blood from the body's lower half to the heart. The emergency surgery saved Hogan's life; at the same time it caused circulatory problems in his lower body. For the rest of his life, Hogan's legs would swell and hurt whenever he walked even short distances.

Injuries from the accident haunted Hogan every day. Vascular problems weakened his legs, and the damage to his left eye would bring on partial blindness and eventually affect his shot making, particularly his putting, due to problems with depth perception. Hogan's left shoulder ached from the fractured collarbone. By the end of February, he had dropped 20 pounds and weighed 117. Doctors wondered if he would walk again. Hogan spent 59 days flat on his back in the hospital before finally being discharged on April 1. Gaunt and frail, he joined Valerie in an ambulance ride to the El Paso railroad station and boarded a train for Fort Worth.

Too weak to walk distances of any length and not strong enough to swing a golf club, he passed the summer working to regain his strength. Many observers believed his return to the PGA Tour was no longer a certainty; Ben believed otherwise. "People have always been telling me what I can't do," he said. "I guess I have wanted to show them."

Hogan knew his recovery was going to be a long haul. In his mind, he didn't think he would ever get back to being the player he was in 1948. For a brief moment, he allowed himself to bemoan his fate. "You work for perfection all your life and then something like this happens," he told reporters. "My nervous system has been shot by this, and I don't see how I can readjust it to competitive life."

It was a momentary lapse. Hogan had a collision with fate; but after being hit by the bus, Hogan hit back. "You can bet I'll be back there swinging," he stated. Valerie was just as defiant. "Ben will be himself again," she said, "bones, nerves, and all."

Jacque remembers being shocked at her uncle's weakened state. "I thought if anybody could come back, he would," she says. "He was determined to come back and play golf."

Where Hogan once spent long hours practicing, he now put in equally long hours trying just to walk. Because the larger veins in his legs had been tied off in surgery, the smaller veins were now carrying more blood than they normally would. To strengthen his legs, Hogan walked daily laps around his living room.

On April 6, five days after returning home, Hogan headed out into warm sunshine, wearing his pajamas, linen cap, and topcoat. It was a landmark day for him, marking as it did his first trip outside. Nearly five months passed before Hogan picked up a golf club in late August. Four months later he headed outside in December to play his first round of golf since the accident. He walked a few of the holes in faltering fashion but relied mostly on a golf cart to get around. A week passed before Hogan, his legs encased in elastic bandages, played his first 18 holes. The exercise took so much out of him that he was forced to go straight to bed.

Named nonplaying captain of the 1949 U.S. Ryder team, Hogan traveled to Ganton Golf Club in Scarborough, North Yorkshire, England, for the matches. Press reports called him "crippled," but the sight of the courageous American practicing his putts excited the Old World. As competitive as ever, Hogan became embroiled in controversy when he questioned the grooves on the clubs of members of the British squad. This was more than gamesmanship; Hogan had a long memory and believed it time to pay back British Captain Henry Cotton for requesting an inspection of Ben's clubs in the 1947 Ryder Cup. No illegal grooves were found on Hogan's clubs, but, when meeting with Bernard Darwin, chair of the Royal and Ancient rules committee, on the eve of the 1949 matches, the British team learned that many of their clubs were illegal. The discovery left Ganton club pro Jock Ballantine spending his evening filing the nonconforming clubfaces.

Hogan was irked by the Brit's fascination with the Americans bringing 600 steaks, six hams, 12 sides of beef, and four boxes of bacon to the tightly rationed UK. "Every time I pick up the paper I read about that meat," he snapped. "I can't even find any golf news. Next time I guess we'll have to leave our clubs at home and just have a meat show."

When British reporters told the American captain that meat was a big story because of rationing, Hogan didn't soften his stance. "Maybe so," he said, "but you don't go around reporting what Lord so-and-so had for tea or lunch or dinner. I don't get your angle. Those steaks and hams have been in your papers for 12 days."

Spurred by their combative captain, the Americans staged a second-day rally to earn a 7–5 overall victory. By the following January, Hogan's determined rehab enabled him to return to the Tour. His comeback electrified the sports world. Herbert Warren Wind thought Hogan's return to golf "amazing and heart-warming." There were few Americans, he said, not following Hogan's progress.

Hogan chose to make his comeback appearance at the 1950 Los Angeles Open at Riviera Country Club in Pacific Palisades, a site where he had enjoyed tremendous success. Thin and frail, Hogan was praised for his return to competition. At the first tee, however, he turned to the announcer. "Just introduce me like you usually would," he said. "I don't want any special attention from the gallery."

Willing himself through a grueling 72 rounds, Hogan led the astonished Snead before The Slammer snaked in a 15-foot putt on the 72nd hole to force an 18-hole playoff. Heavy rains caused the playoff to be postponed until eight days later. Hogan had pushed himself to his absolute limit; his fighting heart could carry his battered body no further. Snead won the playoff 72–76, but Hogan won the admiration of millions. Hogan said the L.A. Open taught him a valuable lesson. "I learned that, thank God, I could still play pretty close to my old form."

Hogan's inspiring story transcended sports. His comeback put him on a different level than any other athlete of his era, his determination displaying a depth of character and toughness. *Hogan* became synonymous with a triumph of the will; he morphed from mere mortal into something more. Jim Murray said fans looked at Hogan like he was John Wayne, a hero who could do no wrong. Golfer Cary Middlecoff believes it was at this time that Hogan took on what Middlecoff called the "miracle man" aura. "Crowds that included a number of his fellow pros would gather around him," Middlecoff said, "and try to watch his every move."

Hogan's comeback was so sensational Hollywood came calling. Like other sports biopics of the era—*The Pride of the Yankees*, *The Stratton Story*, *The Jackie Robinson Story*, *The Joe Louis Story*—Hogan's story went to the big screen. *Follow the Sun* was rushed into production and released in 1951 in part because few believed Hogan could continue his comeback. "Nobody thought he could keep it going," said Venturi. After the L.A. Open, Hogan was in contention at Augusta in his first major since the crash but faltered with a final round 76. The following May, Hogan claimed the first victory of his return, firing a 259 in the Greenbrier Open and winning by 10 strokes. In June, he earned one of the most dramatic victories in golf history, winning the U.S. Open at Merion. Hogan was 16 months removed from his accident, but his body was still feeling the effects. On the final day of competition, he began to wilt in the heat. The final few holes saw his lead—along with his strength and stamina—melt.

Teetering on tired legs and needing to make a difficult shot from the fairway on 18 to save par, Hogan grabbed his 1-iron, the most difficult club to hit. Hogan's drive brought a gasp from the gallery. He made par with a hurried second putt—"I had to go someplace and sit down, my legs hurt like hell"—and forced a three-way playoff. He won easily, blistering Merion with the only round under par. The following April, he hammered Augusta, shooting 8 under to claim his first victory in the Masters.

Merion represented Hogan's rebirth as a champion golfer. "Merion meant the most," he said, "because it proved I could still win."

Hogan's comeback fired the imagination of the public. He had transformed his game and his body, adding 15 pounds to boost his weight to 150. The hours spent rebuilding his ravaged frame during his 11-month recovery resulted in a musculature that impressed fellow pros. They would see him from the back in the clubhouse and were surprised with the muscularity of his legs and thighs. Snead believed the muscle Hogan added from his strength-training regimen helped him maintain length on his drives with less effort.

When Lee Trevino competed against Hogan in the 1960s, he noted that "Mr. Hogan had huge hands" and wrists so thick it seemed to Trevino that Hogan's forearms went straight to his hands. He thought that while Hogan weighed 150 he carried himself as if he weighed 185. Mr. Hogan, Trevino thought, was extremely powerful.

While the mechanics of his post-crash swing remain an example of near-perfect ball striking—swing coach Hank Haney believes Hogan had the best swing the game has ever seen—Hogan told Claude Harmon and friend Marvin Leonard that the damage he suffered to his knees and pelvis reduced his hip turn through the ball and shortened the length of his drives by a dozen yards or so.

Venturi believed Ben never really felt good physically after the accident. Something was different, Venturi said, adding that Hogan knew he had lost something. Valerie knew it too. She thought her husband had been cheated by the accident. Valerie said she and Ben knew he was fortunate that "God had let him live." But there was a sense of loss that enveloped them both.

"He was never the same," says Lisa Scott, remembering her great-uncle in his later years. "He never complained, never said he was sore or tired but you could tell; he moved slowly." As he no longer had regular circulation in his legs, Scott says her uncle "was cold a lot of the time."

The outpouring of sympathy from thousands of fans following his accident served to soften Hogan's hard edge when he was not playing golf. Some saw a "new Ben" and a "mellower Hogan" revealing inner warmth that had been concealed. At the same time, Herbert Warren Wind, who saw Hogan at numerous tournaments, wrote that, whenever the "stench of competition was in the air, Ben was much the same as he had always been, all intensity, all detachment, all business."

Hogan had to be all business to deal with the physical odds facing him. He narrowed his stance, and while his swing became less dynamic it delivered more consistency and control. Middlecoff believed that, while Hogan produced fewer exceptional shots following his accident, he also hit fewer poor ones.

Mike Wright, the head pro at the Shady Oaks Country Club, which Hogan frequented, believed the crash taught Ben something about life that got into his game. It was as if Hogan had something more to play for than titles and trophies. Hogan had a great deal to play for in the 1951 U.S. Open at Oakland Hills. He was seeking his second straight Open victory—a record-tying third in as many attempts—and in his mind, fourth overall, as he always counted his victory in the 1942 Hale America National Open.

"Having been around him it's easy for me to understand how he came back," says Devlin. "He's among the most tenacious players ever, probably top one or two."

Hogan was a champion who came back a greater champion, wrote Herbert Warren Wind. He ruled the golf world in sharply creased gabardine slacks, cotton shirts, golf shoes custom made by renowned Peal & Co. Ltd. in London, and a driver's cap ordered from Cavanagh's on Park Avenue in New York, the prestigious hat shop that outfitted presidents and princes, entertainers, and underworld bosses.

Confronting the champion was a course created by legendary designer Donald Ross and transformed into a snarling, sneering monster by renowned par buster Robert Trent Jones.

2

DONALD ROSS
LINKS THE OLD
WORLD TO THE NEW

Oakland Hills has bewitched and bewildered many of the greatest golfers since the celebrated South Course was formally opened on July 13, 1918.

For that, golfers can look to course architect Donald James Ross and his mentor, the legendary Old Tom Morris, whose heritage extends to the acknowledged home of golf and his own birthplace—St. Andrews, Fife, Scotland.

"Donald Ross," states Glenn Diegel, chairman of the Oakland Hills Country Club's Heritage Committee, "was one of the great architects of the golden age of golf design."

Born in 1872 to a family of modest means in Dornoch, Scotland, north of the Highlands, Ross was the son of a stonemason. His humble home still stands at number 3 Saint Gilbert Street in Dornoch. The motto of the Ross clan is Success Nourishes Hope, "Spem Successus Alit" in the Scots' native tongue. The Ross tartan ran contrary to tradition. Whereas dress tartans were more vivid in color and hunting tartans more understated, the Ross tartan favored bright colors for hunting and subdued colors (pale yellow, light blue, green, and pink) for dress. For a time, tartans were banned in Scotland along with highland dress. The Prescription Act of 1747–1782 followed in the wake of the Scottish rebellion in 1745, and the only legal tartan during that time was the Black Watch, worn by Scottish natives still loyal to the British Crown.

Ross would write that all he was and would become he owed to his upbringing in Dornoch. His love for his hometown was evident in a rare interview in 1935 in which he stated that when he was growing up in Dornoch he thought of life in that Scottish village as very hard and narrow. Life in Dornoch, he recalled, was limited to work and church.

"The older I get," he said as a 63-year-old in 1935, "the more I can feel myself turning back to their way of thinking. At least they never compromised with honesty."

Donald and his brother Alec refined their golfing skills on their home course. History shrouds Royal Dornoch Golf Club like the morning mist from its North Sea location that glazes the course and the beach, or the dew that glistens on the fairways and greens at dawn. The first written record of the Dornoch links appears in 1616 and is predated in Scotland only by St. Andrews (1552) and Leith (1593).

The Dornoch Golf Club was founded in 1877 and served as the successor to the Sutherland Golfing Society, whose members took the links at Dornoch and Golspie. Dornoch at one time boasted the fifth-longest course in Britain. In 1901, Mr. and Mrs. Andrew Carnegie presented the prestigious Carnegie Shield to the club to be bestowed upon the champion of an annual competition each August. The Carnegie Shield is recognized as one of the world's more magnificent trophies, its beauty enhanced by pictures of Dornoch Cathedral, Skibo Castle, and the former Bishop's Palace, now the Castle Hotel. Five years later, Dornoch received a Royal Charter from King Edward VII, giving birth to the Royal Dornoch Golf Club.

Ross grew to love golf as it was played in Dornoch, and he and Alec developed swings that were rhythmic and graceful. Donald became a carpenter's apprentice in his mid-teens and in time was hired at his home course as club maker, greenkeeper, and professional. An accomplished golfer, Ross competed in the 1910 British Open and placed eighth, earning him additional notoriety throughout the British Isles. Ross's success on the links of Dornoch, which sits hard by the sea on the east coast of Scotland, caught the attention of Donald Sutherland. The club secretary groomed Ross for the role of greenkeeper at the links and club professional.

In 1893, Ross headed to celebrated St. Andrews to serve as an apprentice to Morris. Ross had first observed Morris seven years earlier when Old Tom had revamped various holes at Royal Dornoch. Morris, 72 years of age when Ross arrived, had first earned fame by winning the Open four times from 1861–1867 and in 1862 set the mark for the largest margin of victory in a major championship at 14 strokes. It was a record that stood for more than a century until Tiger Woods won the 2000 U.S. Open by 15 strokes.

Morris was more than a great golfer; he designed courses throughout the British Isles. Modern golf owes much to Morris not only for his many course designs but also for his numerous innovations. He created the concept of aiding turf growth by top dressing the greens with sand. Before Morris, bunkers were left largely unattended and could be truly hazardous; Old Tom introduced the idea of actively managing hazards. He introduced yardage markers and was the first to manicure greens with a push mower. He widened the fairways at St. Andrews to accommodate increased play, established separate tees on each hole, and improved the greens. It was Morris who created the famed plateau greens, which are still in use today at Royal Dornoch. For these reasons and more Morris is recognized as the father of modern greenkeeping.

Ross learned firsthand from the master for two years and then returned to Dornoch as pro and greenkeeper. Five years later, he crossed the Atlantic confident of linking the Old World to the New. The time spent with Morris at the "Home of Golf" served to influence the young Ross regarding his thoughts on the best way to design golf courses.

Old Tom never went to Oakland Hills, but his influence can be seen in the design of his apprentice. Ross adopted his former boss's modern idea of placing hazards so that shots could be routed around them. He also learned the duties of a club pro. Working in the shop of renowned club maker David Forgan, Ross built golf clubs and molded golf balls from gutta-percha. Ross returned to Dornoch in 1893 to become club pro and greenkeeper and six years later established himself as the person in charge of the links.

During his time at his beloved Dornoch, Ross met Harvard Professor Robert Willson, who was vacationing in Scotland. Impressed with

Ross's talents, Willson convinced him that, even though golf had been played in the United States for only a decade, the sport had a limitless future in the New World. Ross shocked his Dornoch neighbors when he gave up his annual 300-pound salary and used his life savings to set sail for the States.

Though Ross left Dornoch behind, it remained with him the rest of his life. He returned more than once to his birthplace, where many of his relatives remained, and he designed and built a house in his adopted hometown of Pinehurst, North Carolina, which he referred to fondly as his "Dornoch Cottage." Ross felt at home in Pinehurst due in large part to its considerable Scottish population.

Ross first set foot on U.S. soil in 1899 and, courtesy of Willson, had employment waiting for him as club pro and greenkeeper at Oakley Country Club, outside of Boston, in Watertown, Massachusetts. Ross recognized that, with his knowledge relating to golf, he was in the right place at the right time to pursue his passion.

Growing up in Dornoch, Ross may have believed for a time that his destiny lay in being a stonemason like his father. Ross knew of Andrew Carnegie, the Scottish orphan who had sailed across the sea and made a fortune by melting iron and coke into steel. Thousands of other Highlanders set sail for the promised land across the pond. The offer Ross received to find out what he could achieve was too alluring to turn down. Ross had read about American businessmen and how absorbed they were in making money.

"I knew the day would come," Ross once recalled, "when the American businessman would want some game to play, and I knew that game would be golf. I knew there'd be a great future in it. I came to grow up with a game in which I had complete confidence."

Ross brought to the colonies a conservatism that saw him maximize the terrain as nature had sculpted it. The young designer was determined to use the environment as he found it. This frugality worked in his favor, golf course budgets being as thin as the occasional reed found in the marshy areas near greens. Designers who could lay out a course for a low fee and low construction costs were hired. Ross kept costs to a minimum. He wanted each hole built so that it wasted none of the ground at his disposal.

Ross redesigned the rudimentary course at Oakley with such success that he was sought out to design other courses in the area. One of those whom Ross met was James Tufts of the American Soda Fountain Company and founder of the Pinehurst Resort. Tufts had purchased land in south-central North Carolina, his goal being to transform the sand hills into a winter resort as a getaway for those wishing to escape the harsh New England winters. Tufts's rural tract, accessible by rail only, was called Pinehurst.

Convinced by Tufts in 1900 to accompany him on a trip down south, Ross accepted the position of director of golf at the modest pro shop at Pinehurst Resort. It was a title he retained until his death from a heart attack in 1948. Ross spent summers in New England and winters in North Carolina. When he was commissioned by Tufts to design Pinehurst's first four courses, it was at that moment that golf history changed forever.

Ross developed his course designs from the sand hills. Richard Tufts, James's grandson and an associate and friend of Ross, thought Ross's bunkering on older courses profuse. Richard Tufts believed that Ross realized in later designs that undulations, swales, and grass bunkers called for more types of shots. It was then that Ross began framing greens with bunkers. Because green size was determined by the amount of traffic a course expected, most greens were small. Ross recognized this and reduced the advantage enjoyed by those whose strengths lay in the putter and short game.

In 1905, Alec and the 32-year-old Donald sat for a photo on the porch steps in Pinehurst. The ever-present golfing tam was pulled low on Donald's forehead, and he was nattily attired in his Harris Tweed jacket, white shirt, and dark tie. High button shoes rather than spikes were the style, and it's likely that the golf clubs held by the Ross brothers and at least 10 others in the group photo of 16 men were hand made by Donald.

The first decade of the twentieth century saw Ross set up shop and design and redesign numerous courses. Before he would become known as the preeminent designer of golf courses, Ross established a reputation in the New World, as well as the Old, as a top golfer. He captured the prestigious American classic, the Massachusetts Open, in 1905 and 1911, and the North and South Opens in 1903, 1905, and 1906.

The North and South Open began in Pinehurst in 1903. For many Americans, the Civil War remained a vivid memory, having ended just 38 years prior. Tufts believed a tournament bringing together golfers from the North and South would help soothe the emotional wounds that still lingered. The initial North and South Open occurred a short time before the famed first flight of brothers Orville and Wilbur Wright at Kitty Hawk. Sportswriter Herb Graffis noted that en route to winning the inaugural North and South Open, Ross's graceful swing likely produced a drive that flew as far as the 284 yards the Wright Brothers would cover in their powered aircraft later that year on December 17.

Along with his victories in the North and South Opens and the Massachusetts Open, Ross produced respectable finishes in the United States Open, competing in the National Open seven times and earning four top-10 finishes. Ross's skills stayed with him into his 60s, when his deft touch on fairways and greens allowed him to shoot his age on Pinehurst No. 3.

Ross was hired in 1909 to serve as club pro at Essex Country Club in Manchester, Massachusetts, but four years later the demand for his designs was such that he left Essex to focus fully on course architecture. In 1916, Donald J. Ross Associates was established. That year also saw the founding of a country club that would become synonymous with Ross's name and work. On October 17, Joseph Mack and Norval Hawkins founded Oakland Hills Country Club at a meeting of 46 associates and friends at the Detroit Athletic Club. The first Oakland Hills executive board saw Mack serve as president.

Automobile manufacturing was not only changing forever the face of Southeast Michigan, it was also revolutionizing America's landscape. Detroit had become the automobile capital of the world, and inventors and entrepreneurs teamed to create the industry's most recognized corporate names—Ford, Chrysler, and General Motors. In time, Ford, Dodge, Chevrolet, and other original inventors saw their identities evolve into the industry's most famous corporate names.

On December 20, 1916, Mack, Hawkins, and several investors purchased 450 acres of orchards and rolling pasture that made up the Edwin Miller, William Spicer, and Fran German farms, south of Maple Road, in Birmingham. Their intent was turn the farms into a first-rate golf course where their business associates and friends could meet and greet. They did it by designating approximately 170 acres for the new club and 80 acres for homesites. The first board of directors meeting of the Oakland Hills Country Club was called to order, and 140 new club members paid $250 apiece to join. The club would also own options on an additional 160 acres from the German and Leach farms, situated north of Maple Road.

Work to build the new golf course at Oakland Hills began immediately after the initial board meeting in October. Two months later, Mack provided detailed construction plans at the December board meeting and told club members he had hired the famous course architect from Scotland.

Ross served as architect for many of the Detroit-area country clubs, and his designs are seen in more than 200 courses throughout the state of Michigan. For a quarter of a century, from 1911–1936, Ross designed suburban courses and city courses, lake courses, and rural courses. His earliest designs were private courses at the Muskegon Country Club in 1911 and the Detroit Golf Club in 1916.

When he first visited Oakland Hills in late January 1917, Ross was struck by the stunning topography of the property. Turning to Mack, Ross stated excitedly, "The Lord intended this for a golf course!"

Ross remarked later that he rarely finds "a piece of property so well-suited for a golf course" as Oakland Hills. He took the topographical maps brought to him and laid out a golf course on top. Unlike other architects of his era, Ross did not design his courses to promote a penal system. He constructed bunkers that were well-placed and sensible, rather than penal.

Sensitive as he was to the positioning of trees in the fairway, Ross considered vertical hazards unfair. He avoided using water hazards, considering them an unfair penalty. If water could be used naturally in his design, it would serve as part of the routing to test players. When he found it impossible to not incorporate a pond or stream, he would make the focal point of the hole something other than its water hazard. Ross grew up on the water in Dornoch, but he wasn't fond of incorporating it into his layouts.

A prime ingredient in Ross's design philosophy was practicality. Dirt was moved by means of hand and horse- or ox-drawn carts. The movement of large rocks and stones posed a serious problem. While much of the land he built his courses on was cleared of most rocks, trees, and vegetation, Ross's team still had to gather the boulders and tree stumps remaining in strategic areas. To the cost-conscious Ross, it seemed cost efficient to take the stones found in one area of the course and move them to another area, stack them, and cover them with dirt. He had grown up with these mounds in Dornoch and saw them as a way to challenge each golfer's abilities with irons. These hummocks can still be found on many of Ross's courses, and the humps, hollows, and swales are reminiscent of the Dornoch links.

For this reason, some suggested that there is a sameness to Ross's courses. Critics have also seized on Ross's reserved nature. Author Charles Price has characterized Ross as "a proud, standoffish man, almost egotistically so." Price was referring to Ross being miffed at champion golfer Bobby Jones's decision to work with Alister MacKenzie to build the famed Augusta National Country Club, site of the Masters. Ross believed he and Jones had a handshake agreement to build the new course in Augusta but that Jones chose MacKenzie after seeing his design at Cypress Point on the California coast.

Former *Charlotte Observer* columnist Jake Wade saw the Scot in a different light when the balding, bespectacled architect visited the area in 1945 to work on his Myers Park Country Club layout. "Mr. Ross looks like a banker and indeed must be quite a wealthy man," Wade wrote. "Yet with his dignity and reserve and gentleness of manner and easy, aristocratic touch, he still likes to be known as a golf professional."

Almost forgotten in the celebration of Ross's designs is Ernie Wey, an employee of Bloomfield Hills Country Club. It was Wey who, having offered his services to Ross, oversaw the daily construction of his boss's designs. Working tirelessly to maintain the integrity of Ross's use of land and meet seemingly impossible deadlines, Wey was instrumental in the completion of work on the South Course of Oakland Hills.

Course creation peaked in the Roaring 20s, the rollicking decade marking the Golden Age as much for Ross as for Babe Ruth, Jack Dempsey, Bill Tilden, and Bobby Jones. Ross often worked on 8 to 10

course layouts simultaneously, and he bossed a stellar crew of construction supervisors. Ross aides James Harrison, Walter B. Hatch, Henry
Hughes, Walter Johnston, and James B. McGovern made certain the
master's designs were meticulously followed. When Ross discovered,
usually via examination of photos, that something was amiss in a tee
box, bunker, or green, he would have the finished product redone. By
the 1930s, Ross's empire encompassed some 3,000 men working on as
many as 25 courses at a time.

Because his course layouts were so revered, Ross barely finished one
design before being called upon to start another. His courses attracted
European royalty, star athletes, celebrities, and U.S. presidents. William Howard Taft shot a desultory 17 on the 17th hole at Kebo Valley
in Bar Harbor, Maine in 1911. Perhaps no president appreciated Ross's
course architecture as much as Franklin D. Roosevelt. Stricken with in-
fantile paralysis, FDR went to Warm Springs, Georgia, in 1927 seeking
a cure for his lifeless legs in the waters of the health spa turned treatment
center. Franklin's wife, Eleanor, stated that, when he had the use of his
legs, golf had been her husband's favorite game. After contracting polio,
FDR never again played golf, but he loved to watch the sport and talked
of it often during his visits to Warm Springs. Roosevelt knew of Ross
and requested that he create a layout for Warm Springs. The aristocrat
worked closely with the architect, helping design a course now known as
the Roosevelt Memorial Golf Course.

That the physically disadvantaged could enjoy golf on a Ross course at
Warm Springs was made possible by Roosevelt's generosity. Though the
health spa operated at a loss, FDR covered the expenses out of his own
pocket. Roosevelt's dedication to finding a cure for polio was realized
10 years after the president's death in 1945 from a cerebral hemorrhage.

Fifty years after FDR's passing, one of his successors in the Oval Of-
fice, Bill Clinton, arrived at Warm Springs to try his hand on the Roosevelt–Ross layout. Ross's courses weren't restricted to U.S. presidents.
Baseball Hall of Famer Babe Ruth and comedian Jackie Gleason, the
"Great One" of *The Honeymooners* fame, were frequent visitors to Ponce
de Leon Golf & Conference Resort in St. Augustine, Florida.

Tom Turley caddied for Ruth in 1940 and tells how the Babe handed
him a small, square, unlabeled bottle that was filled with a dark liquid.

"This is medicine," Ruth told Turley. Throughout the afternoon, Ruth drove towering shots off the tee, and, with nearly every shot, Babe blistered ears with profanities. Turley remembered Ruth's rockets as being "dangerously wild," and the two spent a lot of time searching for his missed drives in the woods. Once in the woods, the Babe would ask for his "medicine," which Turley thought smelled like rum. On the 11th tee, Ruth bought a round of Coca-Cola for the group, the four caddies included. The Babe then mixed his "medicine" with his Coke.

Ross's courses attracted golfing royalty as well. On March 13, 1947, a foursome of Ben Hogan, Byron Nelson, Sam Snead, and Jimmy Demaret gathered to compete on the South Course of the Ross-designed Daytona Beach Golf Club in Florida. Demaret shot a course record 63, Hogan and Snead tied for second with 67s, and Nelson finished fourth at 69.

Leaning on what he learned in Dornoch, Ross made the crowned green his trademark. He made certain every break and slope met his approval. Some of his courses were distinctly more difficult than others, and he likely designed them for championship play and thus made them more challenging. So it is with Oakland Hills's South Course, which Ross built around the 10th and 11th holes; the architect would call these holes the finest consecutive par 4s he ever designed.

Work on the South Course began on March 25, 1917. By the following autumn, construction was largely concluded, with only the finishing touches to be administered. Spring 1918 saw the South Course's construction complete. Ross's original plan had par for the South Course at 35 out and 37 in. The second hole was the lone par 5 on the front nine, while the back nine listed par 5s on 12, 14, and 18. Holes 5, 8, and 10 were designed by Ross to have additional back tees, thus creating three additional par 5s for a course that could play 37 out and 38 in. This adjustment pushed par from 72 to 75.

Ross's stamp as an architect was naturalness. To golfers and course architects, Ross's bunkers appear to have been built not by the hands of man but by the hands of nature. He was like MacKenzie, who designed some of the best courses in the world and wrote, "The chief object of every golf architect or greenkeeper worth his salt is to imitate the beauties of nature so closely as to make his work indistinguishable from nature itself."

Ross's layouts led to his being considered by most as the Michelangelo of golf. His signature designs include Oakland Hills, Pinehurst No. 2, Oak Hill, and Seminole. He is the master designer whom Nicklaus said set "a standard by which we are all measured today." Ross held to the basic tenant that "Each course must be original."

An environmentalist, Ross would walk the land multiple times to get the routing dictated by nature. Ross's beliefs in minimalism and simplicity rang true in his designing of Oakland Hills. The 11th green of the South Course was fit into a natural saddle between two hills. Ross found that Oakland Hills's topographical formation "could hardly be surpassed" and the area available was so expansive he was able to lay out a "very open and roomy course."

Along with the expansive area, Ross found the soil to be of sandy loam quality, which he believed the best kind for developing golf turf. He designed Oakland Hills to be a course that boasted holes of "every type and length," thus demanding from golfers all types of shots. It was an aspect important to Ross, who deemed that "each course must have strategies."

Ross knew that the rolling character of the fairways at Oakland Hills meant golfers would be confronted with "varying instances demanding perfect control of the strokes to achieve satisfactory results."

The approach shot to the par-4 16th called for the bold golfer to take the long carry to the green. The less proficient player would attempt the shorter carry to the left and then play to the green with their third shot.

The length of the South Course—6,620 yards for tournament play and 6,400 for general play—was laid out by Ross so that the 1st tee, 9th green, 10th tee, and 18th green were all close to the clubhouse. Completed in August 1922, the clubhouse contains 24 rooms and baths for overnight accommodations. Its designer, C. Howard Crane, was a club member and also the architect of Michigan landmarks Orchestra Hall, the Fox Theatre, the Capitol Theater, and several other Detroit theaters. The total cost of the clubhouse soared to $650,000, more than $300,000 over budget.

Ross's design for Oakland Hills arranged for a variety of tees at each hole. Aware that the USGA had under construction the changing of the par distance, Ross took precautions in planning the holes so that they could be lengthened to the distances required under the new ratings.

"Gil Hanse is one of the best modern architects, having recently restored Merion, Winged Foot, and L.A. Country Club, among others," says Diegel. "He said the Ross design of the South Course was grand in scale, fitting the land that Ross chose in 1917."

In 1918, Mack hired Walter Hagen as Oakland Hills's first club pro; Hagen's salary was $300 per month plus profits from the sale of golf equipment. "Sir Walter" was one of the great barnstormers in sports history, a dashing and debonair gentleman standing six feet tall and sporting slick, black hair. "The Haig" would arrive for golfing exhibitions donning a dinner jacket and brandishing a brunette on one arm and a blonde on the other. Leggy Ahearn, who caddied for Hagen, told writer Gay Talese that, when The Haig came to the clubhouse in the morning still wearing the tuxedo from the night before, "I knew we were in for a bad day."

In 1919, Hagen represented Oakland Hills and shot a 301 to tie Mike Brady in the U.S. Open at Brae Burn Country Club in Massachusetts. Hagen beat Brady in the playoff, 77 to 78, to earn the second of his eventual 11 majors. Some state that Hagen should be credited with 16 major titles, second only to Jack Nicklaus's 18, since he won the Western Open five times in an era when that event ranked behind only the British and U.S. Opens among the premier tournaments in the world. Ever the bon vivant, The Haig spent the night before the U.S. Open playoff with Al Jolson, the famed jazz performer, who was in town for a 10-week run in the play *Sinbad* at the Boston Opera House.

Hagen resigned as club pro at Oakland Hills in 1920, and on his advice, Brady was named his successor. That same year, L.L. Bredin claimed Oakland Hills's inaugural Men's Club Championship, and Worden Hunter placed second. In 1921, Mabel Hawkins defeated Violet Hanley to win the first Women's Club Championship at Oakland Hills.

Ross designed Oakland Hills's North Course in 1922, and it was built under the supervision of Hatch. The North Course opened May 13, 1924, three weeks prior to the start of the U.S. Open on the South Course. The 1924 Open remains historically significant not only because it marks the first major championship ever played at Oakland Hills but also because it is the first U.S. Open in which the USGA allows golfers to use steel-shafted putters.

Playing in his accustomed analytical, cautious style, Cyril Walker won the 1924 Open at Oakland Hills in an upset, shooting 74, 74, 74, 75 for a 297, which beat defending champion Bobby Jones by three strokes. Playing to a length of 6,874 yards and a par 72, Oakland Hills provided a tough test for a major, Walker's winning score being 9-over. Ross's course also claimed its first big-name victim—Bobby Jones. The 10th hole wrecked the reigning champ, lost six strokes to par over the four rounds of the tournament. No. 10 would cost Bobby Jones his chance at repeating as U.S. Open champion.

The 1924 Open was the first of nine majors—six U.S. Opens and three PGA Championships—held on the South Course through 2019. Three years after holding its first major, Oakland Hills's tournament history was burnished a bit more with the hosting of the U.S. Women's Amateur in 1929. Glenna Collett downed Leona Pressler four and three for the fourth of her eventual six amateur titles. Oakland Hills thus played a role in Collett claiming an incredible 16 consecutive tournament victories from 1928–1931.

Thirteen years passed before Oakland Hills hosted its second major— the 1937 U.S. Open. Acclaimed golf architect Albert W. Tillinghast, asked to survey the South Course and offer ideas for improvement, arrived at Oakland Hills in 1936.

"This course needs nothing more to prepare it for the Open," Tillinghast reported. "What it needs is to be left alone." Oakland Hills, he added "is one of the finest golf courses, not alone in this country, but in the world."

Joe Dey Jr., executive director of the USGA, did not agree with Tillinghast that the South Course should be left alone in advance of the Open. Dey suggested to Oakland Hills club member and respected amateur golfer Chris Brinke that par be increased on the eighth hole to five and reduced on 14 to four. These adjustments, Dey noted, would provide a balance of two par 5s per side.

Changes were made, and Ralph Guldahl gutted the revamped South Course with rounds of 71, 69, 72, and 69 to set a low-scoring record of 281, two strokes better than runner-up Sam Snead. The 1937 Open at Oakland Hills was the first Open appearance for Slammin' Sam, and his second-place finish was the result of the most dominant player at that time firing a record low.

Oakland Hills remained a par 72 for the 1937 Open, but Ross's layout was expanded to 7,037 yards, making it the first U.S. Open venue to exceed 7,000 yards. The tournament had likewise been expanded, from two days to three, play beginning on Thursday, June 10 and concluding with the final two rounds on Saturday, June 12.

Snead enjoyed an auspicious start, burning up the course with a 69 to tie with Denny Shute for the first-round lead. On Open Saturday, the leaderboard was headed by Ed Dudley, who fronted Snead and Guldahl by a single stroke at the conclusion of 54 holes. The championship round, on a warm, sun-washed afternoon, saw Dudley fall from contention with a 76. Slammin' Sam curled in his final putt to birdie the 18th to card a 71 for the final round and 283 for the tournament.

Playing behind Snead, Guldahl began his charge when he holed a 65-foot putt for eagle on eight. Pausing play by stopping often to comb his hair—"This is how I steadied my nerves," he said later—he followed with a birdie from 25 feet on nine. Guldahl's gritty rally faltered a bit with bogeys on 10 and 11, but he bounced back with birdies on 12 and 13. The final five holes saw Guldahl go even to fashion a 69 and a 281 total that stunned Snead. Guldahl finished two shots better than the Slammer and one stroke better than the U.S. Open record, set the year before by Tony Manero at a much shorter course (6,866 yards) at Baltusrol Golf Club in Springfield, New Jersey.

Guldahl followed his victory at Oakland Hills with a successful defense of his championship one year later at Cherry Hills Country Club in Colorado. It was the second of his three majors and allowed the future World Golf Hall of Fame member to become just the fourth player at the time to win at least two consecutive U.S. Opens, joining Willie Anderson (1903-1905), John McDermott (1911-1912), and Bobby Jones (1929-1930).

The 1937 Open at Oakland Hills featured not only the most expansive layout to that time in tournament history; it also prompted a new rule be put forth by the USGA. Guldahl had carried 19 clubs in his bulging bag when he won the 1937 U.S. Open. The following January, USGA

Rule 4-4 went into effect restricting the number of clubs in a bag to a maximum of 14.

Oakland Hills in 1937 signaled the start of Snead's disappointing finishes in U.S. Open Championships. Over the course of his long career, he placed second four times in the U.S. Open, the only major championship he never won.

In 1940 and 1942, Oakland Hills did its part for the war effort by hosting a series of exhibition matches to raise money for the Red Cross. In 1940, Hagen captained the Ryder Cup team of Guldahl, Snead, Nelson, Henry Picard, Vic Ghezzi, Jimmy Hines, Dick Metz, and Horton Smith against Gene Sarazen's challengers—Hogan, Demaret, Ed Oliver, Billy Burke, Harry Cooper, Lawson Little, Craig Wood, and Sarazen, the latter serving as player/captain. Hagen's Ryder Cup team triumphed 7 to 5.

Two years later many of the same stars returned, albeit on different teams, and the Ryder Club squad, this time headlined by Hogan, Nelson, Demaret, and Sarazen, took a 10 to 5 decision. In 1946 another soon-to-be notable name made his mark on Oakland Hills, 16-year-old Arnold Palmer finishing second in the Hearst National Junior Championship.

The celebrated history of the South Course makes Oakland Hills a national treasure, a masterpiece created by one of golf's immortals. It was constructed more than 100 years ago, and while alterations have taken place, Ross's routing and imprint remain the same. It's a tribute to one of the architect's greatest triumphs and most enduring efforts.

The most prolific course designer of his day was spare when it came to interviews. He resisted all efforts from friends urging him to write his autobiography. One got the impression, Richard Tufts said, that Ross felt he had failed "if his courses did not speak for him more eloquently than he could himself."

In the case of Oakland Hills, Ross's work spoke volumes. It would take one of his disciples—Robert Trent Jones—to turn the master's voice into a Monster's roar.

3

THE SUN NEVER SETS ON A ROBERT TRENT JONES COURSE

Where Donald Ross left off, Robert Trent Jones began.

This was true not only at Oakland Hills but also across America and around the globe. The present and future giants of the golf course design industry first met in 1926 when Ross, already world famous in golf course architecture, arrived in Pittsford, New York, to design two new 18-hole courses at Oak Hill Country Club.

Trent Jones, then a man in his early 20s and living in nearby East Rochester, became friends with Ross and was so fascinated by the renowned designer he subsequently became perhaps the first person to ever set out on a lifetime career as a course architect.

That he succeeded can best be illustrated by the fact that Trent Jones's career lasted more than 60 years and for several decades he was regarded as golf's most famous and prolific architect. During that time, the small, cherubic man who was born in the village of Ince-in-Makerfield, Cheshire—"a long par-five from Liverpool," Gay Talese noted in a 1959 profile—and spent most of his adult life working out of his offices in gritty Montclair, New Jersey—an equally long par 5 from Manhattan.

Even into his 50s, Trent Jones worked 250 days a year creating and constructing golf courses around the globe. Over the course of his life, he traveled an estimated eight million miles by plane, train, ship, boat, and mule in building more than 300 golf courses and remodeling 150 others. His courses can be found in 45 states in America, 35 foreign countries, and every continent save Antarctica.

It was for good reason that the celebrated architect issued a knowing smile when he stated, "The sun never sets on a Robert Trent Jones golf course."

For decades, Trent Jones stood astride the golf world like a Goliath, and testimony to his impact on golf history can be found in the fact that 21 of his courses have hosted the U.S. Open; 12, the PGA Championship; 6, the World Cup; and 47 other national championships. His Valderrama course in Spain was the site for the Ryder Cup, and the Robert Trent Jones Golf Club in Manassas, Virginia, has hosted the President's Cup. As astronaut Alan Shepard hit his famous golf shot on the moon's surface on February 6, 1971, Walter Cronkite told CBS television viewers, "Soon, we'll have a Robert Trent Jones course on the moon for Alan to play."

Just as Joe DiMaggio's 56 consecutive games-hit streak or John Wooden's 10 NCAA men's basketball titles are unlikely to be matched, so too are Trent Jones's totals. More than 50 of his courses are listed on various top-100 lists, and of the top-100 courses in the World Atlas of Golf, nearly one-fifth—17—carry Trent Jones's signature designs.

Beginning with Oakland Hills in 1951, he became the U.S. Open architect—earning the nickname the "Open Doctor"—and between 1950 and 1970 was tasked with redesigning or designing anew more than half of the U.S. Open's venues. His trademarks were easy to see—long, runway-like teeing grounds; expansive contoured greens; and heavy use of water hazards.

Described by Talese as "a moderately tweedy man," Trent Jones had large eyes and a wide, round face that Talese said was "relatively free of pouches, crevasses, or hummocks." Ben Wright did a documentary with Trent Jones and remembers him as "a fascinating man."

That he influenced generations of course architects is indisputable. Sons Robert Trent Jr. and Rees worked for him, as did assistants and field men like Frank Dane, Ron Fream, Tom Jackson, Ron Kirby, Jay Morrish, Cabell Robinson, and Roger Rulewich, each of whom became successful course designers.

It's a coaching tree to rival any in sports, but Trent Jones's influence on golf goes beyond future course architects who worked for the man to include those who didn't. Pete Dye, Tom Fazio, and Jack Nicklaus are celebrity course designers who owe a debt of gratitude to the man who would pal around with presidents, rub elbows with royalty, and kibitz with kings.

Trent Jones's clients included U.S. President Dwight D. Eisenhower, who received a putting green at the White House and a single hole with three different tees at Camp David, site of the president's weekend retreat in Maryland. Removed by President Richard Nixon, it was put back for President Bill Clinton by Robert Trent Jones Jr., a noted golf architect as well.

Trent Jones designed private courses for American royalty like the Rockefeller family of New York, as well as true royals—King Hassan II of Morocco and Aga Kahn. For King Hassan II, Trent Jones created a links course in a cork forest near the beach palace at Skhirat, Ribat. Trent Jones's stunning course at Dorado Beach Golf Club in Puerto Rico carried a price tag for Laurance Rockefeller of a million dollars, the third and fifth greens winding around a yacht basin so that the rich and famous can chip toward the green from their luxurious boats.

The common thread to each of Trent Jones's courses is the extraordinary test it presents. He believed each of his designs should present a stern challenge for golfers. In the hands of course architects that preceded him, most notably Alister MacKenzie and A.W. Tillinghast, layouts were elevated to an art form. In Trent Jones's view, work of art be damned; he demanded his courses confront golfers with a personal challenge that he compared to combat.

"Golf," he stated, "is a form of attack and counterattack. It offers a golfer his personal challenge of combat. He attacks the course and par; the architect creates fair pitfalls to defend its easy conquest. The architect calls on his ingenuity to create a hole that will reward only achievement."

Robert Trent Jones Jr. agrees, comparing golf to chess in that the architect assumes the role of defender against the golfer, who is attacking the course. Viewing golf as a chess match between architect and player emphasizes the need for short- and long-range strategies.

Trent Jones Jr. says his father's redesigns were necessary to deal with the modern game. "Steel shafts had come in, players were adjusting, and courses hadn't been updated. Elevated greens that were framed with bunkers were a radical change from before."

Trent Jones could look at a piece of ground and know instinctively what makes a challenging hole. There was a flow and rhythm he could feel. He would think how to stake it out and then use logic to make the right choice.

"It's like a jigsaw puzzle," he once said. "But you have to play golf well, too. You have to know the value of shots, how far the ball will go and what it will do."

Trent Jones institutionalized risk/reward shots in golf, and his architecture came to symbolize a heroic battle between man and nature. Tread on a Trent Jones course, and even the best golfers can feel as if they have been suddenly cast in the lead role in an Ernest Hemingway or Jack London novel. Trent Jones had a profound impact on championship golf, as he sought to turn every hole into what he called "a hard par but an easy bogey."

He had his detractors, then and now. The early years of Trent Jones's career saw his designs criticized by golfers as too demanding. Talese called him "as controversial a figure as Frank Lloyd Wright" and one often regarded "as a predatory creature by many of golf's chronic complainers and paranoiacs. They have preferred to view him as a sadistic architect who designs tough courses and then settles back gleefully to watch other people swinging futilely in sand traps, flinging their clubs in frustration, and never leaving the hole with less than a double-bogey."

Trent Jones's layouts were said to favor golfers with powerful swings and were not subtle in their demands. This led to complaints that he designed courses for championship golfers only and not for the less skilled who played for the enjoyment of the sport. His courses have also been critiqued as being predictable—long and brutish, and littered with bunkers, trees, and water hazards. "They all looked the same," Dick Howting says. Critics characterized Trent Jones courses as "long slogs."

Bellerive Country Club has been cited as a modern manifestation of Jones's philosophy. Opened in 1897 as a nine-hole course northwest of St. Louis, it was incorporated in 1910 as Bellerive Country Club, taking its name from Louis Groston de Saint-Ange de Bellerive, the last French commander in America. In 1955, the membership, led by Clark Gamble and Hoard Hardin, moved to a suburb west of St. Louis, Town and Country, and tasked Trent Jones with finding fertile farmland for the new location. Memorial Day, 1960, saw the birth of the "Green Monster of Ladue." Trent Jones, the "Open Doctor," built his newest "Monster" with the U.S. Open in mind. Five years later, his dream was realized, Bellerive becoming the youngest course to host the U.S. Open.

Filled with Trent Jones's staples—backbreaking length, bunkers, trees, water hazards, and an unconquerable par—his youngest "Monster" played predictably tough under a hot June sun. Defending champion Ken Venturi missed the 36-hole cut, as did former champs Arnold Palmer and Ed Furgol. Palmer missed by two strokes, the only time from 1962–1967 he placed outside the top-five finishers in the U.S. Open.

Venturi, his fingers numb from a circulation ailment in his right hand, missed making the cut by 10 strokes. His crippling condition, diagnosed as Raynaud's phenomenon, left his right hand so sore he was reduced to shaking hands with his left. It was the second-straight year Venturi had to battle physical problems in the Open. In 1964, he conquered Congressional Country Club in searing heat that soared to 108 degrees and all but set Bethesda, Maryland, ablaze.

Venturi's dramatic and inspirational comeback at Congressional would not be repeated at Bellerive. His right hand numbed, the reigning monarch took on Trent Jones's Green Monster and shot 81–79. Fighting his disability, the defending champion finished his 36 holes, as he had insisted he would. It was no small feat, considering Venturi's painful condition was similar to the ailment that afflicted Los Angeles Dodgers ace Sandy Koufax at this same time in 1965 and forced the legendary lefty into early retirement one year later.

Among the other past champions in the field, Julius Boros tied for fourth at 7-over, and Gene Littler, eighth at plus-8. Billy Casper (+14) tied for 17th, and Jack Nicklaus (19-over) tied for 32nd. The carnage reinforced Trent Jones's prediction on the eve of the tournament that Bellerive would be the site of some St. Louis blues.

"Those subtle greens are what I call a hazard," Trent Jones said with what sportswriter Jim MacDonald described as a gleam in the architect's eye. "Because of their size, they will be easy to three-putt."

Trent Jones's prediction that his expansive course would favor golf's big guns—Palmer; Nicklaus; reigning PGA king Bobby Nichols; and Johnny Pott, a slugger on a hot streak—failed to reach fruition. Instead, it was co-leaders Gary Player of South Africa and Australia's Kel Nagle who finished tied at 2 over par after 72 holes to force an 18-hole playoff. Nicknamed the Black Knight from Johannesburg, Player appeared to be in control with a 3-shot lead with three holes remaining. The tournament tightened when Player double-bogeyed the par-3 16th hole and Nagle, his pant legs flapping in the breeze, birdied the 17th.

The solidly built Nagle, who stunned Palmer in the 1960 British Open at St. Andrews, parred the 18th after his 20-foot attempt at birdie stopped one agonizing inch from the freshly painted white cup. In position to win and avoid a playoff, Player looked to drain a 28-foot birdie putt but left it four inches shy. Player tapped in for tie, prompting Monday afternoon's playoff between the slightly built South African and the strapping Aussie.

Putting aside any dramatics, Player started fast. He birdied 2 and 3, stayed down on his irons and, following another birdie on 8, built a 5-shot lead. He won by three strokes, 71–74, firmly tapping in his final putt and pausing over the cup in momentary prayer. He had played Trent Jones's demanding course in a most consistent fashion, carding rounds of 70, 70, 71, 71, and 71. That two foreign blokes would "shock the slammers"—as *Sports Illustrated* stated—did not surprise Player. Trent Jones's course was long, but distance, Player stated, is not so important at Bellerive as one might think.

"The foreign players learn to hit the ball straighter," Player said at Bellerive. "In our countries, we have all this rough that you just would not believe, and you have absolutely no chance unless you can hit the ball straight. So we learn to hit it straight first. Then we learn to hit a little harder."

Bellerive has come to symbolize for some the problems with Trent Jones's course architecture. Critics deride the course and contend that, as players and equipment improve with time, the problems inherent in Trent Jones's course design worsen. Hazards that were well placed in the original design now fail to trap modern players.

By the early 2000s, the game's long hitters had tamed the "Green Monster of Ladue" and rendered it a toothless tiger. Bellerive responded by hiring Rees Jones to redesign his father's work. Bellerive's facelift in 2005 was familiar to those who recognize Trent Jones's signature. By deepening the bunkers, adding undulation to the greens and lengthening the course, Rees followed his father's game plan.

A decade later, Bellerive brought back Rees to prep the "Green Monster" for the 74th PGA Championship in the spring of 2013. It was an auspicious event, Bellerive becoming just the third club in history to host four men's major championships—U.S. Open, PGA Championship, U.S. Senior Open, and Senior PGA Championship.

In August 2018, Bellerive hosted the 100th PGA Championship. The men's majors that spring and summer provided a vivid look at different approaches to course design. Augusta, Shinnecock, and Carnoustie boast strategic bunkers, intriguing green complexes, and natural topography that provide a stern test for even the elite golfers. Bellerive's rolling topography might have yielded a similarly interesting test, but it was flattened and manipulated in favor of even fairway lies. Bunkers and hazards flank every hole, forcing each golfer to follow the same line off the tee.

Critics argue that Bellerive asks golfers the same question 18 times: "Can you hit it straight?" Some dismiss this as thoughtless target golf that leaves little room for creative shot making. It's a criticism that echoes the one issued by Deane Beman at the Green Monster's unleashing in the 1965 U.S. Open.

"This (course) is lousy," said Beman, who at the time had won the U.S. Amateur title twice and the British Amateur title. "It typifies modern golf—long holes and big greens and no subtlety. I guess you would have to call me old-fashioned, but I don't see any merit in a golf course like this. It isn't a test of anything except whether you can hit the ball a mile."

Frank Beard likewise found little to enjoy as he trekked Bellerive's layout. "I don't like to play any course where it's not fun," said Beard. "I'm hitting four-woods and two-irons and three-irons all the way around."

Despite Rees's redesigns, some believe Bellerive to be less difficult than when it originally opened in 1960. Andy Johnson writes that, with each passing day, Bellerive becomes a "more distant shell of its identity than it once was." The reason being that what can be difficult today can be easier tomorrow. Advances in golf equipment and in the athletes themselves are responses to Trent Jones's layouts. The ball can be driven farther and straighter than in the past. Thus, what was once a difficult par and an easy bogey is no longer either. Such layouts eventually become obsolete and replaced by better designs.

Ironically, this was the state of the sport when Trent Jones first came on the scene, great golf courses being defenseless against the revolutionary changes in the game, "the lively ball and power-built clubs," as Talese wrote. It was a time when golf was in danger of no longer requiring the skill of Bobby Jones and Walter Hagen.

Trent Jones's philosophy in course architecture was born from being equal parts pragmatist and artist. His early work in the 1930s and 1940s rejected the hard-edged, linear designs of C.B. Macdonald and Seth Raynor, the push-up greens of his idol Donald Ross, and the penalty-laden links golf inherent in the British game. Trent Jones was influenced in part by MacKenzie and fit his golf courses into nature in a way that promoted scenic beauty and a demanding strategy.

By the late 1940s, Trent Jones recognized the advancements in player skills and equipment that made the modern aerial game and realized that many of the old courses were outdated because players could carry the once fearsome bunkers. Believing it was his mission to defend par against power golf, he was determined to add strength to a course by adding length and doubling down on hazards.

The target golf of the post–World War II PGA was all about attack and score. While most course architects ultimately want their attackers to succeed, they prefer it be done with creativity and skill.

Trent Jones saw golf architecture as a means to creating not only palaces of green but also obstacle courses that force golfers to fight for their championships in a pitched battle in which anything can happen. The desperate struggle creates the drama and heroism spectators love to watch, and that's the spectacle Trent Jones sought to create. He designed national courses so that multiple contenders could come to the 10th tee in the final round and each one have a chance to win the championship.

He has passed that belief on, thus extending his influence to new generations of course architects. Robert Trent Jones Jr. echoes his famous father when he says the success of a national championship course is seen when players hit their stride at the end of the tournament.

Born on June 20, 1906, to Welsh parents, Trent Jones and his family immigrated to East Rochester, New York, when he was five years old. He learned to play golf by caddying and occasionally caddied for Walter Hagen at the Country Club of Rochester.

By age 15, Trent Jones was a scratch golfer; at 16 he shot 69 to set a course record in the Rochester City Golf Championship. He dropped out of high school and worked as a draftsman for a railroad company. He posted the best score among amateur golfers at the Canadian Open, but to the surprise of those who knew him and considered him to be anything but a worrier, he began developing stomach ulcers and was advised to avoid tournament golf. Trent Jones remained a fine golfer, shooting in the 70s in his middle-aged years. He was said to rarely become irritated on the course, even when his ball landed in one of the many bunkers he himself had built.

Trent Jones's life changed forever in 1926 when he met Ross in New York and the two future World Golf Hall of Fame inductees became friendly. Trent Jones used his golf connections to gain a special entry to Cornell University. At the same time, he took a job as the first golf professional at Sodus Bay Heights Golf Club in the Sodus Point, New York, area. The course has since been redesigned, but the Sodus Bay Heights Golf Club has preserved two of the greens laid out by Trent Jones as the earliest examples of the young architect's designs.

To prepare for a career as a professional golf course designer, Trent Jones customized his studies to pursue his interest in course architecture. Designing his own program of study, he took courses in agronomy, landscape architecture, horticulture, hydraulics, economics, public speaking, and surveying. While at Cornell, he designed the back nine of what is now known as the University's Robert Trent Jones Golf Course. He would return to Cornell in 1954 as a now-famous alum and complete the front nine.

Concluding his studies at Cornell in 1930, Trent Jones took additional courses in art and then formed a partnership that same year with Canadian golf architect Stanley Thompson. Their firm, Thompson, Jones & Co., had offices in Toronto and New York and helped design courses in Canada, Capilano in Vancouver among them. The work of the two architects profoundly influenced strategic design in North America, helping popularize the belief that courses can undergo a complete redesign rather than the piecemeal approach that was largely accepted and even favored at that time.

Trent Jones struck out on his own in the mid-1930s and returned to America to begin building and designing local golf courses in the States. He would eventually turn course design into a multimillion-dollar business, but it didn't happen overnight. His first four clients filed for bankruptcy, and like millions of other Americans mired in the depths of the Great Depression, Trent Jones turned in 1935 to U.S. President Franklin Roosevelt and the federal government for assistance.

Coming up with what Talese called a "last-ditch idea," Trent Jones, articulate as he was, persuaded officials from the Works Progress Administration—also known as the WPA, one of FDR's alphabet agencies—to have the unemployed work not only on building bridges, dams, and roads but golf courses as well.

Using government labor supplied by the WPA, Trent Jones built six public works golf courses in four years, including Green Lakes State Park in 1936. His first big opportunity came in 1939 when he convinced Thomas J. Watson, chairman of IBM, to construct a company course. The assignment led to an introduction to golf legend Bobby Jones, Trent Jones's boyhood idol.

It was not until after World War II that Trent Jones received his first major assignment and created his initial masterpiece, collaborating with Bobby Jones in 1948 on Peachtree Golf Club in Atlanta. Because of the similarity of their names, the architect distinguished himself from the great champion by reaching back to his Old World roots and adopting the middle name Trent, from the river in England.

Trent Jones designed Peachtree with features that became his trademarks—large tees allowing for several setups; gargantuan greens that were subtly contoured and offered a variety of pin positions; hazards that were unobtrusive; and a dedication, some would say fanatical devotion, to maintaining the land's natural beauty. Swelled by expansive greens; water hazards; and large, flattened fairways, Trent Jones's courses could extend to 7,000 yards and beyond. Peachtree measured 7,400 yards when it opened in 1948.

"In terms of his career, I personally feel Peachtree was his most important (redesign)," Robert Trent Jones Jr. opines. "But Oakland Hills sealed the deal. Oakland Hills made my father. After Oakland Hills, life was better."

Trent Jones was profiled in the *New Yorker* that August by Herbert Warren Wind; features soon followed in *Time* and *Newsweek*. He became the most famous golfing personality not named Hogan. His surgery on outdated U.S. Open courses earned him renown as the "Open Doctor"; Robert Trent Jones Jr. says that, in his father's "remodeling of the old courses, which were not suitable to modern golf," Trent Jones became "synonymous with championship courses."

He also became synonymous with challenging courses. For more than 50 years following its creation, Trent Jones's horseshoe-shaped par-5 13th at the Dunes Club in Myrtle Beach has been reached in two shots just twice. His celebrated South Course at Firestone remains one of the toughest par 70s in the world, a fact made more impressive because it was unveiled in 1960 during the Kennedy administration.

Just as Donald Ross revolutionized course design decades earlier at Pinehurst, Trent Jones's plans at Peachtree led to a new breed of course layout tailored to the playing style preferred by Americans—target golf. The New World style differed significantly from that of the Old World, golfers in the British Isles favoring the bump-and-run game.

Bobby Jones was suitably impressed and requested the young architect redesign the 11th and 16th holes at famed Augusta National Golf Club, home of the Masters. Trent Jones saw that the once fierce bunkers were no longer fearsome. He added ponds so that if a shot landed in the water it's a hazard, a lost ball equaling a lost stroke. Bobby Jones agreed and put a pond in on No. 11 to the left of the green, enlarged the existing pond on 15, and altered the hole on 16.

The design of the 16th runs contrary to Trent Jones's reputation as the monster maker, the short hole considered a delight. Robert Trent Jones Jr. calls it one of the great golf holes in the world. Favoring the use of water as an additional tactical element, Trent Jones put in a pond next to Rae's Creek to make No. 16 more demanding. The result is the challenging hole Trent Jones sought—a difficult par 3 over water. With those bold strokes, Trent Jones returned to Augusta its strength while also adding scenic beauty.

Trent Jones did not invent course architecture; it only seems that he did. His course designs became famous for their innovative use of bunkers, liberal use of water hazards, artistic landscaping, and adroit placement of greens and hazards, all of which demanded a high level of strategy. Falling back on his philosophy that golf is a no-risk, no-reward proposition, Trent Jones designed challenging layouts that favored daring play.

He was a visionary, a man ahead of his time. In the years immediately following World War II, he predicted great changes in his sport. To counter the advances, Trent Jones planned his layouts accordingly.

To succeed in his groundbreaking designs, he employed three landscape architects, three draftsmen, and two civil engineers. His method of operation was a five-step process. It began with Trent Jones's arrival on the site to examine the topography, followed by further examination of the land through photographs taken overhead from an airplane. Trent Jones then took pencil and paper in hand and laid out his course design, in the process solving irrigation and drainage issues. The fifth and final phase was the construction of the land, and for this he and his staff relied heavily on earth-moving machinery. Where Ross relied on men's muscle and horse- and ox-drawn plows, Trent Jones's vast fairways were flattened by heavy machinery, his lakes dug by excavators. Mounds of earth were moved to elevate tees and greens.

Such was the case at Coral Ridge, a Fort Lauderdale, Florida, course owned by Trent Jones. He built a course on sand at Dorado Beach, Puerto Rico; ground granite to form fairways at Pevero in Sardinia; and pulverized volcanic rock into topsoil at Mauna Kea, Hawaii.

It was all part of the signature showmanship Trent Jones brought to his craft, as he designed or redesigned many of the most muscular and intimidating courses ever encountered by golf's greatest players. Baltusrol, Firestone, Hazeltine, Oak Hills, and Spyglass Hill rank among Trent Jones's most formidable layouts, feared for what the pros considered his sadistic use of giant bunkers, creeks, ponds, and undulating greens. He carved a course in the mountains near Bogota, creating a layout that extended beyond 8,000 yards to compensate for the thin air that allowed golf shots to travel 13 percent farther.

Baltusrol remains a classic example of Jones's handiwork. It had hosted a U.S. Open in 1936, and by the late 1940s the club's board of governors hoped to bring the National Open back to its course. In 1948 the board retained Trent Jones to bring Baltusrol into the modern era of steel-shafted clubs and power golf. Trent Jones would oversee the work and be accompanied by legendary Francis Ouimet, who had gained fame in 1913 as a 19-year-old U.S. champion. Ouimet would serve in an advisory capacity to Trent Jones in improving Baltusrol.

Trent Jones lengthened Baltusrol by 400 yards so that it extended to 7,000 yards, added fairway bunkers, and eliminated bunkers that could be easily carried. His most dramatic change came on hole No. 4. He strengthened it by adding some 70 yards and reshaped the bunkers behind the terraced green. To guard the green he added a now distinctive rock wall. Trent Jones's redesign resulted in the "Famous Fourth," a par 3 that not only ranks as the signature hole at Baltusrol but also one of the top-rated holes in golf. The new-look Baltusrol and its Famous Fourth opened for play in 1952, two years ahead of the U.S. Open's return to the club. Members criticized the architect for making the fourth hole too tough, prompting Jones to reply, "Let's go play the hole and see if there is anything that needs to be done."

Along with head pro Johnny Farrell; C.P. Burgess, chairman of the 1954 Open Championship; and a club member critical of his work, Trent Jones headed to the fourth tee. Flashing his 4-iron, the architect sent his ball flying directly toward its target—a hole in one.

"Gentlemen," Trent Jones stated with satisfaction, "I think the hole is eminently fair."

Trent Jones's course designs would become so much in demand that he would work on a dozen or more projects simultaneously while logging as many as 300,000 miles a year. Commercial jets became as much a part of his accoutrement as bulldozers and drafting boards.

As he circled the globe creating tees, fairways, and greens, Trent Jones became the most widely known course architect in the world, the creator of an empirical career that spanned from U.S. Presidents Coolidge to

Clinton. Along the way, he dealt with a huge bear that stole honey from his hut in Canada and a large mountain lion that escaped from a local zoo in Colorado Springs. Trent Jones encountered the lost lion on a new green at Broadmoor Country Club, leading to the ninth hole being known as "Jones' Lion Hole."

His course designs can be found on multiple continents, but he remained rooted in his native European soil. "The shepherds of Scotland began playing along these big patches of grass and dunes," he said. "And the natural bunkers and sand dunes along the linksland were our first traps. Nowadays, when we build a golf course, we're merely duplicating the natural appearance of the linksland."

Wright says Trent Jones told him once that "his entire inspiration came from Scotland." Talese wrote that Trent Jones's preference was to build a course on linksland, the sandy terrain along the coastline being perfect for picturesque courses. At the height of his powers, he was one of 15 recognized course architects in the U.S. but perhaps the only one who could trace his lineage to Scotland, the birthplace of golf. He learned firsthand from Donald Ross, who in turn had learned firsthand from Old Tom Morris. In time, Trent Jones would surpass both of his famous predecessors as the most influential course designer in golf's long history.

When Ross died suddenly in 1948 while updating his Oakland Hills layout for the 1951 U.S. Open, Trent Jones stepped in to pick up where his mentor had left off. Oakland Hills club officials handed Ross's redesigns over to Trent Jones, but the younger man was following his own vision. He issued a redesign that displayed for the first time, in full view, his showman's sense of the Shakespearean theater that is championship golf.

"[The golf establishment's] idea is that galleries are attracted by low scores," he stated in defense of his designs. "What people really want to see are great golf shots under tough conditions. The fans like low scores, but they also want great drama."

Like course architect Alister MacKenzie before him, Trent Jones believed that anything that got people talking about golf was a good thing. Wrote MacKenzie, "Golf is a game, and talk and discussion is all to the interests of the game. Anything that keeps the game alive and prevents us being bored with it is an advantage. Anything that makes us think about it, talk about it, and dream about it is all to the good and prevents the game becoming dead."

Author Geoff Shackelford stated that Trent Jones's redesign of Oakland Hills became the "acclaimed standard for golf course setup. . . . The new setup style reasoned that straight play down narrow corridors would reward the best talent." Narrow fairways would all but eliminate the low scores that embarrassed Oakland Hills when it lasted hosted the U.S. Open in 1937. Shackelford wrote that Trent Jones stretched Donald Ross's original design "like a rubber band, making it longer and tougher but also decreasing the width for play as the band stretched."

Robert Trent Jones Jr. says his father saw the older layouts as "World War I courses with trenches," being overtaken by "World War II aerial bombardment." Golfers were "attacking generals" who now "had to contend with new defenses." The new defenses at Oakland Hills, Trent Jones Jr. recalls, "included narrow targets off the tee and rolling greens."

Having played Oakland Hills, Wright says he has "no faults with that course at all. A golf course to my mind has to be easy at the start and more difficult at the finish."

Trent Jones's style was to give his courses a "signature," and no other course designer has ever produced a more indelible imprint. His style followed him from course to course and was as feared as the man determined to conquer his creations, Ben Hogan.

None of Trent Jones's hundreds of courses, however, ever inspired the sheer terror of his prized beastie—The Monster of Oakland Hills.

4

THE MONSTER OF
OAKLAND HILLS

On November 15, 1950, the sporting world awoke to an ominous warning from writer Marshall Dann in the *Detroit Free Press*.

"Winter snows," he reported, "are about to hide some fearful things which are taking place at Oakland Hills Country Club."

What was happening was that many of the natural designs of South Course creator Donald Ross were being bulldozed into oblivion by the hired hands of architect Robert Trent Jones. Fairways were shrinking fast, and just what was that going on beneath the circus tent on the 16th green of the venerated venue?

Ross had left the greens open in front to allow for the bump-and-run play of his day. Trent Jones, knowing that in an era of high trajectory shots those same greens were now vulnerable, installed steep-faced bunkers. These walls of sand allowed for small glimpses of the putting areas, which snaked between the sandpits in thin strips. The changes taking place on Maple Road in Bloomfield Hills extended even to the sand Ross had used. Because Ross had never thought it fair that a ball would stick in the face of a trap, he used fine gravel rather than sand so shots could hit and roll back. Trent Jones ordered fine sand be used to ensure that the shots would stick.

After witnessing a birdie fest at Oakland Hills in 1937, U.S. Golf Association officials planned a bloodbath for the 1951 Open. It was the first time the USGA had ever contrived to alter a course layout, and the result was a bunker-filled fiend that promised to play long—6,927 yards—and difficult.

"The original Ross design of the South Course was significantly altered by Robert Trent Jones," says Glenn Diegel. "John Oswald, the chair of the Greens Committee, had a lot to do with the setup, along with Joe Dey of the USGA."

The Monster would oblige the USGA's desire for a demanding test, baring its teeth and extending its maws from first tee to last, from sunup to sundown. Trent Jones's rebunkering and ankle-deep dense rough represented a challenge that no one, not even the best golfers of the day, could expect to conquer. The redesign was being done, Trent Jones explained, to separate contenders from pretenders, the latter being those golfers who took advantage of modern conditions to, as he said, "crash their way around easy layouts, posting scores that make them appear like great players." To counter this, Trent Jones would create a course of unsurpassed difficulty, turning the terrain of the celebrated South Course into a torture track.

"Joe Dey looked at the fact that these guys were making mincemeat of the courses, and Trent Jones saw the courses as old and passé," says Dick Howting. "The USGA got together with Trent Jones and said, 'Yeah, you're thinking the way we are. What can be done about it?' And Trent Jones said, 'I'll show you what can be done about it.'"

That Oakland Hills was making headlines again was fitting. Few golf venues have as historic a résumé as the Golden Age course situated on the largest and most prestigious club in golf-crazed Michigan. For decades, Oakland Hills Country Club has been a familiar and respected name on America's golfing landscape.

The two courses—North and South—combine to make Oakland Hills one of the biggest clubs in the Midwest. The famous South Course, designed by Ross, opened for play in 1918. Along with having one of the leading architects of the day as its designer, the South Course also boasted one of the more famous golfers of the time, Walter Hagen, as its first club pro. Hagen had a U.S. Open title to his credit and was one of the more outspoken, and some would say outrageous, sportsmen of the era.

Oakland Hills's South Course is grand in every dimension. The grounds are expansive, featuring great architecture, massive landforms, and superb settings visible in every direction. The sheer size and grandness of Oakland Hills oozes history, tradition, and championship golf in much the same manner the original Yankee Stadium oozed October baseball.

A signature of the South Course is Ross's undulating greens. A misplayed shot to the wrong part of the green can be devastating. Miss a green, and it's virtually impossible to get up and down from the wrong spot. Golfers find the land movement on the South Course to be outstanding, particularly when one remembers that Ross designed the course more than 100 years ago. Those who play the course are amazed at the way Ross utilized the natural contouring of the land. The mounding and various landforms on the five-hole stretch from holes 7 through 11 are considered nothing short of amazing.

With the U.S. Open returning to Oakland Hills for the 1951 championship, Ross knew his 1918 design was outdated. He was preparing to remodel it to accommodate the modern game when he died suddenly. Trent Jones was brought in, and by November 1950 word was spreading that the architect was creating a Frankenstein monster on Maple Road. Conjured up in the minds of the sporting public were images straight out of Colin Clive's 1931 screen portrayal of Dr. Frankenstein in his rainlashed laboratory. The only elements missing were crashing thunder and flashing lightning illuminating stormy night skies.

Fact is Oakland Hills has terrorized golfers long before Trent Jones's bulldozers arrived. In 1924, defending U.S. Open champion Bobby Jones looked to add to his hardware collection in the first U.S. Open hosted by Oakland Hills. His performance on the treacherous 10th saw him shoot 6 over on that hole alone, and paved a path for Cyril Walker to win with a 9 over 297. Bobby Jones would forever call Oakland Hills's 10th hole the toughest he ever played.

Thirteen years later, the U.S. Open returned to Oakland Hills, and the South Course frustrated another Hall of Famer. This time it was Sam Snead, who was playing in his first U.S. Open. Snead played well, but his runner-up finish to Ralph Guldahl, who shot an Open-record 281, set an unfortunate trend for Slammin' Sam. Over the course of his career, Snead will endure four second-place finishes in the Open.

The Open title was the first of two straight for Guldahl, who dominated the tour from 1937–1939. His 7 under 281 raised red flags among USGA members, particularly since it marked such a dramatic difference from the 9-over posted by Walker a decade earlier on the same par 72 course.

"One of the reasons Trent Jones came in was because Guldahl had broken the club record," Diegel says. "That's a reason the setup of the South Course was made very difficult."

Once hired, Trent Jones set about strengthening the South Course. The architect squeezed the fairways, eliminated bunkers that were out of play, and added new bunkers to narrow the tee shot landing zones and entryways to greens. Trent Jones's plan took the South Course from fewer than 90 bunkers to more than 120. He replaced Ross's fairway bunkers on 15 with one that sat in the center of the fairway's driving zone.

To create a more precarious approach shot on 16, Trent Jones edged the green onto a new peninsula in the pond. Par was reduced on 8 and 18 to 4, but the biggest penalty came from an unintended consequence— overseeding around the bunkers with rye grass to hold shots in place. The rye grew thick and fast, steadfastly holding golf balls in its grip.

Jones's radical redesign at Oakland Hills created the modern championship golf course. Trent Jones, aka Doctor Frankenstein, eventually became known as Trent Jones, the "Open Doctor." His work with The Monster led to his being hired to modernize U.S. Open courses at Baltusrol in 1952, Olympic in 1954, Oak Hill in 1956, Southern Hills in 1957, and Winged Foot in 1958.

In a 1951 interview with M. F. Drunkenbrod, golf editor of the *Detroit Times*, Trent Jones explained the reasoning behind his renovation. Oakland Hills remained large and expansive, but Trent Jones's plans made certain the South Course would play far differently than it had in 1924 and 1937.

Trent Jones transformed the former slugger's paradise into a course that placed a premium on position play and accuracy. The architect pointed to the lessons learned at Merion the year before.

"I think the Open at Merion proved that players as well as spectators enjoy a course that is a real test of golf, where every shot must be well thought out and properly executed or there will be a justified penalty," he told Drunkenbrod. "Such a course, as proved at Merion, will produce a real champion."

Trent Jones's purpose at Oakland Hills was to redesign the course to meet the new standards being set by the modern game. Because the ball and equipment had changed radically, courses had to change as well.

"We have attempted to match these changes," he stated, "with new features at strategic locations, creating hazards and pitfalls to make the current Open a test of golfing intelligence and playing skill."

That meant remodeling the South Course and removing the anti-quated features of design that no longer met the standards of modern playing conditions. Recent tests Trent Jones had made during Open Championships proved that the average carry of the entire field was 240 yards. More than 10 players carried 250 yards, but hardly any competitor carried less than 230 yards. What the numbers illustrated, Trent Jones realized, was that course features outside of those limits offered no penal value.

To remedy this, new traps placed at Oakland Hills began at the 230-yard mark. The traps flanked both sides of the fairway, except in areas where natural features made trapping unnecessary. Trent Jones also placed positional and strategic traps in the center or just off center of the fairway, the effect being to demand that a golfer be able to position his tee shot. If a golfer did not want to risk the carry of the trap, there was a target area with an ample amount of room to park a drive.

In an article for the June 1951 issue of *GOLFing* magazine, Trent Jones wrote that, "Areas of calculated risk have been set up demanding that the golfer hit accurately pre-determined target areas on the fairway and at the green or suffer the consequences."

The accent on accuracy, which carried all the way to the putting greens, did not mean that power golf would not go unrewarded if long-ball hitting was controlled. Proof of this was found in the fact that the course, with its revised par of 35, 35, and 70, measured 6,927 yards. The use of middle tees on the 8th and 18th holes reduced par from 5 to 4, and there were now only two par 5s—Nos. 2 and 12.

Favorable conditions could allow the sport's big hitters—Slammin' Sam, in particular—to get home in two on No. 2 and even on 12, though the latter was expected only rarely and only if long hitters were willing to risk the traps guarding the elevated green.

"The topography of Oakland Hills was almost ideal for the development of our plan," Trent Jones told the *Detroit Times*. He agreed with Oakland Hills club pro Al Watrous that Ross's undulating greens were still magnificent.

"The green contouring, while rugged in parts, was extremely adaptable for the new tongue or pin areas we have attached to them," Trent Jones told the *Times*. "New trapping was placed to protect certain pin areas that were open or unprotected, so missed shots will be penalized and well-played ones rewarded.

"The green contours will play a part in offsetting by some extent the benefit of the wedge and the pitching wedge, which have no doubt made the game somewhat less difficult, particularly in the hands of modern first-class professionals."

This was crucial to the redesign since, from under 90 yards, the pitching wedge was making many a missed shot turn into a relatively easy par due to the adeptness with which top pros flicked the ball up to the cup with what Trent Jones called this "magic club."

The contouring of the greens on the South Course would reduce to a point, the benefits of the stroke-saving wedge. Trent Jones noted that the green contouring at Oakland Hills is of a rolling or undulating nature and on some holes the contouring is extremely rugged. On some of these rugged greens, Trent Jones developed new tongue areas of mildly contoured design.

"While this makes the approach putt one of strain," he wrote in *GOLFing* magazine, "when one reaches the ultimate pin area the contouring has leveled out, making for a fair and not tricky putt. . . . We have tried to eliminate anything that could be considered tricky."

From the 169-yard 13th to the 216-yard 9th were a string of four testing one-shotters; the 9th would be played from a tee gouged from the hillside below the old elevated tee. It was on the 12 par 4s that The Monster's significant length would be showcased. Four of the par 4s were of the drive-and-pitch variety. Of the remaining eight holes, No. 2 would be played with a medium or long iron, or at times a wood.

The 8th, the site of Guldahl's famed 40-foot putt for eagle that ignited his run to a title in 1937, would measure 458 yards, its final stages up-hill. The 18th, owning a sharp dogleg to the right following the drive, stretched the tape to 459 yards from the tee to be used for the 1951 Open, and its green was tightly trapped.

The most famous hole on the South Course is 16, which featured a length of 405 yards and a large lake extending to the very edge of the green. The lake would have to be carried with a second shot. The 16th was where Walker forged the birdie 3 that all but clinched the title in 1924.

Trent Jones's renovations removed the possibility of driving directly toward the green as Walker did in 1924 and others managed to do in 1937. Trent Jones expanded the green by extending it out into the lake. A rugged rough would now swing in from the right, effectively changing the line from the tee.

The heavy rough was in keeping with the policy of the USGA for Open Championships. At Oakland Hills, the rough would begin at the 120-yard mark and vary in width from 35 to 50 yards bordering the fairway to the green.

In the green area the rough would be one yard off the edge of the green on the sides and back. The rough would be two inches tall for the first six feet, and five inches tall beyond that point. In the two weeks prior to the tournament, the rough would be allowed to grow to whatever length it may reach during that time.

The 10th hole, which brought about Bobby Jones's downfall, was outfitted with two new traps. This made the hole that doomed the legendary champion even more difficult for the 1951 field.

Trent Jones felt the final four holes at Oakland Hills not only showed the strength of the finishing holes but also provided a general idea of the character of the overall changes.

The 15th was a par 4, 392 yards in length with a dogleg to the left and a trap in the middle of the fairway 250 yards from the championship tee. "This is not a carry trap," Trent Jones wrote, "but primarily a position trap and if the wind is against, it is most unlikely that anyone in the field would carry this trap."

The smart position for which to play on this hole was, Trent Jones believed, to the right-hand side of this trap, although a path was offered between the trap and the woods and an advantage could be claimed by traveling this route. It was, however, as Trent Jones cautioned, extremely dangerous.

The second shot to the green on 15 would be a 3- or 4-iron for a normal hitter and a 5- or 6-iron for a long hitter. The second shot to the crowned green, an inverted saucer-style green, is an exacting one. The green was completely surrounded by traps, and a controlled shot to stay on the green would be required.

The par-4 16th doglegged slightly from left to right. If a shot were missed to the right and went in the rough, Trent Jones said, it was unlikely that any golfer would attempt to carry the water from such a deep rough. Instead, the shot would have to be played short and to the left-hand side.

The green on 16 was a peninsula extending out into the water. Two-thirds of it was protected by water; the left-hand side was completely clear of the water. The left side and the back of the green were both surrounded by traps. The three pin positions most difficult on the 16th are the back right, front right, and front middle of the green. The green position with the mound, Trent Jones wrote, is difficult due to the extreme hazard of going into the water either in the front or on the right-hand side.

"The shot," he declared, "will be a 3- or 4-iron for the normal hitter and a 5-, 6-, or 7-iron for an extremely long hitter. However, with the wind against, the shot can jump two clubs. This will probably be one of the most dramatic holes on the course, as the penalty for going into the water is so severe."

The 17th hole was a par 3, 194 yards, and was called by Trent Jones "one of the finest short holes on the course." The tee was low and the green a good 30 feet above the tee. For most of the Open field, the 17th would require a 3- or 4-wood, and the long hitter a 2- or 1-iron.

The green was protected on all sides by traps, and the key to 17 was the contouring and elevation. The front left-hand side was slightly crowned, falling into the valley on the back left-hand side. The far right-hand side was a terraced-tongue area, guarded by a trap on the back left and protected by a trap on the right.

The 18th, a par 4, measured 459 yards. "A truly great finishing hole," Trent Jones wrote. "I think the championship will be won or lost on this hole."

Because of the tee shot, the 18th was likely the most difficult par 4 at Oakland Hills. The elbow character of the hole demanded the drive off the tee be straight, long, and positioned in order to cut down the distance of the second shot.

The second shot had to be carried onto the green; the bunkering in front prevented it from being bounced onto the green. Trent Jones believed that even a long hitter armed with a 3- or 4-iron would have to play an exacting second shot. The normal hitter, he thought, would play a 3- or 4-wood.

"The green is elevated about 15 feet above the target area," Trent Jones wrote, "and while the key trap is at the front left-hand side of the green, the trapping at the right-hand side will catch any shots that are slightly pushed. The green contouring is undulating in character and the pin positions, both left and right, when the green is fast will make for difficult and trying putting under the strain of a championship. This is undoubtedly a great finishing hole."

He noted that Al Watrous had hit hundreds of balls on the remodeled South Course to prove its values were testing but fair. Privately, Trent Jones told Watrous that if Oakland Hills put their pins as close to the edge of the greens as they did at Augusta for the Masters, "nobody would break par."

"In a nutshell," Trent Jones declared, "Oakland Hills has been redesigned with target areas to be hit from the tee and by second shots on long holes and pin areas to be aimed for at the green. The truly great and accurate shots will earn their just rewards. The slightest miss or badly executed shot will be punished.

"A great champion," he finalized, "should emerge."

Great champions from golf's past agreed. Gene Sarazen called The Monster the "greatest test of golf I've seen in a long time."

Byron Nelson concurred. "This is the way an Open course should be," he stated, albeit from the relative safety of retirement. "It isn't the fearful, tricky thing I'd heard about, but a fair and honest course that will force a man to both play well and think well if he plans on winning."

In his article, Trent Jones wrote that Tour veteran Jim Ferrier, having recently played Oakland Hills, believed the winner of the championship will have played more good shots and fewer bad ones than the winner of any Open Championship he had competed in.

The comments made by Sarazen, Nelson, and Ferrier came in the spring of 1951 and highlighted a public relations push aimed at denying reports that The Monster was unplayable. The previous December, the USGA had briefly suspended construction on Oakland Hills amid reports that Trent Jones's revisions were too severe.

When the contenders for the U.S. Open arrived early at Oakland Hills for practice rounds and encountered The Monster for the first time, their complaints escalated into a crescendo.

"It's a nightmare," said Snead. "Awful. We've got to play it but we don't have to like it."

"Sam Snead was irate," Howting says. "He was flipping out. It was like someone pulled a fast one on him."

Noting the narrow fairways, which in some areas were cinched to a mere 19 yards, Cary Middlecoff told reporters, "You have to walk down these fairways single-file."

Middlecoff was hardly exaggerating. Writer Frank Hannigan, addressing The Monster's extremely narrow drive zones, stated that in some areas these zones "were much less than the general minimum widths—35 to 40 yards—called for in the USGA Championship Manual which guides clubs in preparing for USGA events."

As was his custom when it came to majors and a course he had never played before, Ben Hogan examined it closely to see what obstacles he would seek to avoid. For days he studied The Monster like a scientist studying a new species, finally breaking his silence to speak with reporters.

"First, off the tee there is so little room to land shots out in the real driving range," Hogan said. "Second, if you do manage to land on the fairway, real work is cut out for you to hit the green. Finally, those greens are so large that you're more apt to three putt than two putt."

On top of that, the course "handicaps long hitters by taking away the premium that they've been working for all their lives.

"I contend that straightness and distance off the tees should pay off. But here there is no premium for 275-yard drives no matter how perfectly they're played. You're simply bound to catch trouble on long hits."

The reigning U.S. Open champion declared The Monster the toughest 18 holes he'd ever seen. "If I had to play this damn course every week," Hogan snapped, "I'd get into a new business."

Lacing a long iron over the 18th green during a practice round, Hogan was heard to mutter, "No one can play some of these holes."

Howting says Hogan wondered what was up with Trent Jones and the USGA. "It was almost like they did [the redesign] to him."

Hogan played five practice rounds at Oakland Hills, taking mental photographs to map out his strategy. "He was meticulous in his visualization of his shots," Bruce Devlin recalls. Hogan then steered his Cadillac to a secluded practice range at Bloomfield Hills Country Club to practice hitting high, floppy fades with his 3-iron. As far as Hogan was concerned, Oakland Hills was a driver and 3-iron layout.

Frank Walsh, who had shared the lead after the second round of the 1937 U.S. Open at Oakland Hills, agreed with Hogan. "There aren't many players who have long, high trajectory shots such as Oakland Hills will require in wood play," Walsh wrote in a companion piece to Trent Jones's article in *GOLFing* magazine. "The only players I've seen who were great in this sort of shot are Bob Jones, Bob MacDonald, Bob Locke and Chick Harbert."

Providing a player's viewpoint of Trent Jones's Monster, Walsh penned his thoughts on the revamped South Course:

"There isn't a let-up hole on the course. Seven of the 12 par-4 holes measure over 437 yards. The drives have to be placed in areas about 40 yards wide and trapped from 225 to 260 yards. That trapping calls for every drive being on the beam."

Walsh described the fairways as beautiful firm turf and not the type that allows much run. He thought a high-carrying tee shot that drops lightly to the ground would be required. High second shots would be needed to beat the green's close-in trapping.

Walsh opined that the four par-3 holes were the greatest quartet of par-3 holes on any course. "They'll call for everything from perfect 3-iron shots to perfect drives," Walsh wrote. "Wind will change them a lot between rounds. There are two brutal par 4s on the back nine, the 11th and the 16th. Al Watrous says the 18th is the fiercest hole on the course."

Both Walsh and Watrous believed the greens presented a serious challenge. "When you reach the greens," Watrous said of Oakland Hills, "that's when the game begins."

Walsh thought the large, undulating greens would leave players with a "nerve-shattering" experience. The greens were of uniformly fine texture, wrote Walsh, but the undulations were going to demand a "mighty fine reading."

Ten of the greens were elevated and called for golfers to shoot up to the target. There were no blind holes, Walsh said, "but there may be some blind shots if a fellow doesn't get his woods long and straight."

Hogan told a Denver sportswriter after his practice rounds that the ideal golfer to tame The Monster was "an unusually short driver and an unusually long iron player." Unfortunately, Hogan added, he didn't know of any golfer who fit that description.

"I'm not a machine, only a golfer," Hogan said, "and Oakland Hills was designed for some kind of super golfer that I've never seen yet. I honestly feel this is the hardest golf course in the world. I haven't played them all, but this is the toughest I've ever seen."

In May 1951, sportswriter and Hogan friend Dan Jenkins found the champion hitting balls on the 11th fairway at Colonial. True to form, Hogan only nodded at Jenkins's presence and didn't speak until the writer noticed him doing something he considered rather strange, punching choked-down 3-irons some 155 yards.

"What the hell is *that*?" Jenkins asked.

Not even bothering to look up, Hogan replied, "I need it at Oakland Hills."

To Jenkins, this was an example of Hogan's all-encompassing preparation. Robert Trent Jones Jr. offers another example, recalling a story about Hogan being on the practice range late one afternoon at the U.S. Open. An observer noted that, rather than hitting his controlled fade, Hogan was drawing the ball. Asked about it, Hogan picked up a map of the course, what architects call a "route plan." Without a word he pointed out the numerous holes that were routed from right to left and would require precisely the shot Hogan was perfecting. "His in-depth study of the route plan," Jones Jr. says, "gave him an edge even before the tournament began."

Hogan, ironically, is said to have unwittingly contributed to the making of The Monster. He was practicing his putting near Oakland Hills's rambling clubhouse during the renovation when Trent Jones asked his opinion of the newly installed fairway bunkers on No. 10.

"Too close," said Hogan, puffing on his ever-present cigarette.

Seeing Trent Jones's skepticism, Hogan grabbed his club, teed up, and stroked a drive over the farthest hazard. According to the story, Trent Jones ordered a new bunker be placed at the exact spot where Hogan's drive had landed. In his later years, Trent Jones couldn't recall if that incident actually happened, but if the tale is true, it falls in line with the Open Doctor's diligent study of the pro's driving distances.

Horrified pros, perhaps mindful of Phil Harris's hit song at the time, *The Thing*, took to calling Trent Jones's beastie "The Thing." Other names for the course were "Frankenstein," the "Oakland Ogre," and the "green monster." One sports editor declared it a "golfing rattlesnake."

The first official tee shot had yet to be fired, but The Monster already had the world's top golfers going on the defensive.

5

THE U.S. OPEN
Tiptoeing through Hell

It is the most treacherous of golf's tests, four rounds filled with wasp-waisted fairways; coffee-quick greens; rough that is both thick and dense; and enough bunkers, traps, and hazards to make the U.S. Open an annual battle between man and nature.

"Playing in the U.S. Open," golfer Jerry McGee said, "is like tippy-toeing through hell."

Winged Foot, Shinnecock Hills, Hazeltine, Chambers Bay, Oakmont, Olympic Club. These are the names of U.S. Open courses that have hammered their would-be conquerors and thundered through time. Of golf's four majors, none is more known for a higher degree of difficulty than the one held in mid-June every year.

"Champagne" Tony Lema said playing in the U.S. Open was "torture." *Sports Illustrated* called it "a tournament that knots the nerves and strangles the will as no other golf event can." The U.S. Open has taken the measure of men who rank among the sport's best ever. Bobby Jones, American golf's first celebrity champion, said, "Nobody ever wins the National Open. Somebody else just loses it." The U.S. Open plays so tough it jangles the nerves of many golfers and outright intimidates others. The history of the tournament is that it often breeds in competitors the conviction that they have to play at a nearly superhuman level to succeed.

Jack Nicklaus is well aware of this, having lived to tell the tale of the "Massacre at Winged Foot" in 1974 and Hazeltine four years earlier. "A difficult golf course eliminates a lot of players," Nicklaus said. "The U.S. Open flag eliminates a lot of players. Some players just weren't meant to win the U.S. Open. Quite often, a lot of them know it."

For the Golden Bear, the sound of golfers complaining about the difficulties of a U.S. Open course was also the sound of men who, if not already beaten, were talking themselves out of competing.

If the Masters, played in the Deep South amid the soft spring breezes of April, fragrant azaleas, and pretty pink dogwoods, can be compared to a relatively comfortable cruise, the U.S. Open, warred beneath a scorching sun, is comparable to a crew being battered by a sea witch. Stories of the disasters that have befallen golfers in the green mansions of the U.S. Open are often eerie, even haunting. Survivors of par at these treacherous courses can be scarce. The U.S. Open, it's been said, does not surrender its dead.

Winged Foot in 1974 was a prime example. The opening round on the West Course in Mamaroneck, New York, a suburb that sits northeast of New York City, saw not a single player break par. It became the most infamous massacre on U.S. soil since the Little Big Horn. When it had mercifully ended, Hale Irwin had two-putted on 18 to close out a 7 over 287. Irwin's total was the second-highest winning score in relation to par of any U.S. Open since World War II, Julius Boros having gone 9 over in 1963 in windswept conditions at the Country Club in Brookline, Massachusetts.

The four former U.S. Open champions who survived the cut finished double digits over par. Arnold Palmer played 12 over, Gary Player was plus-13, Nicklaus was 14 over, and Johnny Miller, the 1973 champion who decimated Oakmont in the previous year's final round, limped home at a shocking 22 over par. Miller delivered a parting shot at Winged Foot, calling the rough "ridiculous."

Winged Foot's West Course had become the Wild West. The firm greens confounded the field of 149 players. Nicklaus tapped his first putt of the tournament 30 feet past the hole for a bogey, then followed with bogeys on the next three holes, and was never a factor. The Golden Bear, it's been said, went white faced at the sight of his first putt speeding off the green and murmured that he had never seen such fast greens. Asked his assessment of the finishing holes, Nicklaus was only half-kidding when he stated that the "last 18 of them are very difficult."

Miller struggled early as well. Friday morning saw his ball land in a bunker and require four swings to escape. The demanding setup, with its deep rough and fast greens, produced an average score of 78 in the opening round.

"We were all dumbfounded by how difficult it was," said Irwin. "It was easily the most difficult golf course I have ever seen."

The gritty, hardworking Irwin was known for taming tough courses. Along with winning at Winged Foot, his two prior victories on the PGA Tour had come at Harbour Town, a course called by Dan Jenkins "one of the meanest around."

A former Colorado football player, Irwin's winning strategy was as straight as the putt on No. 9 that put the bespectacled underdog in front.

"I knew the course was difficult," said Irwin, whose final round 73 was 10 strokes over the previous year's total posted by Miller. "I couldn't expect to stay under par. So I decided to play for par and let the others make the mistakes."

Irwin decided something else as well. He would make peace with the beast. "Mr. Monster, you're a good guy, let's get along," he muttered under his breath. "I'm not going to be able to tear you apart, so don't tear me apart, okay?"

Having made his pact with the course, Irwin relied on a hail of low-burner shots. Fellow golfer Lanny Wadkins predicted the man who had a "hole worn through the face of his two-iron" would win Winged Foot. The clerkish-looking Irwin joined a distinguished list of U.S. Open champions who had barely managed to find their way through the clubhouse door but emerged a champion. The list included 20-year-old Francis Ouimet, who stunned Britain's Harry Vardon and Ted Ray at Brookline, Massachusetts, in 1913. Ouimet's win created front-page headlines across the country and helped turn golf from a sport for the wealthy to a weekend obsession for the masses.

The masses at Winged Foot turned out to cheer Palmer, the aging King of an earlier era who was seeking to reclaim the magic once his. Followed by a gallery of 20,000 fans, many of whom made up the foot soldiers of the famed "Arnie's Army," Palmer played as if he was determined to turn back the clock to his halcyon days. His Army responded to Arnie's every move—hitching his britches in his trademark fashion, slashing his way out of sand traps, and ramming home birdie putts.

"Arnie's got it going!" a member of his Army exclaimed.

The 44-year-old legend, looking to fight his way free of the most depressing and enduring slump of his storied career, shouldered his way into a first-place tie with Player, Irwin, and Raymond Floyd at the end of the second round and grabbed the lead in the third with two quick birdies. The graying King was leading the charge to reclaim his crown, and the extraordinary drama was heightened by Palmer's pairing with Player, the little Black Knight from Johannesburg who had won the Masters in April and was harboring a glorious dream of a Grand Slam summer.

For a time during the electric third round the Palmer–Player pairing shared the leaderboard. But as the afternoon wore on Palmer and Player both began to fade. Arnie missed the green on 8 and bogeyed, and he and Player struggled off the tee on 9 and bogeyed again. Palmer sprayed his shots into the woods, into the bunkers, into the ankle-deep rough. Playing with his old panache, Palmer hung in and hung on to save par. He made some putts, missed others, sailed shots over awestruck spectators, and snap hooked drives into the trees before finally finishing bogey-bogey and falling back with a disappointing 73.

Dressed in his trademark black polo shirt and black pants, Player was likewise looking to regain his championship touch, though it was of a much more recent vintage. He had flashed his Masters-winning form in the first round at Winged Foot when he fired a 70 to take an early edge. But his winning ways deserted the Black Knight in a disastrous back nine in the third round that slammed the door on his Grand Slam hopes.

"I'd have to say," Player remarked, "that it was probably the toughest test of golf that I've ever seen."

Tom Watson, a 24-year-old product of Stanford University, made his move on 13 and emerged at day's end as the 54-hole leader with a 1 under 69 that put him at 213. Irwin's 71 left him 1 back at 214, and fate seemed to favor him considering Watson's history in majors. In his brief, two-year pro career, the red-haired, freckle-faced kid had twice held a tournament lead heading into the final round before losing.

History repeated itself on Open Sunday, Watson being brought down with a 6-over 41 on the back nine. Palmer played on. He snaked in a 40-foot birdie putt on 10 to reenergize his Army, and, just when it looked like Arnie was gearing up for one final charge, the Palmer of old gave way to an old Palmer, bogeying three of his last six holes.

Despite nearly collapsing from the sheer strain of it all, Irwin saved par on 17 and secured his victory on 18 with his last low burner of the tournament—this one settling 25 feet from the flag—and finished with a tap-in.

Legend has it that the USGA, embarrassed by Miller's electrifying final round 63 the year before, took measures to "trick up" the course. The USGA denied it, and when asked if the organization was trying to humiliate the game's greatest golfers, Sandy Tatum, chairman of the Championship Committee, shook his head.

"No," Tatum stated, "we're trying to identify them."

What the Massacre at Winged Foot identified, particularly in the public's mind, is the USGA's practice of turning challenging courses into monsters and playing them as par 70s. Palmer, seeking his first major title in a decade, finished tied for fifth, making this his final top-five finish in a major. The Massacre at Winged Foot also claimed Ken Venturi, the celebrated former champion renowned for overcoming brutal conditions. Venturi missed the cut and never again played in a major championship.

Egos weren't the only things bruised in the 1974 U.S. Open. Sam Snead suffered a broken rib in his final practice prior to the tournament teeing off and withdrew. Lee Trevino, Billy Casper, Gene Littler, and Tony Jacklin were former champs who failed to make the cut. Boros, a man who had won two U.S. Opens and was known for conquering tough courses, faltered with a first-round 78 and withdrew due to injury.

"I just didn't play well enough to handle this course," Trevino said before departing the disaster and heading home to El Paso, Texas. "It's the hardest course I've ever seen."

Winged Foot course superintendent Ted Horton said the 1974 Open offered the most consistent, deepest rough in tournament history to that point. He and his crew took pride in that this was the first Open to have uniform six-inch rough.

Miller said the rough actually ranged from 6 to 10 inches. Irwin picked up the grass near the bunkers behind the second green and believed it to be well over a foot. Just a tangled mess, Irwin thought. Horton said golfers had trouble finding their ankles, much less the ball. In a practice round, Jerry McGee drove his tee shot into the rough on 18. Standing in the rough, McGee took a full swing and barely advanced the ball three feet.

Jenkins wrote that the "best golfers in the world . . . were being beaten to death by a marvelous old course."

The U.S. Open, Jenkins added, came down to "which poor soul could merely survive." Despite its picturesque scenery—stone clubhouse, stately elms, and elevated greens—Jenkins wrote that the scenery that will best be remembered is "all of those dead bodies strewn across the suburban landscape."

A decade earlier, in the scorching summer of 1964, the fires of hell had seemingly set ablaze the already brooding, brutal Blue Course at Congressional Country Club in Bethesda, Maryland, when the U.S. Open's Championship Saturday teed off on June 20. A torrid heat wave engulfed the East Coast, creating extremely dangerous conditions as golfers and the galleries tramped the longest layout in U.S. Open history to that point—a staggering 7,053 yards.

Pittsburgh Post-Gazette sportswriter Phil Gundelfinger called Congressional a "long, tough monster." Alfred Wright wrote in *Sports Illustrated*'s U.S. Open preview that he expected golfers by tournament's end to compare Congressional to the original "Monster" of Oakland Hills. Wright likened the demands that Congressional put on golfers to those the English Channel puts on swimmers—"the strength and endurance to make the trip and the courage to persevere when the going seems too rough."

Palmer, one of the pre-tournament favorites, believed the Blue Course to be a "long, tough track." Blistered by blowtorch-like conditions, the hilly par-70 layout played even longer and tougher than expected, in the process taking a terrible toll on golfers and galleries alike.

Advised by doctors to withdraw from the tournament between rounds on Saturday, the underdog Venturi's drama-filled day ran the gamut of emotions. Photographers' cameras clicked away furiously when a missed putt on 18 in the morning round caused the frustrated and physically weakened Venturi to bury his face in his hands. Later that afternoon, and on that same 18th green, the sweat-streaked Venturi was the very picture of elation after he sank his final putt to earn the improbable victory.

Venturi's comeback at Congressional stands with Ben Hogan's Miracle at Merion in 1950 and Tiger Woods's 2008 victory over Rocco Mediate as three of the more inspiring stories in the storied history of the U.S. Open.

Intense heat had created a literal trial by fire. Golfer Tony Lema, though only 30 years old, told reporters he didn't know how he was going to make it through 18 holes. Fellow golfer Bob Rosburg admitted he almost fainted on the 17th tee, which sat in a hollow where the heat was banked at well over 100 degrees. The searing sun sent more than 100 "heat cases" to the Red Cross first aid tent near the first tee.

United Press International reported that it "looked like a disaster area in the Red Cross tent near the first tee as sun-beaten spectators stretched out in the shade on cots."

Venturi had won 10 times from 1957–1960, and challenged for Masters titles in 1956, 1958, and 1960. Injuries suffered in an automobile accident in 1961, followed by a back injury in 1962, put his game, and his life, in a tailspin. By 1964, he was estranged from his first wife, Conni, and nearly broke financially. He seemed a forgotten figure on the PGA Tour, not having played in the U.S. Open for three straight years and failing to receive an invitation to Augusta in 1964.

Down on his luck and depressed over his career, the 32-year-old San Franciscan considered quitting golf and returning to selling cars. Venturi's decision was delayed two weeks prior to the Open when Bill Jennings, owner of the National Hockey League's New York Rangers, invited him to Westchester Country Club in Rye, New York.

Venturi finished third and cashed a $6,400 check that dwarfed his Tour earnings of $3,800 from the entire previous year. Surviving a local sectional qualifier, the former Masters runner-up gained entry into the Open field.

Two weeks later, in mid-June, Venturi arrived at Congressional. In that era, golfers didn't travel with their caddies but had caddies assigned to them via a draw. When Venturi drew Congressional's top caddie,

William Ward, he felt for the first time that destiny could be taking a hand. Playing 7,053 yards, the Congressional in 1964 was the longest par 70 to that point in U.S. Open history.

Raymond Floyd, who was 21 years old when he played the final 36 holes with Venturi at Congressional, recalled pulling on a fresh shirt and having it soaked with sweat in the short walk from the hotel to the car. Congressional Country Club members remembered the heat being so suffocating they struggled to catch their breath; cold water was passed throughout the gallery to keep fans hydrated.

Tied for fourth on the leaderboard after 36 holes, Venturi caught fire at the start of the third round, draining a birdie putt from 15 feet. "Let's get after it," he thought.

Playing as hot as the sunbaked fairways, the temperatures of which rose to an estimated 130 degrees, Venturi shot a sizzling 66 in the third round to move to within two shots of Tommy Jacobs, whose second-round 64 tied the championship record.

Three rounds in the dangerous heat had left Venturi not only severely dehydrated but near death. He told Floyd, "I don't think I'll make it." Venturi grew disoriented amid the scorched conditions. He missed an 18-inch par putt on 17 and by 18 was visibly shaking as he missed a three-foot birdie. He dropped his putter on 18 and struggled to retrieve it. He wobbled, and golfer Jay Hebert worried that Venturi might collapse.

Now suffering real trauma, Venturi had to be escorted back to the clubhouse, where he was packed in cold towels and fed cool water and 18 salt tablets. Lying on the floor next to his locker, Venturi was visited by Dr. John E. Everett, a Congressional member.

"Ken, I recommend you don't go out there. It could be fatal."

"I'm already dying," Venturi gasped. "I have no place else to go."

Pulling on his white linen cap, Venturi ventured back out, staggering into the steamy, stifling heat of Open Saturday; 1964 would mark the last time the final two rounds of the U.S. Open would be scheduled for the same day. Venturi had no memory of walking to the first tee on the fourth round and no memory, in fact, of the front nine, where he fought Jacobs for the lead. Venturi's birdie putt on 9 brought an explosion of cheers from the sweltering gallery, and it's from this point on that Venturi's memory finally returns.

Venturi's determined demeanor, his cap, white polo shirt, gray slacks, and black shoes stirred memories of Hogan at Merion in 1950. Ken's struggle in the steamy cauldron made for compelling viewing, both for those in the gallery and for a nationwide television audience transfixed by the human drama unfolding in front of them. For many, the question wasn't would Venturi win, but would he survive?

Even Venturi had his doubts. He recalled thinking, "Am I going to make it?" Visibly distressed from dehydration, which caused him to lose eight pounds, Venturi labored through the final round. He slowed his pace of play and told Joseph C. Dey, the executive director of the USGA, "If you won't slap a two-stroke penalty on me, Joe, I'm going to slow down."

Spurred onward by playing partner Raymond Floyd, Venturi took it one shot at a time. His mantra became "Fairway, green; fairway, green. Get through the next shot." Some of those shots, Floyd said, Venturi had no business making. "It was destiny," Floyd stated.

Deafening applause followed Venturi to the 18th—"Loudest applause I've ever heard," he said. Walking the fairway for the final time that day led to an emotionally charged scene, Venturi traversing the scorched earth. Had the fairway not been downhill, he doubted he could have made the trek.

Venturi's final putt caused him to throw off his exhaustion long enough to thrust his arms skyward toward the blazing sun. Two weeks removed from quitting the game, Venturi was now on top of the golf world.

"My God," he thought. "I won the Open."

Venturi beat the heat, and 44 years later, Woods battled a balky knee injury that nearly took him to the turf at Torrey Pines. The San Diego spread stretched to 7,643 yards, the longest in major championship history.

Woods had undergone arthroscopic knee surgery several months prior to arriving at Torrey Pines. He had ruptured his anterior cruciate ligament in July of the previous year. He knew he was doing further damage to his knee by continuing to play on it, but decided against surgery when his doctors told him he needed to have the knee reconstructed. Planning to play in the majors, Woods opted for what he called a "cleanup job."

Tiger took time off following the surgery, and when he came back was doing a photo shoot. As he hit a downhill lie, Woods cracked his tibia. Doctors told him he was through for the year, but Woods wasn't so sure. Having competed from July 2007 into 2008 with a torn ACL, he had become accustomed to playing in pain.

Vice president for TGR Ventures Rob McNamara was a regular companion to Tiger on the Tour and spent the week before the U.S. Open with Woods. Tiger's left knee, McNamara said, was "toast." Once Woods fractured his tibia, his practice time was limited to hitting one shot, sitting in the golf cart for a time, and then hitting another shot. He would do this for 45 minutes. According to McNamara, only Tiger's willpower got him through this painful period.

Woods's injuries were known, but the full extent of them was not. Overcoming a bum knee and broken leg—the double stress fracture in his left tibia and torn ACL in his left knee wouldn't be revealed to the public until two days after the tournament—Woods winced in discomfort, bent over in agony following several tee shots, and limped around the course. It reminded golf historians of Hogan at Merion and Venturi at Congressional.

Tiger's Torrey story began inauspiciously with a double bogey in the tournament's first round. Because his injuries made it impossible for him to warm up properly, Woods would double bogey the opening hole in three of the four rounds. At the turn, Tiger was 1 under par, but a double bogey on 14 left him at 1 over 72 and tied for 18th place. Woods's pain was so apparent that many observers, including USGA President Jim Vernon, were amazed that Tiger could finish the round.

Gareth Lord, the caddie for Robert Karlsson, was near Tiger on the 18th tee when he heard Wood's knee crunch after blistering a drive down the fairway. Competitors like Brandt Snedeker noticed Woods wincing on every other shot. Others, like Adam Scott, wondered if it wasn't more a matter of Tiger trying to psyche out other players.

What no one knew was that Woods hadn't walked 18 holes in the two months since finishing second at the Masters. Also not known at the time was that Tiger's orthopedic doctor had advised him not to play because of the risk of permanent damage. Woods would have none of it. Torrey Pines was personal to Tiger. It was the first professional tournament he had ever attended, his father taking him to the San Diego Open Invitational hosted by singer Andy Williams. Torrey Pines is where Woods learned about pro golf; he has fond memories of watching Andy Bean, John Cook, and Mark O'Meara. Because going to Torrey Pines would be like going home, Woods was determined to play the 2008 Open.

Tiger's comeback began in the second round, but it took time. Starting on the 10th, he bogeyed two of the first three holes and added two more bogeys in the final holes on the back nine. It was then that Woods grabbed destiny by the throat. Five birdies led to a 30 on the front nine that was one stroke more than the U.S. Open record for nine holes carded by Vijay Singh in 2003 at Olympia Fields Country Club in Illinois, and by Neal Lancaster in 1995 at Shinnecock Hills in New York and again in 1996 at Oakland Hills.

The tournament turned even more magical on the final holes of the third round. As ocean waves from the Pacific crashed on the shores below, Tiger roared back with a stunning six-hole blitz, carding an eagle on the 13th and 18th and a birdie on the 17th. It led to Woods leading or being tied for the 54-hole lead in a major for the 14th time in his career. Karlsson called Woods's electrifying round the "freakiest" he'd ever seen.

"That back nine was unbelievable," he said. "Just mayhem around us."

Sunday's final round saw Woods and countrymen Rocco Mediate and Lee Westwood jockey for position. The bright, beautiful afternoon offered both a spectacular stage and the kind of high drama reserved for great theater. It came down to Tiger, still gritting his teeth from the pain, and Westwood needing to sink birdie putts on the 18th to force a playoff with Mediate on Monday.

As the poa annua surface tended to get bumpy late in the day, Woods, wearing the iconic bright red polo he reserved for Open Sunday, and Westwood both needed to negotiate tough terrain. Westwood's 15-footer failed to fall. Facing a testing, downhill putt, Tiger fell back on his experiences playing on poa annua growing up. Knowing the green would be bouncy, he changed his stroke, hitting it more with his hands. His 12-footer on the 72nd hole "bounced, hobbled, and wobbled" in the words of fellow golfer Mark Calcavecchia. Tiger thought the ball took forever to break because it was bouncing most of the time, but it found the bottom of the cup.

"The legend of Tiger Woods," Calcavecchia said with some amazement. Woods provided the punctuation for his epic putt, punching the ocean air in celebration.

Tiger's tale continued in the playoff. He rode a par and two birdies on holes 5–7 to an early two-stroke advantage. He increased his lead to three on the 10th before Rocco rallied with birdies on 14 and 15. The latter put Mediate up by a stroke, and Woods was once again left needing a birdie on 18 to tie and force another playoff, this time in sudden death. Tiger's birdie putt tied Mediate at even-par 71, and his two putts in sudden death parred No. 7 and produced his third U.S. Open title and 14th major championship.

It had taken 91 holes, 19 in Monday's extended playoff, but Tiger had triumphed. "I think this one is the best," Woods said, "just because of all the things I had to deal with."

Like Hogan, Venturi, Irwin, Nicklaus, Palmer, and others, Tiger's defining moment had been determined amid the high drama of the U.S. Open. Two-time major champion Zach Johnson, who had missed the cut at Torrey Pines, was at home watching the tournament on TV and was struck by what he saw.

"Tiger hobbling, hobbling, hobbling, occasionally hitting a good shot, making a putt," Johnson said. "Hobbling, hobbling, hobbling . . ."

Tiger had defied his painful injuries, and when it was finally over it was indeed the wobbly Woods who was the last man standing at Torrey Pines. Winning the U.S. Open on a broken leg and torn ACL had pushed one of golf's all-time greatest champions to his absolute limit. "I couldn't have gone much farther," Woods said.

Two-time major champion and TV analyst Dottie Pepper was one of four major champions—along with Woods, Phil Mickelson, and Yani

Tseng—inside the ropes at Torrey Pines. Her up-close and personal view prompted Pepper to consider Tiger's triumph "real Superman stuff. One of the greatest achievements in the history of sports."

Even taking into account the superstar status of Jones, Nelson, Hogan, Palmer, Nicklaus, and Woods, history has shown that more often than not the real star of the U.S. Open is the course itself.

Such was the case at Shinnecock Hills in 2018. Just as the Massacre at Winged Foot followed Miller's footloose and fancy-free performance at Oakmont the year before, so Shinnecock Hills provided a bloodbath to follow Justin Thomas's historic 63 at Erin Hills in the 2017 U.S. Open. The carnage that occurred at Shinnecock Hills was romanticized by many as how the U.S. Open should be.

The tone was established early. Accomplished amateur and promising pro player Scott Gregory suffered through a 92 in the opening round, the first round over 90 in the U.S. Open in the past 16 years. Phil Mickelson sought to play a low wedge and instead sent it through the back of the green. Rory McElroy struggled to blast his ball more than three feet from the high fescue; he also sent an approach shot into a bunker. Jordan Spieth missed a putt from four feet and attempted to hit a wedge onto the green on 11 only to have the ball roll back after he couldn't mark it in time.

Traditionalists celebrated the slugfest between the current crop of top golfers and a course considered one of the country's best. Shinnecock Hill's architectural greatness, topography, and routing force so many different types of shots that it makes for a fascinating test. Add in the type of whipping winds that whistled through the environs on opening day, and conditions became ripe for the battering that golfers absorbed. Even Tiger was not immune. Woods looked to putt on the first green only to have the ball roll back to his feet, a shot reminiscent of Nicklaus's first putt at Winged Foot.

By afternoon's end, Shinnecock Hills had become a bigger story than those playing it, just as it had a decade earlier at the 2004 U.S. Open. The field was unanimous in its criticism of the USGA, complaining that, because the greens had not been adequately watered early in the day, they were crusty, dry, and so fast they were unfair. Players believed the USGA let the greens get away from them. Their beliefs were backed up by the sight of tee shots, chip shots, and putts that failed to stay on the green.

A score of 6 under after two rounds led the tournament, causing USGA officials to toughen up the course prior to the weekend rounds to ensure par. The course wasn't watered before the third round and was left to dry out even further prior to the fourth round. Shinnecock Hills became nearly unplayable. Not only did every golfer fail to break par in the final round; more than a third couldn't break 80. Open Sunday saw photographers snapping pictures of greenkeepers watering the green between groups.

The most outspoken player, Jerry Kelly, openly asked when the USGA was going to "grow a head."

Kelly went on to opine that the USGA was ruining the game and ruining the U.S. Open. "This isn't golf," a frustrated Kelly stated after finishing 17-over.

Cliff Kresge was equally upset. Addressing the media after going 24 over, Kresge asked a pointed question. "Do you like us looking like a bunch of idiots out there?"

Kresge's question could also have been asked at Pebble Beach in 2010, when a shaved bank made a fast green on 14 more difficult. It left approach shots and chip shots treacherous at best, and prompted golfer Ryan Moore to wonder, as Kresge had six years earlier, if the USGA was simply trying to "make everybody look stupid."

The 17th didn't offer much comfort either. It was a long par 3 with a tiny area for hole locations, and many felt the location near the back of the bowl-shaped green to be unfair. Moore gave voice to the belief that the USGA, instead of seeking to make a course difficult, sought to create a spectacle that involved elements of "trickiness."

Moore finished 33rd at 12 over and offered his belief that USGA setups make him hate golf for two months. U.S. Open courses, he said, don't reward good shots like Augusta National does. "I don't under-stand," Moore said, "why you'd have a tournament that doesn't reward good golf shots."

Moore wasn't alone in his complaints. Woods, who finished fourth behind champion Graeme McDowell, called the greens for the U.S. Open "just awful."

If the greens at Pebble Beach in 2010 were awful, the rough at Oakmont in 2007 was dangerous. Playing practice rounds at Oakmont, Mickelson injured his wrist trying to hit out of very thick rough. Mickelson took to wearing a wrist brace during his first two days in the tournament, but his injury proved costly, causing him to miss the cut.

"It is absolutely dangerous," Mickelson said. "It's disappointing to dream as a kid about winning the U.S. Open and spend all this time getting ready for it and have the course setup injure you."

Along with Mickelson, Richard Lee, a 16-year-old amateur and future Tour pro, sprained a wrist and withdrew. Golfer Boo Weekly agreed with Mickelson that Oakmont was "very dangerous."

Fittingly, it took an angel—Angel Cabrera—to subdue the devilish course and emerge as champion, albeit with a 5-over.

Six years earlier, in the 1998 U.S. Open at the Olympic Club in San Francisco, the course again took center stage. This was due primarily to a back-left hole location on the second round. It prompted Payne Stewart to state that the course setup was "bordering on the ridiculous." The USGA admitted it made a mistake with the hole location on 18, but that failed to console Stewart, who lightly tapped an eight-foot birdie putt that missed the hole and rolled 35 feet downhill.

Tom Lehman four-putted the same 18, his putt ringing the cup and rolling nine feet back down the hill, to a surprised Lehman. "The way the USGA set that hole up is unfair," Lehman said. "All the guys I talked to feel the same way."

The USGA listened to Lehman and others and has not used that hole in subsequent Opens at the Olympic Club. Two decades later, the USGA's course setup was once more called into question by pros dumbfounded by the conditions at Chambers Bay in 2015. Hole locations were again a cause for concern, accentuating as they did greens that were severely sloped. The USGA also alternated between par 4 and par 5 on several holes. One of those holes was the 18th, and a TV microphone caught Jordan Spieth, the eventual winner, telling his caddie the 18th was the "dumbest hole I've ever played in my life."

The USGA exposed the poa annua and fescue mix on the greens to warm, windy weather while at the same time withholding water. Because the course had only opened in 2007, the greens had not matured, and they deteriorated rapidly, causing Sergio Garcia, Ian Poulter, Ernie Els, Billy Horschel, Colin Montgomerie, and Ryan Palmer to complain that the Chambers Bay setup was not of championship caliber.

"It is a joke," Ryan Palmer said. "I don't understand it. I just don't know why (the USGA) would do it."

Poulter called the course a "complete farce" and said the greens were the most "disgraceful" surfaces he had ever seen.

The USGA compounded the problems by placing pins on the edges of slopes, this despite the strong sun and wind. Earning late tee times by having played well the first two rounds became a punishment as the final four groups struggled mightily and posted an accumulative total of 46 over par.

Former USGA president David Fay offered insight into the organization's motives when he said the U.S. Open must be regarded as "the world's toughest golf tournament."

Fay added that the USGA always looked to make the U.S. Open setup hard but fair. Sometimes, the organization got close to the edge of what was fair and what wasn't, and sometimes, he acknowledged, "you go over the edge."

There is no question the U.S. Open is golf's meanest major. Scoring is tougher than at any other tournament. Winning scores in the U.S. Open traditionally rank at even par or higher, one reason being recovery shots at Open venues are often missing due to the combination of tight fairways and thick rough. Hacking free of the rough is physically demanding and, as in the case of Mickelson at Oakmont, physically damaging.

Thick rough, fast and firm greens, difficult hole locations, whipping winds, and water hazards create wrecks that attract viewers in the same fashion that people rubberneck at accidents.

Disaster in the U.S. Open comes fast and furious. In 1997 Gil Morgan stood at 12 under before carding 77 on Saturday and 81 on Sunday. In the 2005 Open at Pinehurst, the pairing of Jason Gore and Retief Goosen failed to break 80. Ten years later at Chambers Bay, Dustin Johnson's 82 in the final round wiped out his three-shot lead. Johnson headed to the 18th hole on the tournament's final day eyeing a 12-foot putt for eagle and his first major championship. He missed, but still had a four-footer to force a playoff; he missed that as well. Johnson gained a measure of satisfaction by winning the U.S. Open the following year at Oakmont. In 2006, Winged Foot produced another massacre, high scores littering the 18th.

The U.S. Open sees itself as the defender of par, and while some don't want to watch top players slugging it out with treacherous courses, others understand that they can watch birdie fests throughout the summer and that seeing a bloodbath every June can serve as a compelling counterpart. Fans enjoy watching golfers take apart lesser courses but find intrigue in seeing how those same golfers react when a celebrated course rises up against them.

Watching the world's best battle their way around a brutal course can be captivating. A certain amount of heroism is needed to survive the sand, sun, grass, trees, water, and pressure of the annual summer battle that occurs on U.S. Open courses. *Sports Illustrated* noted as much in its preview of the 1964 Open, stating that those who would win "must play 72 holes knowing that each error they make can hurt them badly. All of this may put tremendous pressure on the golfer, but it fascinates the spectator."

On the eve of the 1951 U.S. Open at Oakland Hills, golfers were indeed preparing to tiptoe through hell. The question in the minds of thousands of fans was who would be the hero who would head into Oakland *Hells* and slay The Monster?

The heralded Hogan swing has launched thousands of imitators. Yet no one has ever completely figured out Hogan's celebrated "Secret." *PhotoQuest Archive Photos*

Framed by a gallery that set records for its size, Ben Hogan putts on The Monster's treacherous greens at the 1951 U.S. Open at Oakland Hills. *PhotoQuest Archive Photos*

Though he was known as a tee-to-green machine, Ben Hogan still found the hazards at times. Here Hogan sends a spray of sand skyward as slashes his ball free of a trap.
Bettman

Wearing his trademark flat white cap, defending champion Ben Hogan prepares to tee off for what he called the greatest round of his life, the historic fourth round of the 1951 U.S. Open. Hogan would shoot a record-breaking 67 on a course he said was the toughest he ever faced, the "Monster" of Oakland Hills. *Framepool*

The record crowd of nearly 18,000 exults on the 18th green after Hogan sinks his final putt and finally brings the "Monster" to its knees. *Framepool*

Surrounded by media members, Ben Hogan flashes his famous smile for writers and cameramen after achieving the impossible and bringing The Monster to its knees.
Bettman

6

PGA TOUR

Showbiz Flair on the Fairways

The golfers who gathered at Oakland Hills for the 51st U.S. Open were as talented a group as any before or since and arguably far more colorful.

The field featured 10 former U.S. Open champions and was headed by Ben Hogan. The reigning champion was seeking his third title in as many attempts, having won in 1948 at Riviera Country Club in Pacific Palisades, California, a course that came to be known as "Hogan's Alley" for his success there in 1947 and 1948. Hogan's horrific car accident denied him the opportunity to defend his title in the 1949 U.S. Open at Medinah Country Club.

The charismatic Hogan was to fans in the 1950s what Bobby Jones was to his followers in the Roaring 20s; what Arnold Palmer was to his Army of fans in the 1960s; what Jack Nicklaus was in the 1970s; and Tiger Woods in the 2000s. Hogan was sartorially vivid, his classic cashmere sweaters giving credence to the fact that there was fashion on the fairways, and the belief that the PGA Tour boasted the best-dressed men on the American sports scene. His flat cap and Sam Snead's straw hat with the colorful bands were trademarks of golf's old guard. Lloyd Mangrum, Tommy Bolt, and Mike Souchak, meanwhile, favored swing-easy alpaca sweaters, available in no less than 50 colors.

The morphology of Hogan fueled the public's fascination with the man and the Tour. Joining Hogan in journeying to Oakland Hills, like so many Beowulf's traveling to Heorot, was fellow monster hunter Snead, the celebrated "Slammer." Owner of what many believed to be the perfect swing, Snead's admirers would come to include Nicklaus, who called Sam's swing "perfect," and Gary Player, who stated that there wasn't any question in his mind that Snead had "golf's greatest swing."

The World Golf Hall of Fame hails Snead's swing as the "archetype of power and grace." The Slammer, discussing keys to his swing, said, "I try to feel oily." When his swing was right, he remarked, "my mind is blank and my body is loose as a goose."

Duke Ellington's famous song—"It Don't Mean a Thing (If It Ain't Got That Swing)"—could have been applied to Slammin' Sam. Snead's sweet swing was self-taught, the Ashwood, Virginia, native using a set of clubs carved from tree limbs. Born May 27, 1912, Snead was the youngest of six children, four of them brothers. His mother, Laura, was at an advanced age—47 years old—when Sam was born. He became fascinated with golf at an early age after watching Homer, one of his older brothers, drive balls across the family's chicken and cow farm. Young Sam preferred to go barefoot, and years later, feeling out of sorts in the 1942 Masters, he reached back to his childhood years and removed his socks and shoes for nine holes on the hallowed grounds of Augusta.

Like contemporaries Hogan and Byron Nelson, Snead started caddying at an early age, in Sam's case age 7, at the nearby Homestead Hotel Old Course in Hot Springs. He fashioned golf clubs from maple tree limbs and used golf balls he found while caddying. Snead's success in golf can be attributed in part to his being arguably the greatest athlete among the game's great champions.

At Valley High School, Snead ran the 100 in 10 seconds flat. In the fall, he was a halfback on the high school football team; in the winter, Snead played center on the basketball squad; and, in the spring, he was a pitcher and outfielder for the baseball team. Snead also played tennis, and he retained his athleticism into his 70s, when he could kick the top of a seven-foot doorway from a dead standstill. Long limbed, supple, and strong, the 5-10, 185-pound Snead moved with a rhythm that seemed almost musical. Not surprising, since he learned to play the trumpet and banjo by ear.

At age 19, Snead became an assistant pro at The Homestead. In 1935, as the nation was emerging from the Great Depression, Snead moved to The Greenbrier as club pro. He joined the PGA Tour in 1936 and earned instant success by claiming the West Virginia Closed Pro tournament. Snead's first full year on the Tour was 1937, which saw him win four times and win a flock of faithful fans as well.

Due in part to the promotional efforts of Fred Corcoran, who billed Snead as a force of nature from the Virginia mountains, Slammin' Sam took the Tour by storm and became the game's greatest attraction. Along with his prodigious power and perfect swing, Snead became famous for a folksy image that featured an ever-present coconut straw hat and homespun humor. Peter Alliss said Snead carried at least six of his hats with him in a polyurethane bag. Each hat had a $100 bill tucked beneath the band. Snead would also tuck money into the hands of those he wanted to tip, namely, waiters and bellboys. "Here boy," he would say, "put that in your hollow tooth."

Long before the advent of modern golf equipment, Snead was hammering drives well beyond 300 yards. The Slammer became known as the "Long Ball Hitter from West Virginia," but he was also an accurate and creative shot maker, popularizing the use of sand wedges for short shots from the grass. Gene Sarazen called Snead "the only person who came into the game possessing every physical attribute—a sound swing, power, a sturdy physique, and no bad habits."

From 1937 until his entry into the U.S. Navy in 1942 for service in World War II, Snead claimed 27 PGA victories, including his first major in the 1942 PGA Championship at Seaview Country Club in Galloway, New Jersey. Snead earned a 2 and 1 win in the match play championship over Jim Turnesa, who advanced via victories over pre-tournament favorites Hogan and Nelson in the quarterfinals and semifinals, respectively. The win was the first of Snead's seven majors and immediately following the event he began his service in the U.S. Navy. Because of World War II, the PGA Championship was the second and last major of the year.

Snead returned from military service to earn six wins in 1946, including the Open Championship at St. Andrews. Because expenses amounted to three times more than the winning purse, Snead, like Hogan, never returned to defend his title. In 1949, Snead claimed nine PGA wins, highlighted by victories in the Masters and PGA Championship. His outstanding season gained for him the Golfer of the Year award.

The Slammer's white-hot winning ways continued with 11 more wins in 1950. Snead's total trailed only Nelson's 18 victories in 1945 and Hogan's 13 in 1946. Snead would always claim that he reached his peak in 1950, when his 69.23 guaranteed him his second-straight Vardon Trophy, awarded by the PGA of America to the Tour player who posts the best scoring average. Snead's scoring mark in 1950 stood as a Vardon Trophy record for 50 years. Slammin' Sam was denied a second-straight Golfer of the Year award, which went to Hogan, despite the latter winning just once, the U.S. Open at Merion, and losing to Snead in a playoff at the L.A. Open.

Snead headed to Oakland Hills having missed out on regaining the Masters title he had failed to defend the year before. His opening round 69 at Augusta tied with Lloyd Mangrum one stroke behind George Fazio. The Slammer's 74 in the second round dropped him into a four-way tie for fifth, but he bounced back with a 68 in the third round to forge a first-place tie with Skee Riegel, one stroke ahead of Hogan. An 80 in the final round finished Snead, and he tied for eighth with Nelson and Johnny Bulla, 11 shots behind Hogan.

By 1951, the U.S. Open was the lone major Snead had failed to win, and his second-place finishes in 1937, 1947, and 1949 were already legend. Snead had his first encounter with the U.S. Open at Oakland Hills in 1937. With a length of 7,037 yards, Oakland Hills was the first U.S. Open layout to surpass 7,000 yards.

Slammin' Sam shot 3 under 69 in the first round to tie with Denny Shute. A 73 in the second round sent Snead spiraling downward into a tie for fifth. The third round saw Snead card a 70 and climb into a tie for second. Snead capped the final round with a birdie on 18, to close at 71.

Ralph Guldahl, playing behind Snead, began his charge by holing a 65-foot putt for eagle on 8 and followed with a birdie on 9 from 25 feet. Guldahl added birdies on 12 and 13, and he played even par on his final five holes, to finish with a 69. His 281 was two shots better than Snead and one stroke better than the previous U.S. Open record set by Tony Manero the year before at Baltusrol.

Ten years later, the St. Louis Country Club in Missouri was the setting for Snead's second heartbreak in U.S. Open competition. Unlike the 1937 U.S. Open, Snead started slowly, and it wasn't until the second round that his name appeared among the leaders. Having shot 1-over 72 in the opening round, Snead followed with a 70 to tie for seventh, three shots back of co-leaders Chick Harbert and Dick Metz.

Snead shot another 70 in the third round to tie with Bobby Locke, one stroke back of leader Lew Worsham. In the final round, Snead rallied from two early bogeys with birdies on 5, 6, and 15. A bogey on 17 left The Slammer needing a birdie on 18 to tie Worsham and force a playoff. An approach shot left him 18 feet shy, but Snead sank his putt to forge a first-place tie.

The 18-hole playoff between the two ex-sailors was held Sunday morning before a gallery of 6,500 fans who saw Snead seize the initiative. With just three holes to go, Snead led Worsham by two shots. Sam struggled on 17, posting a bogey after missing the fairway and then overshooting the green from the rough. On 18, Snead delivered a fine approach shot that went over a bunker and was 15 feet from the cup. Worsham, meanwhile, was 40 feet from the hole on the back of the green. When Worsham's beautiful downhill chip stopped 29.5 inches from the hole, Snead knew a birdie putt would give him his long-awaited U.S. Open Championship.

Snead's putt was poor, his ball stopping 30.5 inches away. As Snead prepared to putt again, Worsham suddenly called for an official to determine whose ball was farther from the hole. A tape measure showed Snead to be an inch outside of Worsham; it was thus still Snead's turn, but The Slammer seemed unnerved by the unexpected delay. Sportswriter Dick McGeorge, covering the championship for the *Toledo Blade*, noted that Snead "looked daggers" at Worsham when Lew called for the measurement. Veteran observers considered Worsham's obvious strategy to unnerve Snead one of the craftiest moves in U.S. Open history.

Jerry Liska of the Associated Press wrote that the harassed Snead was "less steady" than before as he approached his second putt. His nerves "twanging like fiddle strings," according to one report, Snead missed his putt, the ball hitting the side of the cup and squirming off to the right an inch away. Liska later described Snead's putting on 18 as "schoolboy-ish." Worsham now had the opportunity to drain his putt and win the championship. A miss would necessitate a second 18-hole playoff that afternoon. Worsham wasted no time approaching his ball and sinking his putt, his 69 beating the suddenly forlorn Snead by a single stroke after 90 holes.

The sight of Snead stalking off the 18th in despair following a lost opportunity in the U.S. Open stirred memories of 1939. Played at Phila-delphia Country Club, Snead led after the first 36 holes and stood on the 72nd hole needing only par to win the championship. Believing he needed a birdie, Slammin' Sam played aggressively, found a couple of bunkers, and carded a shocking triple-bogey eight that dropped him to fifth place, two shots out of an eventual three-man playoff won by Nelson.

Snead suffered another disappointing U.S. Open finish in 1949 at the first major ever held at Medinah Country Club. The treacherous, 6,981-yard course played to a par 71, and The Slammer opened with consecu-tive rounds of 73. He climbed the leaderboard with a third-round 71 that tied him for sixth place behind front-running Cary Middlecoff. Down by six strokes, Snead continued his outstanding shot making for the first 16 holes of the final round, played late Saturday afternoon, and had an opportunity to force a tie and playoff when Middlecoff, a young, rangy Tennessean, struggled and shot 75.

Thrilling a then-record crowd of 14,000, Snead finished in a furious rush and needed only par for the final three holes to tie. He played 16 in par, and a birdie and par on the final two holes would give Snead a U.S. Open title to go with the Masters and PGA Championships he had won in April and May, respectively. Having won the British Open in 1946, Snead was seeking to join Gene Sarazen as the only winners of the men's Career Grand Slam to that point. Bobby Jones won the pre–Masters Grand Slam in 1930 and remains the only player to claim four majors in the same calendar year. In Jones's case, it was the U.S. Amateur, Brit-ish Amateur, U.S. Open, and British Open. Tiger Woods won the four modern majors—Masters, PGA, U.S. Open, British Open—in a 365-day period, but not in the same calendar year. Tiger's titles encompassed the 2000–2001 seasons.

The 193-yard lake-hole 17th saw Snead's bid for history hit a serious snag when his old-time Open jinx struck again. The Slammer stuck his tee shot on the apron of the green but then rammed his putt six feet past the hole. His next putt rimmed the cup before Snead finally found the bottom of the hole.

Snead's 3-putt on 17 left him in desperate straits and needing a birdie to tie Middlecoff. The Slammer's drive on 18 was down the middle of the fairway, but his 6-iron approach was wide of the green. His par 4 gave Snead a 70, which was the best final-round score among the leaders, but it served only to tie him for second behind Middlecoff, just one stroke separating The Slammer from his most sought-after prize.

Snead's string of agonizing finishes in the U.S. Open didn't deter his determination to destroy The Monster of Oakland Hills. The mark of an exceptional player, he remarked, "is in his ability to come back. The great champions have all come back from defeat."

Champions filled the field at Oakland Hills. Sarazen was a two-time U.S. Open champion, having won in 1922 at Skokie Country Club in Illinois and again in 1932 at Fresh Meadow Country Club in Flushing, New York. One of the world's greatest golfers in his prime, when he dueled Bobby Jones and Walter Hagen in the 1920s and 1930s, Sarazen turned 49 the previous February and hadn't won a major since the 1935 Masters. The latter allowed him to become the first man to win the modern Career Grand Slam and was achieved courtesy of one of the most famous shots in golf history, Sarazen's "shot heard 'round the world."

The shot came on the 15th hole of the final round. Sarazen used a club that was then called a "spoon" because of its concave face and whose loft is a modern 3-, 5-, or 7-wood, to score a double eagle. The shot came with Sarazen trailing Craig Wood by three strokes, and he forged a tie for first place by producing par on the final three holes to force a playoff the following day. Sarazen beat Wood in the 36-hole playoff by five shots. In 1955, the bridge approaching the left side of the 15th green at Augusta was named the Sarazen Bridge, in honor of his "shot heard 'round the world."

Despite his diminutive height, the 5-5 native of New York boasted a reputation as big as Gotham. Sarazen had the pelts on the belt in the form of seven major championships won, and he also laid claim to being a game-changing innovator. In 1929, Sarazen took a tip from baseball legend Ty Cobb and created a weighted practice club. Two years later, Sarazen was learning to fly an airplane from Howard Hughes when he noticed the plane's tail adjusting downward during takeoff. Sarazen said this prompted him to create the sand wedge, which he called the sand iron. He debuted his new club in 1932 en route to winning the Open Championship at Prince's Golf Club. It was this club that Snead later popularized, and it remains a key club in every golfer's bag.

Because it is too valuable for insurers to cover, Sarazen's invention is no longer on display at Prince's Golf Club. Whether the sand wedge was Sarazen's invention remains open to debate. In 1928, four years before Sarazen debuted his sand wedge in the Open Championship, Edwin Kerr McClain had patented a similar golf club. It's possible that Sarazen, struggling with his sand play, had seen McClain's club.

Even in 1951, the man born Eugenio Saraceni to an Italian carpenter in Harrison, New York, four decades earlier continued to favor the sartorial splendor of the Roaring 20s, donning the knickerbockers and plus fours popular in the Golden Age of American sports. While the knee-length knickers had been associated with sports attire since the 1860s, plus fours—trousers that extend four inches below the knees—came into vogue in the 1920s and were the breeches of choice for golfers since they allowed more freedom of movement.

Sarazen was self-taught, using the interlocking grip that was novel at the time. He quit school and was 19 when he turned pro. He changed his surname from Saraceni to Sarazen because he said the latter "sounded like a golfer." Sarazen was the shortest of golf's great champions, but his long-ball hitting belied his smallish frame. Weighing 145 pounds, he was solidly built like his contemporary, welterweight champion Mickey Walker, also a product of the New York Metro area, being born in Elizabeth, New Jersey.

Sarazen and Walker both owned a fighter's mind-set and compact, ferocious swings. Walker was nicknamed the "Toy Bulldog," a moniker that could have applied to Sarazen as well. While Walker went on to win the world middleweight title, Sarazen challenged Hagen to a 72-hole battle and beat the man considered history's best match player.

Sarazen was a devotee of hard work and practice. "The more I practice," Sarazen famously said, "the luckier I get." His efforts paid dividends. The summer of 1932 saw him win both the British and U.S. Open Championships. He played the final 28 holes of the latter in 100 strokes, carding a closing round of 66, which stood as a record until 1960, when Palmer posted a 65 at Cherry Hills to defeat Hogan and Nicklaus. Sarazen's sizzling 66 prompted Bobby Jones to speak publicly of his rival's fierce competitiveness and to compare him to another boxing legend of that era.

"When Sarazen saw a chance at the bacon hanging over the last green," Bobby Jones said, "he could put as much fire and fury into a finishing round as Jack Dempsey could put into a fight." Like Dempsey, Sarazen delighted in competing at a lightning-fast pace. He and George Fazio once teamed to play an entire round at Augusta in just one hour and 57 minutes.

Sarazen and Bobby Jones were born in 1902; Hagen, like Sarazen a native New Yorker, was nine years older. They represented an important link in golf's grand triumvirates, following as they did the British "Big Three"—Harry Vardon, John Henry Taylor, and James Braid—who combined to win 16 Open championships between 1894 and 1914 and set the stage for Hogan, Nelson, and Snead in the 1940s; Palmer, Nicklaus, and Player in the 1960s; the UK triumvirate of England's Nick Faldo, Scotland's Sandy Lyle, and Wales's Ian Woosnam; and the current international "Big Three" of Texan Jordan Spieth, Irishman Rory McIlroy, and Aussie Jason Day.

The highly competitive Sarazen built a rivalry with Jones and Hagen that helped spread the sport's popularity around the globe and for the first time made America the preeminent stage for golf. Yet Sarazen's impact on golf extended far beyond his famous rivalries. The World Golf Hall of Fame notes that, as a "competitor and innovator, Gene Sarazen spanned golf history like no other great American player." He played golf exhibitions around the world and is recognized as arguably the best early ambassador for his sport among American champions. Sarazen's time spent in the sport bridged the eras of Vardon to Jones to Hogan to Palmer to Nicklaus to Tiger.

In time, the carpenter's son became known as "The Squire" after purchasing a farm in upstate New York. Sarazen's bulldog personality was contrasted by the relaxed nature of another former champion in the 1951 field at Oakland Hills. Lloyd Mangrum's "Mr. Ice" moniker was the result of his calm demeanor. His success on the PGA Tour, which he joined in 1937, was the result of a smooth swing that produced a major championship at the U.S. Open in 1946, and close calls in the Masters in 1940 and 1949, and in the PGA Championship in 1941 and 1949.

Mangrum might have won more, but his service in the U.S. Army during World War II produced far greater glory for the product of Trenton, Texas. While training for the Allies' D-Day landings, the professional's position at Maryland's Fort Meade golf course was offered to Mangrum. The job would have kept Mangrum out of combat, and he rejected it. Wounded in Normandy and later in the Battle of the Bulge, Mangrum was awarded two Purple Heart Medals. His injuries in Normandy came when his jeep overturned and his arm was broken in two places. In the Battle of the Bulge, Mangrum endured shrapnel wounds in his chin and knee. Serving as staff sergeant in General George Patton's Third Army, Mangrum was also awarded two Silver Stars and two Bronze Stars.

Military service helped Mangrum put golf in proper perspective. "I don't suppose that any of the pro and amateur golfers who were combat soldiers, Marines or sailors," he said then, "will soon be able to think of a three-putt green as one of the really bad troubles in life."

It seemed appropriate that Mangrum's major championship came after his distinguished service in World War II when he won the first U.S. Open of the post-war years in a 36-hole playoff at Canterbury Golf Club in Beachwood, Ohio. To win, Mangrum had to beat Nelson and Vic Ghezzi in an extended playoff on Sunday, all three having shot even-par 72 over the first 18 holes that morning. Mangrum had lost a four-shot lead in the morning and was now two back of Nelson and Ghezzi at the turn in the afternoon. Mr. Ice kept his cool, and a flurry of birdies gave him a two-shot advantage on 16. He bogeyed both 17 and 18, but Mangrum managed to hold off Nelson and Ghezzi by a stroke.

Mangrum had one of his most impressive seasons in 1948, earning six victories and 21 top-10 finishes. In 1950, he lost in a three-man playoff to Hogan at Merion, but Mr. Ice was on a hot streak when he arrived at

Oakland Hills. He was in the process of being the PGA Tour's leading money winner in 1951 and would also earn the Vardon Trophy for the lowest-scoring average.

Just as Snead's brother Homer influenced his entry into golf, Mangrum's brother Ray was head pro at Cliff-Dale Country Club in Dallas when he hired the 15-year-old Lloyd to serve as his assistant pro. Turning pro at age 17, Mangrum earned his first victory three years later in 1940 at the Thomasville Open. In time, Mangrum mastered the skill of lining low-flying iron shots into strong winds, and he was extremely accurate on and around the greens. Golf aficionado Bing Crosby said Mangrum's game contained "rhythm, balance and style."

Mangrum's style was accentuated by his movie-star looks. His pencil-thin mustache stirred comparisons to contemporaries Clark Gable, Ronald Colman, and Errol Flynn. Owning a gambling approach to golf, Mangrum was as much a swashbuckler in his field as Flynn was in his. It was Crosby's considered opinion that Mangrum had an ideal golfing temperament, extraordinary competitive spirit, and what most folks felt was the finest putting touch in the game.

Mangrum was Mr. Ice, a moniker Cary Middlecoff might likewise have earned considering his glacial pace of play. Instead, the Tennessee-born Middlecoff was called "Doc," a nickname he gained after earning his Doctor of Dental Surgery in 1944. In World War II, he served in the U.S. Army Dental Corps, and after 18 months of active duty, he had filled an estimated 7,000 teeth. At age 26, the Doc decided to give golf his full attention. Middlecoff reasoned that, if he couldn't become a success on the PGA Tour within two years of turning pro, he would return to dentistry.

Middlecoff's original nickname was "The Ghost" because as a youth he was always haunting country clubs in his hometown of Halls seeking tips on playing successful golf. A big boy, Middlecoff relied on his power early on, and while he never had a swing lesson, his prodigious power helped him overwhelm opponents and courses. "I'd give the world to have a swing like that," Bobby Jones once said of Middlecoff.

As a teenager, Middlecoff won the Memphis City Championship and Tennessee Amateur. At the University of Mississippi, he finished first in one tournament by 29 strokes. In 1945 Middlecoff became the first amateur to win the North and South Open, an achievement highlighted by his playing in the final group with Hogan and Sarazen.

In his rookie year on the pro tour following the war, Middlecoff tied the course record in the final round of the Charlotte Open and collected his first winner's check. In 1949, Middlecoff captured his first major, the U.S. Open at Medinah. That same year, Middlecoff and Mangrum set a PGA Tour mark for the longest sudden-death playoff—11 holes—before being declared co-champions of the Motor City Open.

Middlecoff may have had a quick temper, but he was more known for his slow pace of play, coming to a visible stop at the height of his backswing. Middlecoff's languid pace prompted fellow pros to say the real reason Doc gave up dentistry was because no patient could hold their mouth open long enough for him to complete his work.

On the eve of taking on The Monster, Middlecoff's 1951 season was ranking with 1949 as one of his best. He would win six titles in 1951, matching his total in 1949. Tall at 6-2, he overcame the slight handicap of having one leg longer than the other. Much of Middlecoff's success lay in his ability to combine power with accuracy and to complement his strength and length off the tee with an excellent short game.

While Middlecoff was the Golf Doctor—he appeared in a 1947 biographical documentary under that title—Craig Wood was the "Blond Bomber." His nickname was the result of his rugged handsomeness and powerful drives, both of which were seasoned by a father who was a foreman for a timber company—a fitting career for a man named Wood—and devoted outdoorsman.

Born in Lake Placid, New York, in 1901, Craig was taught at a young age by his father to wield an axe. Working with an axe not only developed Craig's hand strength and upper-body physique, it also led to keen eye-hand coordination. All of these attributes would work to Wood's advantage when he turned pro in 1920 at age 18, but life on the PGA Tour proved frustrating at the beginning.

A series of near misses in majors haunted Wood. In 1933, Wood astonished spectators and competitors at the Open at St. Andrews when he muscled a drive that measured 430 yards. But on the first hole of a playoff against friend and rival Denny Shute, Wood drove his ball into the Swilcan Burn and eventually lost by five strokes. In the PGA Championship a year later at the Park Club of Buffalo in New York, Wood suffered another playoff defeat, this to his former student and assistant pro Paul Runyan, aka "Little Poison," in the sudden death that followed the regulation 36 holes in the final round of match play.

The next year, 1935, witnessed Wood losing to Sarazen in the second Masters ever held. Wood fell victim to Sarazen's famous double eagle on the par-5 15th hole in the final round. Emboldened by his dramatic shot, Sarazen rallied to erase his three-stroke deficit, forced a playoff, and beat Wood by five strokes the following day.

In the 1939 U.S. Open at Philadelphia Country Club, Wood was in yet another playoff, a rematch with Shute, and this time the two were joined by Nelson. Shute quickly fell off the pace in the playoff, and by the ninth hole Wood and Nelson were dueling for the title. Wood led by one shot on the 18th, but the Blond Bomber's par was bettered by Lord Byron's birdie. In the second 18-hole playoff the following day, Nelson's 1-over 70 was enough to defeat Wood, who shot 73.

Four heartbreaking playoff losses failed to stop Wood. He was the first man to lose all four majors in playoffs; Greg Norman has since duplicated that feat. But at the advanced golfer's age of 39, Wood broke through in a big way in 1941, becoming the first player to win the Masters and U.S. Open in the same year. In the process, he evened old scores with Nelson and Shute. The Bomber set a record by leading the Masters from start to finish, posting scores of 66, 71, 71, and 72 for a 280, to top Nelson by three strokes. In the U.S. Open at Colonial Country Club, Wood won with a 284 that beat Shute by three strokes.

Wood's Tour contemporaries were happy for him. Snead called him the "nicest guy I think I've ever seen." True to his down-to-earth roots, the Blond Bomber regularly helped other players on the Tour improve their game.

Worsham, the 1947 U.S. Open champion, had recently won the Phoenix Open when he arrived at Oakland Hills. His famous U.S. Open victory over Snead four years earlier could hardly have been more dramatic—a one-stroke win in an 18-hole playoff at the St. Louis Country Club. Worsham's win was historic; it marked the first time the tournament was televised locally. Worsham and Snead were Southern gentlemen who enjoyed a long friendship, frequently fishing and hunting together.

Born in 1917 in Level Run, Virginia, Worsham would become known as "The Chin," for his prominent jaw, and "Honest Lew," for his once assessing himself a penalty stroke after his ball moved on the green while he was playing for the lead in the Texas Open. He and his family moved to Washington, D.C., when Lew was young, and his road to a career as a pro golfer began in 1929 with his caddying at Bannockburn Golf Club in Maryland. Seven years later, Worsham became a shop boy at Kenwood Golf and Country Club. He turned pro in 1938 when he accepted a PGA assistant's position at Chevy Chase Golf Club and a year later became PGA head professional at Burning Tree Club in Bethesda. Worsham served in the Navy in World War II, being stationed with Snead and Jimmy Demaret at Bainbridge, Maryland.

Worsham's first PGA Tour win came in 1946 in the Atlanta Open, and he won the Delaware Open that year as well. The following year was one of Worsham's finest. Like many of those on the Tour in the 1950s, his primary job was as a club pro. He became PGA head professional at Oakmont Country Club outside of Pittsburgh, Pennsylvania, and he asked if he could compete in the U.S. Open in St. Louis before reporting to work. Worsham won the U.S. Open and Denver Open, and finished eighth on the Tour's money list. He also competed in the 1947 Ryder Cup, the first since World War II, and he won two matches at the Portland Golf Club to help the U.S. triumph.

From 1947 to 1962, Worsham played at Augusta 16 straight years. Between 1938 and 1961, The Chin competed in 17 U.S. Opens; he also participated in 15 PGA Championships. Twelve of Worsham's appearances in the PGA Championship came during the years when the tournament was match play, and he succeeded in making the field all but twice.

Bantam Ben, Slammin' Sam, The Squire, the Golf Doctor, Mr. Ice, the Blond Bomber, and The Chin helped make up a gallery of golfers that may have been the most colorful in history. And then there was Titanic Thompson, who while not a Tour pro was an expert golfer who factored into the lives of Hogan, Snead, Runyan, and Byron Nelson and later stars like Lee Trevino and Raymond Floyd.

Born Alvin Clarence Thomas, he was raised not on a riverboat, as would have been fitting given his future as a gambler, but on a farm in the Ozark Mountains. He grew into a gambler–hustler of the first order and was said to be the inspiration for the character Sky Masterson in Damon Runyon's *The Idyll of Miss Sarah Brown*, later made into the musical *Guys and Dolls*. Thompson (he took the name after *Thomas* was misspelled in a newspaper article) earned the nickname "Titanic" when he outhustled a shark named Snow Clark in a Joplin, Missouri, pool hall. The incident occurred in the spring of 1912, around the same time as the sinking of the famed luxury liner. While Thompson was counting his winnings, someone asked Snow the young man's name. "It must be Titanic," Clark answered. "He sinks everybody."

Everybody included noted New York City crime boss Arthur Rothstein, who fixed the 1919 World Series and was shot to death shortly after being involved in a high-stakes poker game that included, among others, Titanic Thompson. It also included Chicago boss Al Capone, who was conned out of $500 by Titanic. Ti's skills were so varied that he was often compared to Merlin the Magician. One of his hustling partners was the famed "Minnesota Fats." Fats thought Titanic a genius, the best "action man" of all time.

Titanic's action included being a golf hustler. He was ambidextrous and gifted with great eye–hand coordination and excellent eyesight. A self-taught golfer, he improved his skills through lessons with club pros and for 20 years played several times per week. He was good enough to turn pro but declined, declaring he would have to take too much of a pay cut. In an era when Tour pros were lucky to make $30,000 a year, Titanic sometimes made that much in a week by hustling wealthy country club players.

Hogan traveled with Titanic in the early 1930s for money games on the side. "The best shot maker I ever saw," Hogan said. "Right- or left-handed, you can't beat him."

Thompson would play and win right handed, then offer to play left handed in an apparent concession while raising the monetary stakes.

Opponents, not knowing Thompson was naturally left handed, would accept. With that, Ti would pop open the trunk of his two-ton Pierce Arrow car, pull out a bag with left-handed clubs, and promptly sink another sucker.

Thompson once bet he could use an old hickory-shafted club and still drive a golf ball 500 yards. The bet was quickly accepted. Titanic won by waiting until winter and then driving his golf ball onto a frozen lake, where it bounced on ice until reaching the required distance.

"Only a fool," Hogan stated, "would play him in a game he suggested."

Snead, a hustler in his own right, said Titanic was "golf's greatest hustler." Thompson hustled big spenders for $20,000 a hole. Titanic wowed not only the locals but also Nelson, who was impressed by Ti's skills, and Hogan, who marveled at Titanic's ability to work his shots, be it slicing a ball between bunkers or hooking it around a tree.

There was no question, Nelson said, that Thompson could have been a star on the Tour. But, Lord Byron added, Titanic didn't have to turn pro. "He was at a higher level, playing for $25,000 a nine while we played for $150."

Even without Titanic Thompson, there was certainly no shortage of showbiz flair on the fairways in the 1950s. In a decade when more golf matches were being brought to the masses via television, the larger-than-life flamboyance displayed by charismatic characters paved the path for the PGA Tour's explosion in the latter half of the decade.

The combination of TV; the emergence of Arnie, his Army, and Palmer's penchant for attacking courses rather than playing them; and a golf-fanatical U.S. president in Dwight D. Eisenhower inspired millions to take up the sport. The eyes of the world were suddenly glued to golfers and the weekend wars they waged against themselves, their opponents, and the great green expanses designed to challenge them.

The high-gloss treatment given by national magazines, such as *Life*, *Look*, and *Time*, to the Tour, to Hogan, to Trent Jones, and to The Monster made the coming collision a much-anticipated, must-see event. In its March 5 edition, which hit newsstands three months prior to tee off at Oakland Hills, *Life* magazine featured Trent Jones's design work at Atlanta's Peachtree Golf Club course in an article titled "Par-Buster's

Nightmare." *Life* noted that Trent Jones planned every obstacle on his courses "with loving care."

The 1951 U.S. Open field of 162 golfers—134 professionals and 28 amateurs—complained openly and loudly that Trent Jones's Monster was, in the words of an Associated Press report the morning of the opening round on June 14, "strictly a series of snares and delusions."

America's sports fans studied the day's newspapers and read stories about the Belmont Stakes; Joe Louis's comeback fight against Lee Savold; the New York Yankees' pursuit of the Chicago White Sox in the American League, and the entire National League's chase of the "Boys of Summer" Brooklyn Dodgers. But it was the U.S. Open that grabbed the biggest headlines. Red Smith of the *New York Times*, the dean of American sportswriters, began his column by declaring that "one of the finest sports stories of recent times will be developing on the outskirts of Detroit this weekend."

Smith called attention to Trent Jones's redesign of Oakland Hills— the venerated writer labeling it "a tightly-trapped meadow"—and to the men seeking to survive it. There was Hogan, whom Smith described as a "cautious competitor these days, who must husband his strength for the big shows." Hogan was returning to defend the title he had won the previous summer in circumstances that Smith wrote were "a travesty of fiction." The memory of Hogan's triumph at Merion was still too fresh to require repetition, but Smith believed that a generation hence "kids will read Hogan's story and wonder whether it could possibly be true, wonder how any man could have the resolution and faith and skill to beat his way back from the cemetery gates, as Ben did, to victory in an athletic event which may be, all things considered, the most cruelly searching test in sports."

Hogan would attempt to defend his title against a field of competitors comprising not just the top players in America but also the best from around the world. The latter included Roberto De Vicenzo, the dashing Argentinian, who, in Smith's words, "never did anything much in North America until last weekend, when he swept like a prairie fire through the Palm Beach Two-Pants Suit tournament at Wykaagyl." In the process of outplaying Mangrum and Australian Jim Ferrier on the rain-soaked, wind-whipped course in New Rochelle, New York, de

Vicenzo, described in newspaper stories as "handsome Roberto" and the "gay gaucho," captured first place in the Palm Beach Open and charmed the galleries as well.

Along with De Vicenzo, there was South Africa's Bobby Locke, two-time champion of the British Open and a man considered by many authorities the finest golfer in the world. Smith saw Locke as both interesting and controversial. If you spotted him in the club lounge, it was unlikely, Smith opined, that you would believe him to be an athlete. Still, Locke managed to "beat the brains out of the opposition." Locke had appeared almost timid when he made his first appearance in the United States several years earlier at the Masters. Locke had just destroyed Snead in an exhibition series in South Africa, but observers who saw him in Augusta took one look at the diffident Locke and decided "Slammin' Sam" must have been severely off his game in South Africa.

At six-feet tall and with a stocky build, Locke was a fairly big man. But Smith saw Locke's "pudgy features" and felt they gave the impression of softness. The square-rigged knickers made Locke look shorter than he was, and, when introduced to his hero Bobby Jones at the Masters, Locke snatched the little white linen cap he wore off his head in a manner that Smith saw as schoolboy-like and "downright comical."

Locke's swing looked choppy and contrived when compared to the loose, graceful swings of America's top pros. Galleries paid little attention to Locke until he reached the greens. Once on the green, his ability to run putts down from long distances captivated galleries. Locke won so much money on the American tour that he was barred by the PGA as a disciplinary measure stemming from a dispute concerning tournament commitments. Smith stated that it was easy to believe the pros were boycotting Locke because "he was a threat to their bank balances."

By the summer of 1951, Locke was back in good standing with the PGA Tour and gunning for golf's big prize along with Hogan, De Vicenzo, and Snead. In the weeks leading up to the 1951 Open, Snead had withdrawn from competition to work out at Oakland Hills. He studied the course and polished his game to get ready for another attempt to grasp the championship that had proven so elusive.

Smith saw Snead as a sentimental favorite and predicted in his column that the galleries would be "watching and rooting" for Snead. Hogan may have recognized the same and on the eve of the tournament, shrugged off suggestions that he and Locke should be favored at Oakland Hills.

"Sam Snead should win this tournament by a mile," Hogan said in the locker room while a stinging rain drenched the big green Monster outside. "Sam has the long driving game adapted to this course and he ought to take it, but don't think I intend to tell him how."

The comment was surprising coming from the usually taciturn Texan, and reporters were caught off guard by what one termed Hogan's "gab-fest" and "unusual talkativeness."

Snead, however, wasn't buying what Hogan was selling.

"Don't believe a word of it," Sam drawled in his down-home country tones. "That's just Ben tryin' to get in everybody's heads like a swarm of wasps. Next thing, watch out, he'll be sayin' the course is really too easy and ought to be toughened up."

Snead was familiar with Hogan's penchant for gamesmanship. When Hogan tried his mind game with Snead at Oakland Hills, The Slammer grinned. "I know what that little man is doing," he said.

For all of the pre-tournament talk about Snead, Hogan, De Vicenzo, and Locke, Smith predicted that some player nobody had ever head of would come barreling in on Thursday, Friday, or even on Saturday with a round that will make the fans forget the favorites for a few hours before he too blows up.

"You can bet on that happening," Smith finalized. "It always does in an Open."

Fans agreed, and a record number were en route to Oakland Hills to witness firsthand what promised to be a dramatic and historic event. The battle brewing between Trent Jones's brooding beast of a course and the world's greatest golfers had the buildup normally found in championship fights.

This was golf, not boxing, but victory might still be decided as much by will as by skill. The one who could impose his will had the best chance of conquering his competitors and the course. Snead believed that winning usually came down to an intangible that couldn't be measured.

"Desire," Snead said, "is the most important thing in sports. No one has more than I've got."

Tommy Bolt wondered about that. When it came to desire, Bolt said Hogan's car wreck made Ben "an even more dangerous critter. He saved everything inside for the titles he wanted most and the rest of the time he just practiced, practiced, practiced."

To a man, Hogan and the field of charismatic competitors who made up the PGA Tour shared Snead's belief that it would take something special, something more than fashion, flair, and flamboyance on the fairways, to win what was being billed as the toughest of all U.S. Opens.

The most treacherous, most torturous course ever created lay in wait.

7

FIRST ROUND

The Monster Unleashed

Thursday's early-morning tee times at Oakland Hills had the feel of the first round of a heavyweight championship fight.

Golfers were grim faced as they approached the first tee. The highly publicized pros realized, as golfer Frank Walsh stated in previewing The Monster for that month's issue of *GOLFing* magazine, "there isn't a let-up hole on the course." Indeed, and that fact had Trent Jones's design causing more nightmares than a Hitchcock film.

Caddie Jack Fowler thrilled at the sight of all the top players coming together at Oakland Hills. There was Sam Snead, with his croquet-style putting; nearby, was muffin-faced Bobby Locke. "They only used club caddies at that time; they didn't have pro caddies," he says. "It was a great experience watching Sam Snead, Bobby Locke."

And, of course, there was Ben Hogan, ready to begin his assault on history and become the U.S. Open's first repeat champion since Ralph Guldahl in 1937–1938 and first to win three Opens in as many attempts since Scotland's Willie Anderson in 1903–1905. Hogan was instantly recognizable, fans spotting his white cap from a distance.

"On Ben it looked great," Tommy Bolt said. "It was Ben. He wouldn't have looked the same without that little white thing pulled down over his eyes."

Fowler noticed something else about Hogan; the man's irons looked smaller than those used by other players. "Maybe," he muses, "that gave his shots a different sound."

The Hawk had a different way about him as well. "He was all business," Lisa Scott remembers. "He was not Mr. Chatty on the golf course; he didn't have time for idle chitchat. When he looked you in the eye, it was like being under a microscope."

Robert Stennett says Hogan's hard stare prompted golfer Deane Beman to state, "Hogan doesn't look you in the eye; he looks you in the pupil."

Hogan's quest to make history was complicated by the fact that he had never encountered a course like The Monster; no one had. Frank Hannigan wrote in *USGA Journal and Turf Management* that The Monster offered "a severe test." *Sport* magazine writer Bill Rives called Oakland Hills "a monstrous trap." A course considered exasperating under any circumstances had been rendered, in Rives's estimation, "almost unconquerable." Future champions Gary Player and Padraig Harrington would claim that only Carnoustie compares to Oakland Hills when it comes to the toughest golf venue in the world.

Yet as Fred Corcoran of the International Golf Association once said, the stronger the course, the better Hogan played. "This has been the story of his life."

The Monster's starting hole was a 440-yard par 4. Hogan narrowed his hawklike gaze. He knew The Monster's layout was a wild one; now, he was facing it in an official capacity for the first time. Hogan studied the fairway bunkers on both sides, which flanked a narrow landing area. He could see that a short, accurate approach shot was critical to an undulating green and would determine the opportunity for a fast start.

A surging, sun-spangled crowd of 9,500—a record at the time for the opening day of a U.S. Open—pushed forward for a better glimpse of the man who would be king. Because of the press of the crowd, many used handheld periscopes to view the champion. Tommy Bolt said Hogan was the only player to get an ovation from fans on the practice tee. He had seen Hogan playing practice rounds before a tournament and noted that "half the gallery was made up of other professionals."

Fans saw the smoke from Hogan's Chesterfield swirl in small circles and cloud his countenance; the champion's chain-smoking stirred thoughts of Tex Williams's hit song from that era, "Smoke! Smoke! Smoke! (That Cigarette)." He was dressed in his customarily conservative style—pima cotton shirt, "the most expensive you could buy in those days," fellow pro Gardner Dickinson noted; buttoned-up cashmere sweater; light-colored pants; white golf shoes; and white linen cap from Cavanagh, one of the very best hatters in the country. The elegant outfit was classic Hogan, who was so conservative in his attire that he was said by Dickinson to have considered gray a loud color. When Dickinson told Hogan gray was *not* a color, the reserved Texan replied, "Oh yes it is."

Hogan knew this was the opening salvo of several demanding approach shots to The Monster's greens. At 510 yards, No. 2 was the second-longest hole on the course and one of just two par 5s in Trent Jones's layout. It was a reachable par with a slight dogleg to the left that could accommodate approach shots to a green that sloped from back to front. Errant shots on the right that were caught by greenside trees and traps would make it virtually impossible to get down in two.

Bunkers surrounded the par-3, 200-yard No. 3 hole. The most dangerous of The Monster's maws sat at the left front of a green that had less undulation than others but had enough subtlety to make par a decent result.

The 448-yard, par-4 No. 4 was difficult enough for par to be acceptable. A tight landing area, with bunkers and trees on the left, presented a tough test off the tee. The risk–reward on this hole was that for those looking to cut the dogleg they would benefit from a short downhill approach to an accessible green. Straight putts and realistic runs at birdie— a rarity on The Monster—were possible due to a putting surface that sloped back to front.

No. 5, a par-4, 437-yard bunker and tree–lined hole, featured a narrow landing area and a creek that could be reached from the tee. Undulations on this green were severe; a missed approach shot would leave golfers eyeing a bogey or worse.

The 350-yard No. 6 was the shortest par 4 on Trent Jones's course. Accessible to some tee shots, the elevated green, one of the course's deepest, was contoured and well bunkered and sloped from back to front.

No. 7 was a par 4 that stretched 381 yards. The fairway sloped and tilted toward a small pond to the right; to the left was a trio of bunkers. The player who opted to lay up would need to accurately deliver a second shot to the green. A missed shot would catch bunkers on both sides and leave a limited amount of green to work with. The green had fewer contours than other holes, and the putting surface had a subtle slope from back to front.

Teeing off on the par-4, 458-yard No. 8 required taking aim on a narrow landing area that was guarded on both sides by bunkers. The bunkers on the left were particularly dangerous; finding them would force the second shot to be a layup. Flanked by bunkers, the contoured, elevated green sloped from back to front. Putting from below the hole would be the best option to card a difficult birdie or respectable par.

No. 9 represented the second of four outstanding par 3s. The 216-yard hole had an undulating green that was one of the more difficult in The Monster's makeup. An elevated terrace on the left side of the green and a crown in the middle of it made a birdie two a miracle. Instead, three putts were more likely on this hole than any other.

Three bunkers guarding the landing area off an elevated tee on the 448-yard, par-4 No. 10 threatened to turn birdies into bogeys. Danger lurked beyond the landing area. The fairway sloped sharply to the right, and The Monster would grab drives from the middle of the fairway and thrust them into the right rough. Bunkers left and right guarded against an uphill second shot. A slight ridge ran through a large, flat green. Despite this, the green on 10 was one of the few at Oakland Hills that could accommodate a two-putt par.

Though the fairway adjacent to the right-side bunkers on 11 provided a great landing area, the margin for error on the 407-yard par 4 was small. Short approach shots led to a narrow, deep green that was guarded on the front and sides by humongous bunkers. Because the back of the green was up to five feet higher than the front, downhill putts were capable of racing right past the hole and off the green.

The Monster's roar was menacing on No. 12, a par 5 stretching to a length of 566 yards. A tee box sitting some 40 feet above the fairway signaled the start of the longest hole on the course. To tame the monstrous length, one had to navigate a slight dogleg to the right, potential trees on that same side, and a cluster of fairway bunkers on the left. A more troublesome bunker sat 65 yards in front of the green and would come into play for those who chose not to go for it in two. Approaching an elevated green, players would face cavernous bunkers guarding the front and right of the green. From front right to back left ran a deep crest, and players putting from the wrong side of the crest had to deal with a demanding two-putt par.

A short par 3 on 13 followed the lengthy par 5 on 12. At 169 yards, it was the shortest hole in The Monster's layout. A bogey threatened any shot not hit within 10 feet of the pin. Bunkers all but encircled the green, and at the front of the green was a deep bowl three feet lower than the back terrace. Golfers struggling to recover from the encirclement of bunkers and keep the ball on the upper terrace would find themselves at the mercy of The Monster. The correct club selection was a must to make par or birdie.

Signaling the start of arguably the five most treacherous finishing holes in golf history, the 447-yard, par-4 14th featured a fairway flanked by trees and bunkers on both sides. Bunkers also guarded the front of a green that sloped from front to back. Even if on line with the pin, a second shot could easily find its way through the green and into rugged rough. Once on the green, players would encounter enough subtle breaks to make birdies on this hole rare.

A large bunker located in the middle of the fairway and thick woods lining the left edge made the 392-yard, par-4 No. 15 a risk–reward hole. Players had two strategies available to them on 15. They could choose to stay to the right of the bunker, where they would face a longer approach shot to a green protected by yawning bunkers. Their other option was to choose to split the fairway between bunker and trees in an effort to face a shorter second shot. Once on the green, golfers would negotiate a putting surface that was one of the more treacherous on Trent Jones's course. Straight putts on 15 would be rare.

The Monster's signature hole was No. 16. The par-4, 405-yard design featured the most challenging second shot on the course. A wide-open fairway led to a broad but shallow green that was nearly completely surrounded by four bunkers and further guarded by a large pond to the right. An approach shot that avoided the pond also had to take the surrounding bunkers out of play. A ridge that ran front to back on the green was enough to make a two-putt par respectable.

The No. 17 hole represented the last of The Monster's par 3s and at 194 yards was the second-shortest distance on this course. In terms of left to right location, the pin would be visible, but because of the green's 30-foot elevation, players could not see how far, front to back, the pin was located. This helped make for another difficult par. Bunkers protected virtually the entire front and sides of the green, and another bunker was located at the back of the green. Due to the large ridge that split the green, hitting the tee shot on the same side of the pin was crucial. Shots that were on the wrong side of the ridge or long could lead to a bogey or worse.

Oakland Hills's No. 18 offered a finishing hole that was demanding and exacting. It began with a tough shot off an elevated tee typical of Trent Jones's courses and concluded with the difficult green The Monster was infamous for. The par-4, 459-yard hole, the third longest on the layout, featured a dogleg right framed by fairway bunkers right and left. Another bunker, elevated and shallow, awaited players on their approach shot. In the middle of the green was a bump that ran from front to back. A scary three putt was a possibility for those putting from the wrong side of the ridge.

On a course created for theater and high drama, the 18th offered a fitting final act. Trent Jones called it a great finishing hole for a series of great holes, which would in the end produce a notable champion. His nightmarish layout completed, the renowned architect stood back and admired his handiwork.

"Let's see them tear that apart," he said.

"My father was happy with the result," Robert Trent Jones Jr. remembers.

Trent Jones had followed the directive of John Oswald, the chairman of the Oakland Hills Greens Committee, who believed that the star of the 1951 U.S. Open should not be Hogan, Snead, Sarazen, Locke, or any golfer, but the course itself.

"The Open is the greatest title there is," Oswald, known as Big John, told USGA executive director Joe Dey. "The course should be so hard nobody can win it."

Given the green light to modernize the masterpiece, Trent Jones concocted a course that achieved his objective, which was to give the pros "the shock treatment."

The Monster's menacing design and a par shaved from 72 to 70 brought cries of protest from PGA Tour members. "Oh, how they howled!" Trent Jones would recall with relish. Snead, a veteran of the 1937 U.S. Open at Oakland Hills, took one look at the redesign and remarked, "No resemblance now to the course as it played in 1937."

Snead's fellow pros termed Trent Jones's monster "impossible" and a "grotesque nightmare." Sportswriters in Detroit covering the U.S. Open believed the wails of anguished golfers were loud enough to be heard in nearby counties. Golf writer Dan Jenkins heard the cries coming from Oakland Hills and said "more than one golf writer thought he had died and gone to Quote Heaven."

Oakland Hills was the Oakland Ogre, the Green Monster, a Frankenstein. Renowned *New York World-Telegram* sports cartoonist Willard Mullin provided the moniker that would endure when he named it "The Monster." Writer Lincoln Werden of the *New York Times* told readers the course was "enormously difficult" with a "controversial par 70."

Robert Trent Jones Jr. remembers his father welcoming the publicity. "He told us, 'If they're talking about me in the papers, I'm ahead of the game.'"

Jack Fowler, hauling the clubs of former U.S. Open champion Tony Manero, recalls the pros' complaints. "A lot of them were whining," Fowler says. "The undulations of the greens had them shaking their heads. A lot of their complaints were aired and there was no defense of the course [from the players]."

The USGA wasn't interested in complaints. The blue-jacketed fathers of American golf toured Trent Jones's design and declared it a suitable test of championship golf. "It is exacting but not unfair," Championship Committee chairman John D. Ames told reporters. "You can't expect to have your cake and eat it, too."

Trent Jones's course was getting more publicity than the golfers, and he added fuel to the fire by publicly challenging the greatest players in the world.

"I predict no man will break par for the 72 holes," Jones said after his tightening and trapping included adding 66 new hazards to Donald Ross's design. "I would take 284 and sit in the clubhouse perfectly satisfied to let the others shoot at it."

Jenkins thought it a good idea. Oakland Hills, he wrote, was "the kind of course where you could lose your feet in the tall, brutal rough. . . . And on those frequent occasions when the golfer would find himself on the wrong side of the green, there was usually something between his ball and the cup, either the Sahara desert, played by a yawning, intrusive bunker, or the Himalayas, played by the fierce undulations of the putting surfaces."

To slay Trent Jones's creation, correct course strategy and club selection were absolute musts for those wishing to make birdie or par and avoid bogeys or worse. Hogan was known for his ability to analyze courses through a smoky stare and choose the correct club to execute his strategic attack.

Jimmy Demaret, Hogan's colorful playing partner, said once that watching Hogan pick his club "amounts to watching one of the greatest club selectors in golf." Among the clubs in Hogan's quiver were drivers, persimmon and laminated. They were tipped, with zero bulge and roll. Most golfers of that era favored solid blocks of persimmon. But Hogan, forever experimenting with equipment, found laminates worked fine; his clubs featured layers of wood—mostly maple—glued together.

The bottom of the shaft was driven through the clubhead—"tipped," as it were—to ensure even more stiffness. "Bulge and roll" is the side-to-side, up-and-down curvature along the wood face, a nineteenth-century invention that corrected for mishits. Because he didn't mishit much, Hogan went without bulge and roll, the reason being that, when he mishit, he wanted to know it.

Demaret said the 14 clubs in Hogan's bag included a driver, 3-wood, 4-wood, 2- through 9-irons, pitching wedge, sand wedge, and putter. He generally didn't carry a 1-iron after it had been stolen following his famous shot at Merion in 1950, but he did bring a 1-iron to Oakland Hills. Demaret believed Hogan knew exactly what each club would do for him and used his analytical mind to take into consideration contributing factors such as wind, distance, obstacles and hazards, and condition of the course.

In the era of Hogan and Demaret, a general guide for selecting the correct club read as follows:

Driver, for distances from 240 yards to 275 and up; brassie, 220–265; 3-wood, 200–250; 4-wood, 200–225; 1-iron, 180–215; 2-iron, 175–205; 3-iron, 165–200; 4-iron, 155–190; 5-iron, 1455–180; 6-iron, 135–170; 7-iron, 125–160; 8-iron, 115–150; 9-iron, 105–140; wedge pitch, edge of green to 105 yards; and sand wedge, edge of green to 40 yards.

It was indeed a general guide. A player who did not command great power could find, for instance, that a 2-iron simply wasn't enough club for them to hit 190 yards.

Demaret branded Hogan a conservative in choosing his clubs. *New York Times*'s famed columnist Red Smith believed the near-death accident had forever altered The Hawk's strategic plan of attack. Demaret noticed that, on approach shots, Hogan sought to make certain he was short of the green rather than fly over it. Hogan was well aware of the difficulties that lie behind the green, and to avoid such problems, he would aim for the front of the green and a two-putt par.

Demaret recalled a round of golf with Hogan at the Colonial Country Club in Fort Worth when Hogan's caddie bragged to the other boys in the caddie yard that he knew "more about this course than Hogan does."

From the first hole to the 18th, Hogan's caddie kept advising the extra club.

"You'll be dead to the pin with the four."

Hogan responded each time by asking for the club under it.

"I'll take the five," The Hawk would say, and then drive his shot to the apron of the green.

"He would've been right up to the hole with the other club," the boy muttered to Demaret. "He's a champ and this is his home course, but he keeps using the wrong club!"

Demaret laughed. When Hogan reached into his bag for a particular club, Demaret knew it was a safe bet The Hawk had analyzed the area he was shooting at and had done so with what his playing partner called a "telescopic eye." Hogan carefully planned his shots prior to attacking, so much so that he was criticized at times for taking too much time with his shots. Some critics called Hogan the "surveyor," a nickname he resented as much as he did "Bantam Ben."

"That's a brutal word to tag on a golfer," Hogan said of being labeled a surveyor. "When I look a course over, I'm trying to figure it out. I want to know what's going to happen when my shot hits the ground. I want to check the grass as well as the distance to the green or my particular objective."

Hogan was an expert on grass. He knew the different types—from the Bermuda grass greens found in his home state of Texas to the seaside turf on courses down South and out West—and what the ball would do on each type of grass.

Hogan's calculating mind made him, in Demaret's opinion, the Tour's top strategist in the 1950s. "He is the master attacker of even our toughest layouts," Demaret wrote at the time, "because of his ability to think out a course."

When necessary, The Hawk would pace off the distance from where his ball was to the spot where he calculated it would come down. At the same time he was doing that, Hogan would examine the grass and every bunker, shrub, tree, and undulation along the way. If The Hawk looked to carry a bunker or attempted to launch a shot over trees to save ground on a dogleg hole, he made sure he knew what was behind those obstacles. "He knows," Demaret stated, "what's going to happen on the other end of the shot."

Yet even Hogan couldn't quite figure out The Monster. Golf historian Herbert Warren Wind believed Hogan was "bothered and confused" by Trent Jones's layout. This wasn't just a golf course; it was a green god, its grandeur matched by its grimness. Hogan had played five practice rounds prior to Thursday's opening round and his computer-complex mind had yet to come up with a way to slay The Monster.

"I can honestly say I don't know yet how to tackle it," the champion told reporters. "Almost every fairway has a pinpoint driving area. Miss it and you're in trouble. You can't get out. You lose a shot."

Hogan's confusion on how to attack The Monster may have been for public consumption; privately, he seemed to have some definite ideas. He had made an early appearance at Oakland Hills and caught the attention of Al Watrous. The Oakland Hills club pro had seen someone on the upper tee, and no one, not even a member, was allowed to even walk across it much less hit shots off it. Not realizing who was on the other end of the range, Watrous yelled at the solitary figure.

"Get off the tee!"

As he got closer, Watrous recognized the man.

"Hogan," he said. It was the first close-up Watrous had of Hogan's way of hitting a golf ball. He had never seen such skilled shot making by any player. The Hogan Watrous witnessed was in the process of establishing a game plan. "I've never been on a course in all my life that I couldn't figure out some way to play," Hogan said. "Usually two rounds are enough."

Yet The Monster was something even Hogan couldn't comprehend. "I've played five rounds here and I still don't know how to play Oakland Hills."

Or did he? A practice round yielded a 69 even though Hogan missed a short birdie putt on 18. His game plan began to crystallize when his long-iron approach to the 18th green sailed past the putting surface. It was then that Hogan realized that iron play, particularly long irons, would be key to defeating The Monster. Distance off the tee, Hogan told a writer, would be less a factor at Oakland Hills than distance with the long irons.

To hone his game for the challenges presented by Trent Jones, Hogan spent a day at Bloomfield Hills Country Club hitting an assortment of 3-iron shots with a focus on high, soft cuts. Trent Jones's strategic placing of bunkers caused Hogan to realize that taking the bunkers out of play was essential to victory. The way to do that was to use long irons to tame a course in which half of the holes measured at least 437 yards. With three of the short holes reaching 200, 216, and 194 yards, 12 of the 18 holes would be played with long irons.

Recalling Hogan's "Miracle at Merion" the year before, achieved as it was with long irons, sportswriters believed golf's little big man was one of the best bets to triumph at Oakland Hills. Associated Press sportswriter Will Grimsley saw Hogan, Snead, and Bobby Locke as the favorites. Grimsley cited the "big question marks curling above the heads" of each.

Could Hogan, the "miracle comebacker," return from semi-retirement and become the third triple winner in U.S. Open history?

Would Locke break American dominance and become the first foreigner to take the prized title since big Ted Ray of England in 1920?

Could Snead snap his longtime jinx and finally win the U.S. Open? It would seem fitting since Oakland Hills was the site of Snead's U.S. Open debut.

Grimsley contended in his preview that, if any man could conquer the rugged Monster, it would be Hogan or Locke, "those two nerveless competitors who are rated the finest and shrewdest shot makers of modern golf." Grimsley thought the expected duel between Hogan and Locke provided the most intriguing feature of the 51st U.S. Open.

Smith saw Snead as the sentimental favorite of the fans; Grimsley believed it would be Hogan but noted that Locke shaped up as the top challenger. Locke was earning a lucrative living, Grimsley wrote, by "beating the knickers off America's best pro campaigners." The British Open king had few peers when it came to putting, and Locke owned the accuracy and acumen that would serve him well at Oakland Hills, where there was a heavy price to pay for missed shots.

"No amateur or outsider will win this one," Trent Jones stated. "It will take a sharp-shooting, level-headed old pro to do it."

Locke was among the more level-headed, sharp-shooting pros in the world, and it was for these reasons that sportswriter Harry Grayson didn't see Snead or Hogan as the favorite, but Locke. He was coming off consecutive British Open Championships in 1949 and 1950, posting four rounds in the 60s and final scores of 283 and 279. The latter, recorded at Troon in Scotland, represented an all-time low in the royal and ancient Open Championship.

Despite his celebrity, Locke was less than well liked on the PGA Tour. Wrote Grayson, "Old Muffin Face with the fluid swing wins their money—and keeps it." Bolt said Locke nearly one putt the pros into the poorhouse. When Locke was winning every week, said Bolt, American pros were "thinking of ways to get him back to South Africa."

Grayson believed the slick South African was the man Hogan had to beat on the "famous and tricked-up Oakland Hills course." Locke's short game was remarkable and would adapt well to Oakland Hills, where The Monster's fairways pinched in the drive zone, curbing the big hitters. Locke also had a flair for pitching to the correct part of the green, where the emphasis is on accuracy. Grayson rated Snead behind Locke and Hogan, and also felt that a host of others—Lloyd Mangrum, Cary Middlecoff, Lew Worsham, George Fazio, Jim Ferrier, Herman Barron, Al Brosch, Chandler Harper, Henry Ransom, Johnny Palmer, and Porky

Oliver—were superb shot makers who could take the title. Grayson pointed out that there wasn't a bad golfer in the field at Oakland Hills.

In anticipation of a record crowd at Oakland Hills, the USGA announced that first prize would be raised from $2,000 to $4,000 and that prize money for the tournament was being increased from $12,000 to $15,000.

As golf's top stars assembled for Thursday's opening round, they teamed up with their caddies. Hogan's caddie was Dave Press, a teenager who fibbed about his age in order to get the job. Press was 13, and at that time boys had to be 14 to caddy. At 5-10 and 150 pounds Press was big for his age; he was roughly the same size as Hogan. In that era, professionals did not travel with personal caddies as they do today. Every day, Press hitchhiked 20 miles from his home in Hazel Park to Oakland Hills. He told Associated Press sportswriter Harry Atkins that every caddie at Oakland Hills wanted to carry Hogan's clubs and that he got the coveted job because he drew The Hawk's name from a hat.

Unlike Hogan's caddie at Colonial, Press held the bag and did not offer advice. Press learned, as Dick Collis did in the World Championship of Golf later that summer, that Mr. Hogan played golf as if he were, in Collis's words, "in an isolation box." Hogan's lack of communication with his caddies was unique not only when contrasted with modern pros but also with those in the 1950s. Collis said Snead asked for his assistance in choosing a club on every hole in 1949 and 1950. Hogan sized up courses on his own; Collis called it an "eye to brain" method.

For the 1951 World Championship of Golf, Collis had the 30th pick in the player draft, and despite hearing that Hogan wasn't going to play in the summer spectacular, Collis still chose Hogan. He learned quickly that Hogan rarely asked for assistance. Over 72 holes, the champion asked Collis for his opinion just twice. Otherwise, Hogan's brief communication was to not shag his short-iron practice shots until they came to rest; he wanted to check their spin.

Speaking of Press, Hogan would tell *Royal Oak Tribune* sports editor Dayton Perrin, "Dave stuck to his knitting, and that's as it should be. Not once did he tell me what club to use. He was a fine boy, a quiet boy. That's the way I like them."

Hogan would tell Press to grab the shag bag and meet him at the car. Be discreet, Hogan said, so no one would notice. Hogan was discreet about something else as well. Though Hogan endorsed MacGregor equipment, Press soon learned that the champion played Spalding golf balls. Hogan told Press when MacGregor made a ball as good as Spalding's, he'd switch. When a company rep met Hogan on the putting green at Tam O'Shanter Golf Club in Chicago, Collis recalled Hogan raising "holy hell." Hogan handed the rep 12 boxes and told him if he ever gave him golf balls like that again he wouldn't play their ball.

Press confirmed that Hogan had MacGregor irons in his bag but noticed that his woods were virtually impossible to identify because they had been modified so many times in Hogan's workshop. For his tee shot on No. 1 at Oakland Hills, Hogan gripped a driver. The wind this day wasn't a factor; it would neither help nor hinder tee shots. Fans seeing Hogan for the first time craned their necks to get a glimpse of the man they had read so much about.

Hogan teed up his ball, waggled, and drew back his driver. Writer Marshall Smith, covering the Open for *Life* magazine, captured the essence of watching Hogan's heralded swing up close. From the tee, Smith wrote, the tight-lipped, businesslike Hogan swung his famously rigid clubs with remarkable authority and accuracy.

Herbert Warren Wind believed Hogan's swing was not picture perfect. "But when he had the time to tune it up properly and the physical reserve to maintain it as he wanted it, was so functional and assertive that it had a smooth, efficient, kinetic beauty of its own."

Chuck Kocsis, the low amateur at the U.S. Open in 1934 and again in 1937, watched Hogan's swing up close. Kocsis felt that, in spite of the praise and glorification given it by the press, Hogan's swing was not in the same category as that of Snead or Bobby Jones for fundamentals or rhythm. "It was a repetitive swing," Kocsis said of Hogan, "grooved from hours and hours of practice."

He thought any good golf instructor viewing the swings of Hogan and Snead would promote Snead and express reservations regarding Hogan. All of which was fine with Hogan, who was concerned with championships, not aesthetics. "I wanted a functional swing," he said.

"The primary purpose in a tourney is to shoot the low score, not have the prettiest score."

Hogan was said to be a low-ball hitter. Colonial locker room attendant Frank Holland, who shagged balls for Hogan, thought the champion's iron shots sometimes rose no higher than a 10-foot ceiling. Hogan's drives whistled like the liners hit by his contemporary, Ted Williams. The Kid and The Hawk met two months before at the 1951 Masters when the Red Sox were in Augusta for a spring exhibition game. Hogan was sitting on a locker room bench when Williams approached him and shook hands. Upon leaving, Williams turned to Fred Corcoran, who had been introducing the ballplayers to golfers, and said of Hogan, "I just shook a hand that felt like five bands of steel."

Sportswriter Al Barkow of the *New York Times* knew it sounded ridiculous to say, but he called the effect Hogan had on everyone who watched him play "mesmerizing." Those who missed seeing Hogan in person, Barkow stated, will never get the real sensation. "Film doesn't capture the Hogan aura," he wrote.

The Hogan aura and mystique are still so strong that even now fans see him as a golfing machine that regularly produced shots of near perfection. Hogan was human, and he proved fallible in this, his first official meeting with The Monster. Hogan's club selection and course strategy failed him in the opening round. He continually chose the wrong club and wrong approach to deal with The Monster's gun-barrel fairways and wheat-like rough.

Hogan's miscalculations began on the first fairway. He stood, hands on his hips, deciding whether to pull from his bag a 2- or 3-iron to the green. Five days of practice had provided in Hogan's adding-machine mind what he believed to be the proper calculations. His internal debate on the first fairway Thursday convinced him that the 2-iron was the proper club. He waggled once, then sailed the ball 10 yards over the green.

"Just bad thinking," he admitted later. "I used the wrong club."

The Hawk's errors in judgment were indicative of his confusion. Gene Gregston, who knew Hogan and is one of his biographers, wrote that Trent Jones's layout produced a course "that offered Hogan's wits the most baffling battle yet." The Hawk would go through his usual machinations—examining the lie, sizing up the type of grass and the wind—and then calculate the correct position on the green to place his approach shot to set up the best possible putt. But his careful calculations went for naught.

"Like a stupid ass," he said, "I'd be on the left side of the green rather than the right."

Finding himself on the wrong side of greens and fairways was only part of Hogan's problem in the opening round. He put himself over the putting surface on a couple of approaches and on one occasion left himself a long, downhill chance and three-putted. Practice rounds had convinced him to revert to his old center-shafted blade putter, and he bent the blade "open" more than before. But his clubs couldn't save him this day. Time and again, Hogan made the same miscalculations, surprising the record crowd following his every step. In an effort to stay behind the bunkers, he clubbed down off the tee, but that strategy failed because it left him long second shots into the greens. Hogan's failures infuriated him; he flicked his still-burning cigarettes down with such force they bounced off the sunlit ground.

Every shot The Hawk made took into account a multitude of factors—proper club selection, length of backswing, slice or hook, hit the ball high or low. Inwardly, he wrestled with what type of shot he would play and which club he would play it with. The Monster was so demanding that it allowed only one right answer for each shot, and as Marshall Smith wrote in his tournament coverage in *Life* magazine, "Hogan didn't get it." The Hawk's six extra shots—the result of his six errors in judgment—were proof of that. "The place puzzled him," wrote Gregston.

Lincoln Werden wrote in the *New York Times* that Hogan was "a bit ruffled by his failure to solve the course." Hogan was indeed frustrated that he shot 39 on the front nine and 37 following the turn, including a horrendous 2 over par 6 on the final hole. He managed just two birdies while compiling six bogeys and finished five shots off the lead. It was the highest first-round score he had endured in the U.S. Open since 1939.

Beneath his white cap, Hogan's face was pale. His shoulders slumped, his head hung toward the ground. The sight stunned fans, but reminded them that Hogan, a golfing immortal, was still a mortal man. The Monster turned him inside out in this first round; yet Hogan remained customarily tight lipped. "He was a man of few words," Lisa Scott remembers. The champion was bitterly self-reproachful in the postmortem. "That was the most stupid round of golf I have ever played."

In their room at the Detroit Sheraton that night, a still angry Hogan told Valerie, "I made six mistakes and shot 6 over. You can't steal anything out there."

"He was just furious," Valerie recalled to sportswriter Dave Anderson. "He thought the course was just too difficult, too unfair."

Round 1 had gone to The Monster, a fact seized upon by the nation's sportswriters. The pros had not only failed to conquer the Ogre of Oakland Hills; they had been dealt a historic defeat, a fact made clear by the Associated Press in its opening paragraph:

"Golfdom's mighty masters . . . took their worst shellacking from par in modern history Thursday."

The opening day proved that Trent Jones, hired for the strict purpose of toughening Oakland Hills, had succeeded. Hogan and the field realized that the targets Trent Jones had left them to shoot at had been narrowed to the width, in Marshall Smith's words, of a couple of billiard tables. "Trying to hit them from 250 yards away would have been difficult with a .22 rifle, let alone golf balls," wrote Smith.

Throughout the first day, The Monster discouraged the big hitters, the very attributes pros spend their lives striving to become. The field was forced instead to improvise, to adjust their game to the hellish layout. Their collective strategy was to play short off the tees and stress the second shot.

Trent Jones Jr. says the beauty of a hazard is that, while golfers may not be in difficulty, the possibility of difficulty is what worries them. Bobby Jones gave voice to this when he stated, "The value of any hazard is oftentimes more psychological than penal."

Wily old Walter Hagen, a spectator at Oakland Hills, agreed with Jones. The Haig saw the psychological effects The Monster was having. "This course is playing the players instead of the players playing the course," Hagen said. "It really is a monster."

By afternoon's end, Snead had stumbled home with a 1 over 71 for the first-round lead. In the words of the Associated Press, The Slammer had "held the Oakland Hills ogre by the horn for 14 holes—being 3 under par at that point—but then he was struck with an attack of old putting jitters."

Hogan's pre-tournament statement that Snead should win the tournament appeared prescient as "Slammin' Sam" slammed The Monster with a 34 on the front nine before taking a 37 on the back. Carding five birdies and four bogeys, Snead's opening-round lead was reminiscent of his first U.S. Open at Oakland Hills.

With a little luck, The Slammer could have had a five-stroke lead. He played safe on just three occasions in the opening round—when he recorded a par on No. 5 with a 1-iron tee shot; when he went with a spoon, or modern wood, to birdie No. 6; and on 18, when he hit two iron shots for a par 4.

The Monster had its moments as well. It trapped Snead on No. 3 and forced a bogey four. The rough on 10 caused The Slammer to drop a stroke; he then missed an eight-foot eagle putt after covering the 12th in two. He recovered on the next two holes, canning birdies on 13 and 14 with a pair of 12-foot putts. Snead totaled 30 putts on the round.

Snead was still within range of a startling 3 under 67 when he approached the tee on No. 15. The Monster caused a double bogey on 15, its sandy bunker burying Snead's iron and its terraced green doing terrible things to a four-foot putt. Bogeys followed on 16 and 17 as The Slammer was over the green on both holes. The 16th was a replay of 15, sand and another missed four-footer, while the 17th saw The Monster's deep rough snag Snead's strong iron. The 3 under Snead owned three holes earlier was now 1 over, The Monster having turned Slammin' Sam's 67 into a 71.

So difficult was The Monster that Chandler Harper, the 1950 PGA champion, struggled to 7 over after 14 holes and did what many of his brethren likely thought of doing—picking up his ball in what the Associated Press described as "utter disgust." Harper refused to turn in his card, stating "To hell with it" as he left The Monster's lair.

Al Besselink, the 27-year-old fledgling pro from New Jersey, and the blond, bull-shouldered Clayton Heafner of North Carolina each shot 72 to tie for second place. Called "Bessie" by fellow Tour members in the 1950s, Besselink was born in Merchantville, New Jersey. The son of a sign painter, Besselink grew up in modest surroundings and initially made his name in golf when he became the first University of Miami golfer to claim a national tournament. Besselink captured the prestigious Southern Invitational Tournament twice before graduating in 1949 and turning pro later that year.

True to the Tour's nature in 1951, Besselink played to the galleries. Some golf historians see Bessie as his era's Greg Norman. Like Norman, aka "The Shark," Besselink had colorful nicknames—the "Prince of Merchantville" and the "Dapper Adonis." Bessie played golf with a gambler's flair and charmed the galleries with grand gestures. He once played the final four rounds of the third round of the Colonial Invitational in Fort Worth with a red rose stuck between his teeth. Bessie had snatched the rose from a bush on the 15th hole and brandished it to show his appreciation for, in his words, the "loveliness of Texas women in general and Fort Worth women in particular." The next day, Besselink was presented with 50 roses from female fans.

Ever the gambler, Besselink once bet $500 on himself at 25:1 odds to win a tournament and claimed $22,500. For the same tournament, Bessie sank a 6-foot par putt on 18 to win by a single shot and earn a wheelbarrow full of $10,000 worth of silver dollars. He donated half of the $10,000 to the Walter Winchell–Damon Runyon Cancer Fund. He regularly bet Hogan and Snead; that the latter owned the first-round lead at Oakland Hills didn't surprise Bessie. He considered Snead the greatest golfer who ever lived.

Gambling allowed the Prince of Merchantville to live like King Farouk. The PGA Tour didn't pay much in the 1950s. Besselink estimated he earned less than $10,000 a year on the Tour, yet he spent $100,000 every year. A favored scam of his hinged on how he fared in his early rounds in a tournament. If he fell from contention, Bessie tanked Saturday's third round in order to have an early tee time Sunday. The early start meant he would not have to deal with wind, pressure to win, or spike marks on the greens. Bessie would find a bookie and bet his final-round score against the top 10. He'd beat nine of them by shooting 68 and earn more money than the winner.

Bessie reveled in his roguish lifestyle. He was a friend to the rich and famous of Hollywood and the movers and shakers of Washington, D.C. One of Bessie's rules of life was to hang around the top of the deck. Tall at 6-3 and with blond, wavy hair combed straight back and a classic Roman nose, the Dapper Adonis donned the Technicolor clothes popularized by his friend and mentor, Demaret. Bessie's language was as colorful as his clothes; he spiced his New Jersey accent with the salty vocabulary of a sailor.

The incandescent Bessie burned by day and night; he dated movie stars and married a millionaire. Bing Crosby introduced Bessie to Terry Moore, a starlet of the 1950s. He was the subject of newspaper columns written by Winchell and Red Smith; one story on the dashing gambler was headlined "Bessie Swings Off Course Too."

Besselink befriended Hogan and Snead, and the Prince of Merchantville spent time with American royalty like President Eisenhower and ring legend Joe Louis. Besselink won the Joe Louis Invitational in Detroit and gave the host a pair of blue and gray suede Foot Joys. Bessie and the Brown Bomber both wore size 12D. Louis told a friend, "Put these in my locker. Give the boy 200 bucks."

Besselink remembered Louis having tremendous respect for Hogan, whom he called "Mr. Ben," and recalled the Brown Bomber being a decent golfer, the champ capable of shooting 72. Bessie excelled at wedge play; he believed a wedge had to have the correct loft, grip size, swing weight, and shaft. Arnold Palmer once drove behind Besselink and, at some point between Pensacola and Baton Rouge, spied sparks shooting from beneath Bessie's car. Palmer realized Bessie was using the highway to grind a wedge.

The Dapper Adonis would become an international celebrity, taking his winning ways from North America to Venezuela; Bogota, Colombia; and Madrid, Spain.

Tied with Bessie was Heafner, a fierce, fiery competitor. The bulky Charlotte native had tied for second in the 1949 U.S. Open, tied for fifth in the 1949 PGA Championship, and tied for seventh in the 1950 and 1946 Masters. From 1941–1953, he would earn seven victories, but Heafner's impact on the PGA Tour extended far beyond golf.

Heafner proved to be a pivotal figure in Charlie Sifford breaking golf's color barrier. He played matches with Sifford and counseled him on key issues. Prior to the 1951 Open, Heafner had last won at the 1950 Carolinas Professional Golf Association Championship.

Among the 10 competitors two shots back of Snead and one behind Besselink and Heafner was Locke, who, according to press reports, "explored every trap and every stretch of rough" on The Monster and finally scrambled to a 73.

Sportswriters were likewise scrambling as they sought to find the last time par had so completely confused the top shot makers of their era. Snead invoked the help of heaven and Dame Fortune to deal with the devilish design and its multitude of bunkers, awkward doglegs, and severely undulating greens.

"The angels," drawled The Slammer, "will have to be riding smack on the shoulder of the man who wins this one. If you're lucky, you got it."

Sportswriter Jerry Liska wrote that not since the 1934 U.S. Open at Merion, when three 71s tied for the lead on the par-70 course, had golf's "supreme event undergone such huffing and puffing as marked [Thursday's] opening round in which Snead's 1 over par 71 was the best effort wrenched from Oakland Hills' terrifying course."

So terrifying was it that it was determined The Monster had forced the field to not only play defensive golf, but to shoot an average score of 78 in a staggering first round. One-third of the field was over 80. The Monster proved dominant in its first official meeting with its competitors; its brutal par defeated would-be conquerors by a resounding 162–0.

Diminutive Paul Runyan, nicknamed "Little Poison," stayed in contention early by striking the monstrosity with more woods than irons to shoot 73 and join a crowded field in third place. Included in that group were Locke, Sam Bernardi, Al Brosch, Sammy Byrd, Ernest "Dutch" Harrison, Charles Klein, Johnny Palmer, Lyman "Smiley" Quick, and Denny Shute, each an interesting personality who brought their own unique strategy and style into their battle with The Monster.

Byrd is the only major league player to have won a PGA Tour event. A teammate of Babe Ruth and Lou Gehrig on the New York Yankee teams from 1929–1934 and a World Series champion in 1932, Byrd was a late-innings pinch runner for Ruth and was referred to as "Babe Ruth's legs." A son of the South, Byrd was born in Georgia and grew up in Alabama. He batted .274 in his eight-year Major League Baseball career and compiled a .975 fielding percentage while playing left, right, and centerfield.

Byrd left baseball in 1936 for the PGA Tour and earned six victories from 1942–1945. He claimed a combined five additional championships in various Pennsylvania and Michigan tournaments.

Byrd lost the 1945 PGA Championship to Byron Nelson, 4 and 3, in match play. He also placed third and fourth in the 1941 and 1942 Masters, respectively. The man who served as Babe Ruth's legs also served as Ben Hogan's teacher. Byrd taught Hogan a swing lesson that had been first taught to him by Babe Ruth. It was a drill that forced Hogan to keep his upper left arm connected to his core through his swing. Byrd and Ruth remained friends after their Yankee years and regularly played in a foursome with Joe Louis and famed sportswriter Grantland Rice throughout the 1940s.

Ernest Joseph "Dutch" Harrison was a pro golfer for 45 years, one of the longest careers in PGA Tour history. A native of Conway, a tiny town 30 miles north of Little Rock, Harrison was known as the "Arkansas Traveler." Harrison's travels carried him far and wide, and his winning personality allowed this sharecropper's son to become friends with the rich and famous. Hogan, Arnold Palmer, Jack Nicklaus, Bing Crosby, Bob Hope, and Jim Garner were some of the celebrities Dutch hung out with, and true to his Southern upbringing, he would address each as "Mister," as in "Mister Ben," Mister Bing."

Harrison began his pro career in 1930 amid the Great Depression and survived financially by playing "money matches" in addition to tournaments and exhibitions. Dutch earned nine top-10 finishes in majors, including third-place finishes in the 1939 PGA Championship and 1960 U.S. Open. His 18 PGA victories and 25 career wins included the 1939 Bing Crosby Open and 1958 Tijuana Open Invitational. In 1954 Dutch finished fourth in the Masters and earned the Vardon Trophy for lowest-scoring average.

That Harrison, a future member of the PGA Hall of Fame, never won a major was a fact that baffled many, even his friend Hogan.

"He was a heckuva good golfer, and I might say he didn't win as much as he should have," Hogan said following Harrison's death from heart failure at age 72 in June 1982. "I thought he was a lot better player than his record showed. He should have won more of the major tournaments."

Harrison may not have won majors, as many expected he would, but he was one of golf's all-time hustlers, and he hustled some of the game's more notable names—Arnold Palmer and Lee Trevino among them. Harrison's hustling ways began at an early age. He started caddying at age 12 to get out of working around the home, which included picking cotton in the fields and getting paid 50 cents for every 100 pounds. "Caddyin' beat choppin' wood and doin' farm chores," Dutch would later drawl, and by age 14 he was traveling around the greater Southwest. He grew to be a big man, 6-3 with a top-heavy build like Babe Ruth. Those who shook hands with Dutch were surprised at their soft, supple feel; they had none of the many calluses that marked Hogan's hard hands.

In an era when golfers were defined in part by signature shots— Snead's drives, Hogan's fade, Locke's draw—Harrison's skill with a golf club allowed him any shot he desired. Asked once what club to use to hit a certain type of shot, Harrison grabbed his 5-iron and executed a series of shots that varied from a soft lob that traveled 80 yards to a drive that flew more than 200 yards. Dutch's deft touch was needed against a Monster that appeared to be too tough to be attacked and overwhelmed.

Known as "Little Johnny," "Smilin' Johnny," and "Jovial Johnny," Palmer was a son of the South like Harrison. A native of North Carolina, Palmer claimed seven victories on the PGA Tour and 18 wins total. He turned pro in 1938 and played the PGA Tour from 1941–1958. Little Johnny was a jitterbug renowned for his short game. His best finish in a major came in the 1949 PGA Championship when he placed second to Sam Snead; a year earlier he overhauled Hogan in heavy rain to win the *Philadelphia Inquirer*'s fifth annual invitation golf tournament in Whitemarsh, Pennsylvania.

A B-29 tail gunner in World War II, he flew 29 missions over Tokyo. The Associated Press called Palmer a "professional to fear in any tournament" and said the stocky, wire-haired Palmer owned "a blue-chip finishing punch that left the best U.S. shot makers hanging on the ropes." His short game, solid and on occasion sensational—he set the course record at the Canadian Open in 1952—was his weapon of choice against Trent Jones's brute.

Lyman "Smiley" Quick was a hustler in the mode of Dutch Harrison. A combat Marine in World War II, the chunky Illinois product turned pro in 1946 and produced one PGA Tour victory and six wins in all. His Tour win was a shared title with Sam Snead, Jackie Burke, and Dave Douglas in the 1950 Bing Crosby Pro-Am at Pebble Beach.

Considered one of the finest amateur golfers in Southern California, Quick earned his fortune hustling Joe Louis out of his ring earnings. The Brown Bomber was enamored of the green expanses; Louis's upset loss to Max Schmeling in 1936 is said to have happened in part because of his time spent on golf courses rather than in the ring. Late in life, Louis sometimes played 45–54 holes in a given day.

Reputed to be a four handicap, Louis became the first black man to play in a PGA-sanctioned event when he teed off in the 1952 San Diego Open. Good as he was, Louis was no match for Smiley, who laughed all the way to the bank with an estimated quarter of a million dollars of the Brown Bomber's money. It was enough for Quick to brag that the money he won from Louis allowed him to afford two Los Angeles apartment houses and several sports cars. The slick Quick knew how to trick. A smiling assassin, Quick was a veteran shot maker, and he brought his gambling, hustling style to bear against the beastly layout.

While Smiley was a self-promoter, Denny Shute was so quiet and unassuming he sometimes had his wife, Hettie, accept his winnings on his behalf. Shute's successes were enough to earn him induction into the World Golf Hall of Fame. Nicknamed the "Human Icicle" because of his cool, methodical play and even-natured temperament, Shute had the distinction of being the last man to win back-to-back PGA Championships until Tiger Woods in 1999–2000.

Like Woods, Shute was born to play golf. The son of an English pro, Shute received his first set of golf clubs from his father when he was just 30 months old. He won his first West Virginia State Amateur title in 1923 and, after turning pro, peaked in an 11-year span from 1929–1939. He declined to play tournament golf with as much frequency as his fellow pros, prompting Snead, the all-time wins leader, to state that if Shute had played more, "he'd of been the equal to me."

Byron Nelson saw enough of Shute to remark that the reserved champion was "a lot better than people realize."

Unerring with his iron play, Shute won three majors, the first coming when the Human Icicle refused to melt amid the white-hot pressure of a playoff with Craig Wood in the 1933 British Open at St. Andrews. Shute followed with consecutive PGA Championship victories in 1936–1937. He totaled 12 PGA Tour wins and six additional victories.

As was his custom, the slender Shute relied on his precise chipping and putting to finesse The Monster and make up for his lack of distance off the tees.

Tied at 75 were Mangrum, Roberto De Vicenzo and top amateurs Bo Wininger and Chuck Kocsis. Five strokes off the pace set by Snead were Hogan and Cary Middlecoff. Disgusted as he was with his round, Hogan found little solace in the fact that four fellow past champions—Lawson Little (1940), Craig Wood (1941), Worsham (1947), and Middlecoff (1949)—had likewise been mauled by The Monster and shot 76. Like them, Hogan was in danger of descending into the Dante-like depths of Oakland *Hells*. Left unsaid at the time was that Hogan's 76 was still two shots better than the average score of 78.26.

The first-round carnage complete, The Monster's victims were already piling up. Just one day into the tournament, Trent Jones's fearsome layout had the best golfers from three continents looking like dead men walking.

"This course," said Hogan, studying the 76 on his scorecard, "is a monster."

8

SECOND ROUND

A Torturous Test

Robert Trent Jones reveled in what he saw as the "psychological shock suffered by the world's ranking golfers" when they encountered The Monster.

The architect had adhered to the orders given by the Oakland Hills's club membership to "toughen it up and make it memorable." That he succeeded was undeniable; Trent Jones had, in fact, created a scarier monster than Mary Shelley ever imagined.

Even the normally unflappable Bobby Locke was taken aback. "Toughest I've ever seen," Locke told M. F. Drunkenbrod when asked his opinion of Oakland Hills.

Sam Snead knew as early as the first practice round that The Monster would offer a torturous test of golf. Slammin' Sam's moment of clarity came when he and two others walked side by side down the first fairway.

"Two of us," Snead drawled, "were in the rough."

The first round reinforced what Trent Jones believed he already knew. "For the first time in many years," he said, "the course the Open was played on completely caught up with the players."

Modern players, he stated, had been getting away with playing courses that, with few exceptions, had been designed in the 1920s or even earlier. Those courses, while classic, had been tailored for the clubs, the ball, and the playing conditions of that time.

Those courses had been sufficient to test the champions of their era—Bobby Jones, Walter Hagen, and Gene Sarazen. But they had lost their testing abilities. Steel shafts and a wound ball enabled the modern masters—Snead, Ben Hogan, Bobby Locke—to produce shots that were not possible with wood shafts. The added length of their drives carried them safely beyond the trapping designed to punish poorly hit tee shots. Golf was no longer the game of Jones, Hagen, and Sarazen. Younger guns playing a brand of golf unfamiliar to the aging legends had replaced the greats of yesteryear. Hogan demonstrated as much to Trent Jones when he laced his practice drive over a hazard during the reconstruction of Oakland Hills.

Trent Jones knew the modern power game brought shots, be they on line or off line, so near the greens that pros had little difficulty dropping a wedge shot on to them. The combined advantages caused par to lose its meaning. It was bound to happen, Trent Jones said, considering that correct shot making had lost its intended meaning.

Having conducted tests, Trent Jones accumulated enough data to arrive at values he believed were a true reflection of the playing skills of the field that would test Oakland Hills. The result was a rugged par 70 that presented professionals in the 1951 U.S. Open with a task as difficult as had been faced by golfers in 1924 in the first U.S. Open at Oakland Hills. Having played circuit layouts that saw a sprayed tee shot followed by a wedge leave players putting for birdies, they were now confronted with a course that demanded accuracy and delivered penalties for errors in shot making or judgment.

"The field was thrown into utter confusion," Trent Jones remarked with relish. Oakland Hills had become a land of confusion. Golfers of great reputation, most notably Hogan, were tottering home with rounds high in the 70s, some in the 80s. They issued loud complaints—the golf equivalent of crying "Foul!"—but Trent Jones insisted there were no trick holes at Oakland Hills. The architect pointed to the fact that there was no particular hole on which all players struggled; each had played poorly on any hole where he had failed to execute or exhibited faulty reasoning.

Hogan's first round was a prime example of both. Errors in judgment and missed opportunities led him to 6 over par 76 and left him five shots off the pace set by Snead. Walter Hagen applauded the decision-making being forced upon players by The Monster. "It was nice to see the golfers placing their shots for a change," he said. "The man who wins here will be the player who knows what he can do, and tries to do it."

Hogan knew what he could do and began doing it in the second round. Having soaked his legs in Epsom salt and wrapped them in Ace bandages, he limped out into the morning sunshine and humidity and back into battle with The Monster. Hogan thrived on conquering courses; his calculating approach seemed able to solve any golf problem posed to him.

The 1948 U.S. Open offered a vivid illustration of The Hawk's powers of concentration. He had been paired with friend George Fazio, the latter holing out a 4-iron second shot on a par-4 hole. The gallery reacted with a roar, and yet at round's end Fazio's eagle was nowhere to be found on his card. Hogan wouldn't record it. So intense was his focus on his own game that he claimed he hadn't seen Fazio's shot or even heard the crowd's reaction.

Dan Jenkins, one of the many writers at Oakland Hills covering the U.S. Open, considered Hogan a fascinating study, particularly in tournaments and even more so in pressure-cooker, career-defining moments. He would watch Hogan walk toward the fairway or green with a slight forward bend as if he were heading up a hill. The Hawk studied each shot intently, as if it were a mathematical problem so complex that only Hogan could solve it. The champion would take a deep draw on his Chesterfield and attack the problem with a swing Jenkins called "flat and flawless."

Hogan didn't completely solve the problems posed by Trent Jones's Monster course in his second round, but he did slice three strokes off his previous round, shooting a dicey 73 that put him at 149. His driver was his primary weapon; he believed it to be the most crucial club in his bag, critical for both accuracy and distance. He knew the quality of his drive off the tee determined his attack on the approach shot. Convinced that under pressure a soft shaft could fail him, Hogan opted for a stiff, strong shaft.

"Stiff shafts allowed him to control his shot more," Bruce Devlin says. "If he was using a softer shaft he couldn't control it as much."

Devlin favored a softer club shaft than Hogan and remembers Ben poking fun at clubs he compared to buggy whips. "When we played rounds together he would walk around to my bag, pick out a club and say, 'I see you're still playing with the buggy whip.'"

Taking his clubs in calloused hands, Hogan employed the Vardon grip. Named after Harry Vardon, who popularized it en route to winning a record six British Open Championships from 1896–1914 and the U.S. Open in 1900, the Vardon is an overlapping grip favored by the majority of pro golfers since the start of the twentieth century. Though it was named for him, Vardon adopted the grip from Scotland native Johnny Laidlay, a two-time British Amateur champion credited with inventing it.

The overlapping grip sees the pinky finger of the bottom hand—the hand placed lower on the club, in the case of a right-handed player like Hogan, the right hand—between the index and middle fingers of the top, or lead, hand. Hogan friend and author Jody Vasquez noted that Hogan altered the Vardon grip slightly, and, in order that he would hold his clubs the same way for every swing, the bottom side of the grips were raised by a piece of cord installed beneath the rubber. The placement of Hogan's right hand was designed to cure his hook and produce the renowned fade.

Spectators at Oakland Hills studied the man and his swing. In his address to the ball, Hogan's left shoulder was higher than his right to block out the left side of the fairway. His feet were positioned five to six yards wider than the width of his shoulders, and he dug his golfing shoes, with their extra spikes, into the ground. He pulled his right foot back, his right toe pointing straight ahead. He opened the club starting back—some believe this was the Secret—and tucked his right elbow into his body. He employed more downswing than most as he turned his left hip as quickly as he could, the lateral movement of his left hip toward his target allowing Hogan to delay his release. He drove his clubhead toward the target, his head not moving until his ball was in flight. Hogan's hands finished high, his left elbow around and behind him.

The mechanics of Hogan's swing impressed British journalist and author Louis T. Stanley. Known as "Big Lou" for his tall and corpulent frame, "Lord Trumpington" for his home near Cambridge, or "Lord Louis" for his outspoken opinions, Stanley aired his thoughts with authority and named Hogan, "without hesitation" golf's most impressive shot maker. Stanley cited the "machine like precision" with which Hogan lined up his shot, the "effortless swing" that appeared incapable of going awry, and the "cold concentration" that combined to make Hogan's swing the "ultimate model."

Hogan's stylish, substantive swing improved his opening-day total, but he still played much of the second round with a frown; beneath the brim of his cap he looked grim. His eyes were fixed straight ahead, down the fairway, Herbert Warren Wind noted, "like a man heading for a spot in the woods where he has marked an errant shot."

Laboring beneath the burdens of summer heat and missed shots, Hogan trudged the course stiffly. He would stand beside his ball, hands on hips, cigarette jutting from his lips as he studied the lie, examined the emerald grass, and factored in the summer wind. He took his time, his mind filing through all of the possibilities. Other players went through similar motions, Herbert Warren Wind wrote, but it was Hogan who gave the strongest impression that he was "genuinely thinking about what he was doing." Tommy Bolt believed Hogan knew more about hitting a golf ball "than any five of the top golf professionals in the world."

Hogan knew at Oakland Hills that he couldn't hit the ball as he normally would; Trent Jones's layout wouldn't allow it. As author Robert Sommers noted, on any other course, if the hole were cut on the left of the green with bunkers guarding against a direct attack, Hogan would drive to the right side to gain a better shot at the pin. This approach, however, wasn't believed to be feasible in light of the tight fairways.

Continuing his conservative strategy against The Monster's fortified interior, Hogan clubbed down off the tee to avoid the trapping bunkers. If he was missing the bunkers, he was also missing opportunities a frontal attack would have afforded. Hogan's frustrations increased, and Wind noticed that, on such occasions, Hogan's grin became ironical and his eyes widened until they seemed to be "a full inch in height." As always, he remained close lipped.

Bolt knew Hogan wasn't one to waste words. "He wastes as many words as he does golf shots," Bolt said. Robert Trent Jones Jr. walked alongside Hogan on several courses and recalls his silence. "Hogan didn't say anything," he remembers. "He was insular, polite but taciturn."

Biographer Curt Sampson wrote that Hogan's smoke, silence, and detachment "resembled a Catholic Mass on Easter Sunday, but without the altar bells."

When Hogan departed from the final green, he was no longer on The Monster's highway to hell, but he remained infuriated by what he considered a "completely ridiculous" layout. "I've been lacking my power of concentration," Hogan acknowledged to reporters surprised at his admission.

What Hogan wasn't lacking, even though he was 9 over for his first 36 holes, was his ball-striking skills. Al "Red" Brosch was one of Hogan's playing partners in the first two days and thought Hogan the luckiest man he'd ever seen. While Brosch battled his way through a series of uphill, downhill, and sidehill shots on opening day, every one of Hogan's second shots came from a level lie. It wasn't until the second day that Brosch realized Hogan was playing his shots from the same spot as the previous day.

Hogan, however, remained frustrated with his performance. "He shot a 76 in his opening round and as his rounds went on he got better," Dick Howting says, "but it was not as good as it could be."

By his admission, Hogan never thought his golf was as good as it could be. He told *New York Times* writer Al Barkow he dreamed of playing the perfect round of golf—18 holes in one. In his dream, Hogan aced the first 17. But his drive on the 18th lipped out, and he carded a two. When Barkow asked how he felt about that, Hogan said he was angry. Angry at shooting 19, Barkow asked? Hogan issued a slight smile, leading Barkow to believe Hogan had some perspective after all.

Hogan had little perspective when it came to The Monster. He believed Trent Jones's layout to be "probably much too hard" for the majority of players in the field. Through 36 holes encompassing 322 rounds, Hogan was correct in his assessment. The sullen brute of a course had surrendered just two par 70s—Dave Douglas, who rebounded from his first-round 75 and would be Hogan's playing partner on Open Saturday, and Big John Bulla, who rallied from his opening-round 80.

Trent Jones saw the high scores as mistakes made by the professionals in their strategy. "The boys who are not underclubbing are going to be in the payoff," he predicted. "Anyone playing it safe is at too much of a disadvantage fighting the chips and putts on these green contours. And if they are in the rough it's much better to be closer to the pin."

Ralph Hutchison, the public address announcer at this U.S. Open and the pro at the Saucon Valley Country Club in Bethlehem, Pennsylvania, took issue with what Oakland Hills authorities had done to their South Course.

"It was one of the most unfair courses that I have ever seen," he told sportswriter George Kirchner of the *Lancaster New Era.* "They did just about everything possible to keep any guy from scoring, and in my mind they certainly overstepped the boundary lines."

Hutchison spoke of greens that were fast one day and slow the next, the condition of the bunkers guarding the traps, the placement of the traps, and rough that was unusually high and deep.

"I saw Lawson Little in rough practically up to his waist and with a wedge he was just about able to hit his ball back to the fairway," Hutchison said. "You can appreciate this when you consider that Little is a husky guy who can wallop a golf ball."

Turning his attention to the tight fairways, Hutchison said that, while the width is established under USGA rules, authorities placed traps inside instead of outside the fairways to get around the rule. "Thus, without violating any rule," he said, "they were able to narrow the fairways and make the course all the tougher."

The course was tough enough in Round 2 to make Snead's lead disappear as swiftly as a campaign promise. He followed his 71 with a 78 and complained bitterly that poorly raked traps had cost him four strokes. What had also proved costly was The Slammer seeking to slice his way free from The Monster's thick rough; his collapse was the biggest story of the second round. Snead's struggles were mirrored by a number of pros scrambling to make the cut for the reduced field of 55. The cut came at 152, which at 12 over was the highest at any major since the 1930s.

Douglas's par 70 put him one shot behind golf's bad boy, Bobby Locke, whose two-day totals of 73 and 71, for a 144, headed a leaderboard that saw 15 players crowded together between first and ninth place. Sensational amateur Francis "Bo" Wininger was alone in third place at 146. The red-hot novice from Northfield, New Jersey, shot a 71, a four-stroke improvement over his first-round total.

Wininger's solid showing stirred recollections among U.S. Open historians of Johnny Goodman in 1933. Goodman outdueled Ralph Guldahl by a stroke to win the U.S. Open at North Shore Country Club in Glenview, Illinois. It was the lone major won by Goodman and remains the last time an amateur finished first in golf's toughest tournament.

Wininger, a former Oklahoma A&M student seeking to make history and match Goodman's feat from 18 years earlier, was followed by a group of five players—1947 U.S. Open champion Lew Worsham; two-time PGA champ Paul Runyan; Al "Red" Brosch; Clayton Heafner, who was built like an NFL linebacker; and Charles "Chuck" Klein—who were tied for fourth at 147. Tied for ninth at 148 were 1941 U.S. Open champ Craig Wood, Julius Boros, Jimmy Demaret, Fred Hawkins, George Kinsman, Henry Ransom, and Earl Stewart.

Among the 10 players knotted at 149 were two preeminent talents and pre-tournament favorites—Hogan and Snead. Four past U.S. Open champions failed to make the cut after being mauled by The Monster. Billy Burke, who won his only major when he defeated George Von Elm in a marathon 72-hole playoff—the longest in U.S. Open history—in 1931 at Inverness Club in Toledo, Ohio, shot 77s his first two rounds and carded a 154 that was 14 over par. Lawson Little, the 1940 champ, likewise won his lone major in a playoff, this over Gene Sarazen at Canterbury Golf Club in Beachwood, Ohio, but shot 76 and 79, for a 155, at Oakland Hills.

Tony Manero staged a dramatic final-round rally to claim the 1936 crown on the Upper Course at Baltusrol Golf Club in Springfield, New Jersey, but found The Monster an unsolvable problem, shooting 77 and 79, for a 156. Manero's missing the cut meant his caddie Jack Fowler would be free to follow Hogan for the final two rounds.

Sam Parks Jr., the 1935 champion, was no stranger to difficult scoring conditions. Severe weather caused scores to soar in the 1935 U.S. Open in Oakmont, Pennsylvania. Parks managed to win by two shots over Jimmy Thomson; like Burke, Little, and Manero, the U.S. Open would prove to be his only major championship victory. And like those three, Parks struggled mightily against The Monster, going 79 and 79, for a 158.

Locke succeeded in momentarily taming the beast of Oakland Hills with flawless iron play. The Associated Press reported that the "chubby British Open champion" rifled his approaches to every green and putted for birdies on all but three holes. Shooting 36 on the front nine and 35 on the back, Locke secured his one-stroke lead over Douglas at the tournament's midpoint mark.

Smiling broadly and outfitted in his customary colorful attire—baggy knickers, linen dress shirts, four-hand knotted neckties, flat white cap, and white buckskin shoes—Locke played the gallery like a maestro. Following a good shot, he would smile and tip his cap to fans; poor shots failed to faze him. "Shaky, very shaky indeed," was Locke's lighthearted response after missing a short putt.

Locke's laissez-faire approach extended to his life off the course. He played the ukulele, was a singer, and was reputed to be one of the Tour's top partiers. Big, brilliant, and fun loving, Locke finished fourth or higher in each of his three prior U.S. Open appearances. Considered by many to be Hogan's top competitor when the tournament opened, Locke lived up to his billing.

Locke learned golf as a youngster in South Africa by reading a Bobby Jones instruction book. Unlike the masterful Jones, the golf swing Locke displayed at Oakland Hills was not a work of art. Author Charles Price wrote that Locke employed a "long, meandering backswing, at the top of which he collapsed his left side." Locke adopted an inside-out move that almost always produced a hard right-to-left draw. The result was that he would slap the ball into a long, sweeping arc that started out far to the right but hooked back to his target. Price said Locke "hooked every shot in the bag, including his putts."

Locke considered his golf swing to be a natural one and thought the swings of Americans unnatural and demanding constant practice. Like Francis Ouimet before him, Locke felt there was a danger to practicing too much, leading a golfer to leave his best game on the practice fairway. Gene Sarazen agreed and said a golfer had to be physically fresh to play a good game. Hogan was the only player Sarazen knew who had the physical and mental stamina to play great golf after expending maximum concentration and power in practice. It exhausted Sarazen to watch Hogan practice, and there were times when he felt Hogan left his best strokes on the practice range.

"They talk about Mr. Hogan's work ethic, but it wasn't work for him; it was his passion," Robert Stennett says. "He loved it."

Unlike Hogan, Locke did not seek perfection in his swing. When he heard a fellow pro remark that "Locke's trouble is that his left hand is weak," Locke quipped, 'Don't worry about that. I take the checks with my right hand."

Bad Boy Bobby did indeed cash checks at the expense of American golfers. His journey to the States began in the aftermath of Snead's winning the 1946 British Open. It was the first one played since 1939 due to World War II, and it led to financier Norbert Stephen Erleigh sponsoring a tour for Snead in South Africa. Locke, who in 1935 had been befriended by Erleigh as a teenage amateur, would be Snead's competitor. The two toured the country dueling in 16 matches; Locke won 12, Snead two, and two were ties.

The sports world was astonished that the American golfer was defeated by what writers said was a "man from the jungle." In time, the golf world came to know Locke's imperturbability under pressure and his proficiency with his putter. American pros and the U.S. press gave him the moniker "Old Muffin Face." Expressionless as he was, Locke's excellence on the green places him among the best putters in history; Gary Player believes his fellow countryman the best ever.

"Very early in my career I realized that putting was half the game of golf," Locke said. "No matter how well I might play the long shots, if I couldn't putt, I would never win."

Trent Jones's course demanded the kind of careful, testing shots foreign-born players were used to. This made The Monster a course that seemed to fit Locke, whose tactics reminded golf historians of Horton Smith, the native of Springfield, Missouri, who was nicknamed the "Joplin Ghost" and won the inaugural Masters championship in 1934 and claimed the prestigious title a second time two years later. Like Smith, Locke looked to avoid gambling on an imperfect shot that could leave him in trouble, preferring instead to rely on his near-perfect putting.

The image of Locke on the green at Oakland Hills fascinated fans. He addressed his ball holding an old, rusty-headed putter, and his stroke imparted such topspin that his ball advanced with end-over-end rotation. Locke's goal was to use the front and two sides of the cup to guide his shot into the hole. Just as he shattered the illusion that American pros could not be beaten, Locke destroyed another widely held belief that success in the short game was a big reason for the Americans' superiority over foreign-born players. He could putt as well or better as any American.

"I am never short on a putt," Locke stated. *"Never."*

Locke's success at Oakland Hills was not a surprise. Four years before he dueled The Monster, Bad Boy Bobby arrived in America and stormed through the States like the Liberators he flew out of Foggia, Italy, as a member of the South African Air Force in World War II. Flying more than a hundred missions left him looking leathery; Herbert Warren Wind thought Locke's face markedly altered by his wartime service. He appeared much older than his 29 years. Wind wrote that Americans seeing Locke up close for the first time did not see a boy wonder but a big-boned, confident man. Of the 15 U.S. Tour events he entered in 1947, Locke finished first six times; second, twice; third, once; and top seven on four other occasions. He was the most successful invader on U.S. soil since Harry Vardon; galleries loved Locke's accent and attire.

Locke met and became friends with Bing Crosby and Bob Hope in January 1948 at the famous Crosby Clambake, held in January to kick-start the winter Tour. Locke fancied himself a crooner like Crosby, that is, once he had sampled several beverages of choice. "I've never been very good," he admitted, "but after six or seven Pabst Blue Ribbons, I begin to sound reasonable."

Locke may not have been much of a singer, but his fondness for fashion rivaled that of Jimmy Demaret. Pro golfer Dean Hutchison was a boy when Locke made a memorable first impression in 1948. Bobby wore dark blue plus fours, pale blue stockings knitted by his mother, and brown-and-white golfing shoes with no laces. One of Locke's shoes had a loose spike so that when he walked he made a click-click-click sound still memorable to Hutchison decades later.

In 1949, Locke was banned from the American Tour. The PGA said it was because he had failed to play several exhibitions and tournaments and had done so without explanation. Skeptics believed the PGA was banning the South African from the American Tour because he won too many tournaments and too much money. Claude Harmon, the 1948 Masters champion, said the PGA blackballed Bobby because of his success. "Locke was simply too good," Harmon reportedly said. "They had to ban him."

The ban was removed in 1950, and Locke returned to the States. He also returned to his winning ways on U.S. soil, emerging victorious in the 1950 All American Open in Chicago by beating Lloyd Mangrum in a playoff. The win proved particularly pleasing to Locke, who acknowledged that, apart from being World War II veterans, he and Mangrum had little in common. Physically, Locke could not have been more different than Mangrum, whose pencil-thin mustache and dark hair parted down the middle gave him the appearance of a matinee idol. Mangrum's respect for Locke was given voice when he praised his playoff rival's putting prowess. "Locke," he stated, "was able to hole a putt over 60 feet of peanut brittle."

Once again, Locke was laughing all the way to bank. "I just can't say how nice it is to be back in the States," he crowed. American pros did not roll out the welcome mat for Locke's return. They chafed at his maddeningly deliberate pace of play.

After two rounds of dueling The Monster, the calculating Locke led a screened field of 55 competitors into what would be a grueling fight to the finish. To the huge throng at Oakland Hills, Locke's game looked as old-fashioned as his attire. Herbert Warren Wind noted that Locke's much-discussed swing exaggerated the inside-out arc, and while there was "nothing crackling about his hooky woods, they went a long way and they ended up on the fairway." Nor was there anything crisp about Locke's irons, but as Wind wrote, "they were accurate."

Locke may have looked like a tintype from the Roaring 20s, but by the midpoint of the tournament he had roared into the lead. While Locke was a known talent, the unheralded Douglas was an unknown underdog who had seemingly come from nowhere to challenge Bobby.

The tall, thin iron-shot ace from Newark, Delaware, Douglas had a golfing pedigree. His grandfather, David Douglas, managed a golf course near Edinburgh, Scotland. In 1911, Dave's father Alex immigrated to the United States at age 22 to be the club maker for James Thomson, the pro at the Philadelphia Country Club. Dave was born seven years later in Philadelphia and learned the sport at the Rock Manor Golf Club in Wilmington, Delaware, where his father was serving as club pro.

Dave and future fellow pro Ed "Porky" Oliver grew up together in Delaware and competed against each other in much the same manner that Hogan and Byron Nelson had been friendly rivals in their formative years in Texas. Douglas and Oliver physically resembled the lead characters in the long-running "Mutt & Jeff" newspaper comic strip. Mutt was the tall character, Jeff his half-pint companion. Creator Bud Fisher described his two characters as "two mismatched tinhorns."

Douglas, who lettered in basketball at P.S. du Pont High School, would grow to be one of the tallest, thinnest golfers on the PGA Tour, stretching to 6-3 and weighing just 154 pounds. Oliver, meanwhile, was nicknamed "Porky" due to his 5-9, 240-pound frame. As teenagers, Douglas and Oliver traded course records and came to be known as the "Thin Man and the Fat Man"; as a team they set several tournament records in the Delaware area. They also competed against one another in highly publicized matches, Dave and his dad dueling Oliver and Wilmington Club Pro Alex Tait.

Dave gained confidence from his golf experiences and finished as low amateur in the Philadelphia Open and Lake Placid Open. In 1938, the 20-year-old Douglas qualified for the National Amateur. He turned professional that year when he accepted the assistant pro job at Newark Country Club in Fort Wayne, Indiana. He returned to Delaware in 1940 and became the pro at the Newark (Delaware) Country Club. That same year, Douglas qualified for the U.S. Open. Ironically, it was the tournament in which Oliver was disqualified for starting his round prematurely.

In 1945 Douglas joined the U.S. Army and spent 18 months serving aboard a hospital ship. Leaving the army following his two-year stint, Dave assisted his father at Rock Manor and began giving golfing lessons at night at the Boulevard Driving Range in Wilmington. By the end of 1947, Douglas was ready to test his game on the winter tour. His first PGA victory came in his third attempt when he won the Orlando Open in 1947.

An incident at the Orlando Open illustrated Douglas's desire to mark his place on the Tour. Playing with fellow unknowns Ellis Taylor, who would eventually claim eight Delaware Amateur titles; Vic Catelino; and Otto Greiner, Douglas was in a foursome playing ahead of Snead. Slammin' Sam hit into their group several times, and, when one of The Slammer's second shots rolled between Catelino's legs, Vic suggested they let Snead play through.

"We will not," Douglas stated. "He's no better than we are."

Douglas backed up his words by firing a final-round 66 to force a playoff with Jimmy Demaret and Herman Kaiser. Douglas demonstrated a demeanor as relaxed as that of Locke, shooting a 71, which tied Demaret, and winning the $2,000 in prize money by draining a five-foot birdie putt on the first hole of sudden death.

Douglas's dramatic victory over Demaret did not translate immediately into more wins. For the next 18 months, he labored in relative obscurity. Still, he built a reputation as one of the more likable players on the Tour. His lean, lanky frame and elongated swing produced a hook similar to Locke's in its consistency, and, like Locke, Douglas earned the admiration of his fellow pros for his ability to save par with his putter.

Douglas's skills were on display in the 1949 Texas Open. Rounds of 65, 72, and 66 put him firmly in contention and placed him in the final threesome, where he once again ran into Snead. This time, however, Slammin' Sam wasn't following Douglas but leading him. A gallery of 7,000 crowded the competitors. Douglas, who was not used to being followed by such a large gathering, delivered a bogey on the first hole but then carded seven straight birdies en route to a 65 and his second tournament title. Members from the crowd surged forward in celebration, lifted Douglas on their shoulders, and carried him off the 18th green and to the clubhouse. Douglas signed so many autographs that it took him more than 15 minutes to travel just 100 feet.

Still, victories and prize money remained elusive—he ranked 17th in earnings in 1948—and, by the time he teed it up at Oakland Hills, Douglas was contemplating quitting the Tour. Yet his smooth swing produced a par 70 in the second round and punctuated some of The Monster's mystique. It also earned Douglas some of the recognition he deserved.

The 28-year-old Wininger (he pronounced his name as "Y-ninger") was born in Chico, California, in 1922. His family moved to the Midwest, and Bo played on the same high school baseball and football teams in Commerce, Oklahoma, as Mickey Mantle, though Wininger preceded the future New York Yankees superstar. Like Mantle, Wininger was considered one of the more sturdy sportsmen Oklahoma has produced.

Fans saw in the debonair Wininger a man owning thick, wavy hair and a love of fast cars. Herbert Warren Wind stated in a *Sports Illustrated* article in 1955, titled "Bo Geste," that Wininger "has one arrant idiosyncrasy: he drives an automobile as if he were a shady European prince who no longer gets his kicks from chamois hunting and chemin de fer."

Jack Nicklaus had a memorable encounter with Wininger in Las Vegas when Bo was pro at the Desert Inn. Following a round at the Sahara Invitational, Wininger drove Nicklaus to the latter's hotel one night, gunning his Shelby Cobra to 115 miles per hour as he raced through the streets of Vegas.

"Bo, slow down!" Nicklaus exclaimed.

"Oh, I'm just having some fun," Wininger laughed.

"Bo, slow down!"

Nicklaus said later he was as scared as he's ever been that night in Wininger's car.

Wininger's need for speed led to what became known as the "Mobile Incident." In the winter of 1953, one year after joining the PGA Tour, Wininger and his golfing pals finished the Baton Rouge Open and steered their cars east to the St. Louis Open, the next stop on the pro calendar. At 10:00 p.m., Wininger was driving alone toward Mobile when he saw fellow golfers Art Doering, Bill Ogden, and Freddy Wampler racing along at 75 miles per hour.

Wininger leaned on his accelerator and passed his pals. Checking his rearview mirror, he saw a car's headlights gaining on him. Believing it was Doering, Ogden, and Wampler, Wininger leaned on his accelerator a little more. He soon realized that the car gaining on him was not his golfing buddies but the local police.

Wininger pulled over, and, when his friends saw the situation he was in, they too stopped. All four golfers were booked for speeding and led to a combination court and jail similar to the tiny Mayberry courthouse on *The Andy Griffith Show*, which would air in the early 1960s. The judge, an old dirt farmer, arrived in an angry mood at being dragged from his bed in the dark of night. He fined each golfer $20, prompting Wininger to assume the role of spokesman for the group.

Hoping to play on the judge's sympathies, Bo began by stating that $20 was an awful lot of money for touring pros like themselves. Professional golf, he said, was just about the hardest way for a man to make a living. Every week, they motored from tournament to tournament hoping to scratch out a living. Each of the four golfers fined was having a hard season; their putting was awful. They were heading to St. Pete hoping to earn enough money to afford a bowl of chili and a motel room roof over their heads.

Wininger's tale of woe succeeded in softening the judge, who said he would lower the fine from $20 each to $17.50 for all four. Bo thanked the judge and then proceeded to pull a bill from his wallet.

"Judge," Wininger asked, "you have change for a hundred?"

Wininger and his fellow pros were progressing at a much slower pace as they navigated the tough terrain of Oakland Hills. Struggling at every turn, they drove into traps and rough and failed to crack par. Two days into the tournament and even the most dedicated golf historian could not recall when more than 300 rounds of the U.S. Open had failed to reveal a subpar score.

Writers and historians covering the tournament did realize that it had been 41 years since a foreign player had captured the U.S. Open—Ted Ray winning at Inverness in 1920—and 18 years since an amateur, Johnny Goodman, accomplished the feat. But after 36 holes Locke and Wininger were hoping to see history repeat itself.

Later that night, in New York City, Hogan's friend, former heavyweight champion Joe Louis, scored a sixth-round KO of Lee Savold. Some 630 miles west of Madison Square Garden, another legendary champion pondered his chances of victory.

"It would take two subpar rounds for me," Hogan said. "Even that might not be enough."

It would take a miracle to card consecutive subpar rounds, and The Monster had all but ruled out miracles. Nor was Locke known for surrendering leads or succumbing to the pressure of a major tournament.

The twin peaks seemed too much, even for a miracle man who built his reputation on overcoming obstacles. Heading into Saturday's climactic 36-hole grind, Hogan appeared all but out of it. With 15 golfers ahead of him, The Hawk did the mental math of what it would take to win. The numbers were not promising.

"I'm afraid it's out of reach," the despondent champion sighed. "Even two subpar rounds might not be enough. I'd have to be Houdini now. It would take 140 to get the lead, and how can anyone shoot 140 on that course?"

Day turned to dusk as the last group of golfers reached the final hole. They sent their shots to the green on 18 through the filtered sunlight of late afternoon. Later that night, friends of Hogan told him that he might win with a pair of 69s. He frowned, his mouth a hard line. His words were those of a man experiencing a chilling inner doubt.

"It seemed too much," Hogan recalled thinking, "on this course."

9

THIRD ROUND

Fire in the Iceman

Open Saturday dawned bright and brilliant in Bloomfield Township, Michigan.

"Texas weather," Ben Hogan grinned, and it was so pleasant it prompted Herbert Warren Wind to comment that it was "a lovely June day."

Hogan's enormous popularity and the endless publicity surrounding The Monster drew nearly 18,000 fans to Oakland Hills, at the time a record attendance for one day at the Open. Hogan was paired with Dave Douglas, an angular native of Newark, Delaware. Prior to their round, the pair posed for a photo that showed the 6-3 Douglas to be a half-foot taller than the Texan. The odd couple donned similar light-colored polo shirts and slacks, and, when the photographers' flashbulbs popped, both men issued smiles masking their apprehension at facing The Monster.

Bobby Locke, the leader heading into this third round, attracted a sizable crowd. Fans surrounded Locke, whose white cap, white shirt, white pants, white socks, and white shoes reminded Herbert Warren Wind of the White Rabbit in *Alice in Wonderland*.

Locke spent the morning round moving at his usual funereal pace and struggling to stay free of Trent Jones's bunkers. But as was his wont, Locke recovered with what Wind called "remarkable finesse." The British Open champion was making the shots he needed to make, and Wind had the distinct impression the White Rabbit would continue to do so.

Locke would sail his shot far out to the right, and the Oakland Hills gallery would gasp as it watched the ball come back and land in the center of the fairway. On The Monster's greens, Locke would hit a 20-foot putt, and, even before the ball was halfway to the hole, Bad Boy Bobby would be tipping his hat to fans. Said Sam Snead, "He wore out his hats tipping them."

Any competitor looking to catch Locke at the 54-hole mark was going to have to produce a round of the first order. From the crowd of hopefuls stepped Hogan. He had spent the night diagnosing in his mind the menacing Monster. It was a devilish design, so intimidating it demanded defensive golf from the best players. The first two rounds had proved that even long hitters like Snead could not consistently carry the new hazards. It seemed The Monster was simply too tough to be attacked and overpowered.

Unable to play their power game, golfers were left trying to thread narrow openings with perfectly placed shots. Those unwilling to adopt that risky strategy played shorter off the tee, but their plan was not foolproof since it still left them with longer approaches.

Faced with a seemingly unsolvable scenario, the field played it safe. Using fairway woods and irons off the tee, they abandoned their accustomed attacking style in favor of a cautious approach. That strategy failed as well. With 75 new traps along the fairways and another 75 around the greens, The Monster was succeeding in taking from the field first one weapon and then another, and snagging the slightest slice or hook.

"Did you ever see such a damned, stupid golf course in all your life," one frustrated golfer fumed. "What's this Jones trying to do? What the hell's that trap doing on the fairway on the 15th?"

It appeared no one could handle Oakland Hills. Writer Ben Rives believed The Monster had "baffled the cream of the world's golfers." Gay Talese called it "a weekend of diabolical madness" for tournament pros.

That presumption included Hogan, one of the greatest attacking golfers ever. Puzzled by the deceptive layout, The Hawk was playing defensively. He spent the first two rounds seeking safe shots, and his strategy left him 9 over par at 76 and 73, for a 149. He was in 16th place, five shots behind Locke, and it was noted that Hogan's usually sharp analysis was failing him. To many observers, the champion's chances of defending his title were negligible; Hogan himself had doubts. But, as he soaked his weary legs on the eve of Open Saturday, he came to a conclusion. Playing it safe had played to The Monster's strength. Hogan knew he needed to change tactics; The Hawk would have to attack.

Historically, the 36-hole final-day format was known for creating confusion and anxiety and for being a breeding ground for rumors. Staggered starting times left some players finishing their morning round just as the early starters were into their afternoon round. The overlap often obscured the significant occurrences of the early round as the attention of the golfers and the gallery laser focused on the final 18 holes.

Hogan began his morning round 90 minutes ahead of Locke. The man the Scots would later call the "Wee Iceman" for his cold efficiency, excited the huge crowd early. Casting aside his cigarettes and aiming his approaches at the pins, Hogan began coolly pummeling the beast and posting red numbers—indicating birdies—on the first two holes. The Hawk continued to electrify the crowd, carding another birdie on the 5th for three on his first five holes. He was at 3 under, the finest start all week.

Observers at Oakland Hills would remember Hogan's war with The Monster as a palpable thing; they could feel his fury. The Monster roared back on the 380-yard 7th hole, its brook that extended into the right side of the fairway catching Hogan's tee shot. The Hawk lost a stroke but regained his edge on 8, his 35- to 40-foot (eyewitness estimates vary) birdie putt banking in off the back of the cup. Hogan added a par on 9, bloodying the brute with a magnificent 32 that put him at 3 under at the turn.

Wreathed in smoke and with a gleam in his eyes—"They were the eyes of a circling bird of prey; fearless, fierce; the pupil no more than a dot in their imperious center. They were not the eyes of a loser," Jim Murray wrote—Hogan followed with a string of pars through 13. With The Monster reeling and a round of 67 in sight, fans flocked to see a surging champion intent on making golf history. Because this was prior to the practice of roping off the course from tee to green, fans were permitted on the fairways. They hurried across the course in arm's-length pursuit of their hero, who hobbled along in customary self-containment.

"He wrapped himself so tightly in his own business out there that he hardly knew who his playing partners were," Tommy Bolt said. "He only knew when his turn came to hit."

The gallery following the tournament leader was not immune to the Hogan mystique. He was teeing it up on the 14th as Locke was playing the nearby No. 5 hole. When Locke's crowd learned that Hogan was at 3 under, nearly half of them bailed on Bobby to watch Ben. Hogan handed back one stroke on the 14th, overshooting the green, which tilted slightly away from the approach, and, chipping back weakly, needed three to get down from the edge. Fans emitted an audible gasp when the champion, reputed to have ice water in his veins, misfired on a four-foot putt and two-putted for bogey.

The huge throng followed Hogan to 15. The Monster, still baring its teeth, struck back at its tormentor. The 15th was problematic, a dogleg swinging to the left and stretching to 392 yards. Seeking to avoid the bunker Trent Jones had placed in the middle of the fairway—a hazard many saw as homage to the Principal's Nose bunker on the 16th hole at St. Andrews—Hogan looked to stay to the left. He attacked with his driver but hurtled his ball to a bad lie in heavy rough on the right.

It was the kind of miscalculation that haunted Hogan in the opening round. As he had on Thursday, the champion compounded his mental mistake with a physical miscue. Unable to get a full swing at his ball because of the dense rough, Hogan hooked his approach shot in a small parabola that sailed across the fairway and into the opposite rough. Another feeble shot brought Hogan out of the rough but dumped him into the outrageously placed bunker protecting the green. He blasted out of the whitish sand, sending a spray skyward, and two-putted for a devastating double bogey.

Hogan's dream had become a nightmare. He had lost three strokes and was now at par.

After holing out for his disastrous 6, Hogan stood motionless on the green, hands on his hips. His sequence of shots—rough, rough, trap, short, and two putts—was stunningly bad. The champion stared darkly into the distance for several seconds—it was this glare that prompted Cary Middlecoff to call Hogan "The Hawk"—before dropping his head and stalking to the 16th tee.

Sensing that his great round was unraveling and facing one of the most testing holes on the Tour, Hogan fought back. He ripped a frozen rope to the right of the fairway, his ball rolling to a stop inches shy from rough that ran to the edge of the pond. Foreshadowing the risk–reward approach he would favor at Cherry Hills in the 1960 U.S. Open, Hogan attacked a pin positioned on a slice of green perched precariously over a pond.

It was a high-risk shot, but Hogan's nervy plan called for constant attack. Besides, he was still angered by the 6 he had just taken on 15. With the cup set to the right of the green, Hogan took aim on a spot most of his competitors considered unplayable. He spun his shot into the green, the ball stopping just five feet from the flag. The daring shot sent Hogan's followers into frenzied delirium. He followed with a par, but The Monster rose up on 17, forcing Hogan to take a bogey when he missed a four-foot putt.

The bruising back and forth between man and Monster continued on 18, Hogan producing par for a 1 over 71. It was an excellent score, the second best surrendered by The Monster to that point. But as Herbert Warren Wind wrote, it was also a disappointing one. Hogan had been on the cusp of carding a round so dazzling it might have taken the heart out of his competition and all but slain The Monster. Instead, the fiendish creation still had fangs, and the field still had hope that Hogan was human after all.

Hogan's round was three strokes better than the 74 posted by Locke and brought Ben to within two shots of the lead, with 18 holes still to play. Jimmy Demaret's par 70, just the third of the tournament, allowed him to tie Locke for the lead at 218. Julius Boros and the small, ageless Paul Runyan were both one stroke back at 219. Hogan, Douglas, and Clayton Heafner followed at 220.

Having lost four strokes to par over the final five holes of his morning round, Hogan shuffled off the course and headed to the locker room for lunch. His mood and visage darkening, Hogan limped off with a labored gait that moved one writer to comment that the champion "looked like a man condemned to die."

There was still a battle ahead, and competitors would have half an hour for a quick lunch before heading back into the bright sunlight. Not enough time for Hogan to soak his shattered legs as he needed to do at the end of 18 rounds. Glenn Diegel notes that Hogan "had lunch with his wife on the veranda." Ben munched grimly on a roast beef sandwich and washed down his sandwich, bouillon soup, and an aspirin with his customary glass of ginger ale.

Writer Marshall Smith observed that the champion chewed and swallowed his food mechanically, as if it had no taste. He ate in complete silence, seemingly unaware of who sat beside him and the multitude of crowded tables on the veranda overlooking the golf course. Hogan was struggling, Smith thought, to get himself in the proper frame of mind to win the Open. Smith thought it a manufactured mood that The Hawk had developed with much practice.

The tension of this Open had moved from the course to the clubhouse. Aware of Hogan's mood, reporters offered questions in hushed tones. Breaking his silence, Hogan said this thing that Trent Jones created was more than just a golf course. The Monster had a personality; it was a dangerous and formidable opponent. The course presented a problem that demanded to be solved. Barely containing his cold rage, Hogan cursed not only the course but his own game as well. He seethed at the thought that he had The Monster reeling in the third round but let it survive.

The Associated Press agreed, stating in an early report that "Hogan lost a chance to overhaul the leaders in the U.S. Open Golf Championship today when his game crumbled at the finish and he shot a 71 on the third round."

As the 54-hole standings were being posted, Hogan seemed only mildly interested in the scores produced by competitors; Locke, Demaret, Boros, Runyan, Heafner, and Douglas were all in contention.

Demaret took on The Monster with his trademark wit and wristy fades. The first of golf's show business stars, Demaret was colorfully clothed and quick with a quip, as much an entertainer as an athlete. Fellow Tour member Jackie Burke Jr. said Demaret was a "jet-setter before there were jets."

Dan Jenkins noted that Demaret's attire offered a rainbow of colors—aqua, gold, lavender, orange, pink, and red slacks; and maroon, checked, plaid, polka dot, and striped sports coats. Demaret's outfits for his three Masters victories were salmon pink; chartreuse and brown; and canary yellow, the latter coming on a glorious Easter Sunday. Herbert Warren Wind took to calling Demaret "The Wardrobe."

Demaret would give shoemakers a swatch of his snazzy slacks so they could create matching saddle oxfords. Demaret defended his garish outfits. "If you're going to be in the limelight," he would say, "you might as well dress like it." He lived for the limelight. A former nightclub singer, his baritone voice led Grantland Rice to call Demaret the "singing Texan." When he won the 1950 Masters, Demaret grabbed the microphone and began crooning, "Do you know how lucky you are?"

Demaret not only could sing; he was a first-class comedian as well. Bob Hope called him the world's funniest amateur comedian. Exiting his plane following a turbulent flight to Japan for the World Cup golf tournament, Demaret remarked, "Lindbergh got eight days of confetti for less than this!" Demaret's Technicolor style and personality are said by some to be the reasons golf enthusiast Bing Crosby invented the pro-am. When snow covered Pebble Beach in the 1962 Crosby, Demaret quipped, "I know I was drinking last night but how did I get to Squaw Valley?"

Demaret's impact on golf went beyond crooning and comedy. The native of Houston, Texas, was a three-time Masters champion. Born in 1910, the fifth of nine children, he spent much of his youth playing golf barefoot and caddying on sand greens. His lifelong love for matching colors came from his father, who was a painter and a carpenter.

At age 17, Demaret was hired by Jack Burke Sr. to be the assistant pro at Houston's River Oaks Country Club. One of his tasks was to babysit Jackie Jr., who would grow up to be a fellow Hall of Famer and partner with him in founding Houston's Champions Club.

Initially splitting time between golf and singing, Demaret joined the Tour full-time in 1938 at age 28. His breakout season came in 1940 when he won six straight tournaments, including his first Masters. His best year came in 1947, when Demaret won his second Masters, six tournaments total, led the Tour in earnings, and claimed the Vardon Trophy.

Demaret, like Snead, is one of the best golfers ever to not win the U.S. Open. He came close on several occasions, finishing second by two strokes in 1948, when Hogan won at Riviera in Pacific Palisades. Demaret turned 41 the month before the U.S. Open at Oakland Hills, but was still on top of his game, as evidenced by his 1950 Masters championship and third-place finish in the 1950 PGA Championship.

After carding 74s in his first two rounds at Oakland Hills, the stout Demaret's strong arms allowed him to employ a wristy swing that emphasized low fades with little effort and produced par in the third round. Hogan, knowing Demaret's shot-making skill, particularly under adverse conditions, called him the "most underrated golfer in history."

"This man played shots I hadn't dreamed of," Hogan said. "I learned them. But it was Jimmy who showed them to me first."

If Demaret was underrated, it was because his love of the good life prevented him from winning more tournaments than the 36 he eventually did. Golfer Henry Cotton captured the essence of Demaret when he said, "He loves golf, but no more than a good time."

While Demaret was "The Wardrobe" Boros bore the moniker of "Moose" for his physical size (6 feet and 200-plus pounds), strength, and nonchalant manner. He took on The Monster with a relaxed, rhythmic swing that produced a 71 in Round 3 following 74s in the first two rounds.

Boros was said to be one of the few golfers not intimidated by Hogan, and it's likely that the man who combined flawless technique with a well-banked inner fire was also not intimidated by Trent Jones's creation.

Born in 1920 in Fairfield, Connecticut, to Hungarian immigrants, Boros didn't turn pro until age 29. A former accountant, Boros soon earned a reputation among Tour members as a brisk worker. Boros never took a practice swing nor tarried like Locke, and his reasoning was simple. "By the time you get to your ball, if you don't know what to do with it, try another sport."

The effortless ease Boros exhibited on a golf course was the result of a discovery made during his military service—he had a bad heart. Yet, despite the calm he displayed, Boros admitted he was as nervous as the next man when faced with apprehensive situations. "It felt like razor blades in my stomach," he said.

The Moose's motto—"Swing easy, hit hard"—reflected his game. He hit with power, but his swing was free of strain and technically sound. Fellow Tour members considered Boros to be all hands and wrists, and the future Hall of Famer played the third round at Oakland Hills with the deft touch of a surgeon. He is believed to be the first player to successfully use the flop shot—an arcing soft lob from the high grass to the green—and did so in an era before the highly lofted wedges became prevalent.

Boros brought all his attributes to bear on The Monster. Playing with grace and control on fairways and greens, Boros's sweet swing parachuted his iron shots so that they landed with a softness that was unique. He dealt with The Monster's deep rough with a soft, slow swing, feathering his shots with wonderful accuracy.

"He was the most relaxed guy," Herbert Warren Wind wrote. "He seemed to have no nerves, and that made him very dangerous. Julius was one of the few players who could stand up to Hogan. He was never scared by him, and at that time, that was pretty hard not to be."

Wind thought Boros to be a man of "considerable sophistication. He moves his cigarette and phrases in a way that recalls Humphrey Bogart but you would never know that watching him in competition."

Boros was like Locke in that he was poker faced in his duel with The Monster. He impressed the Oakland Hills galleries as an efficient, rather than an arresting, sportsman. His short game was solid, if unspectacular, but he drew praise from fellow Tour members for being at his best in a big tournament. Boros's big hands carried his club through a languid-looking swing that saw him slide his club subtly into the ball. He loped around the Oakland Hills course, disguising his apprehension and the razor blades in his stomach behind a fluid swing and placid demeanor.

Tied for fifth with the bulky Boros at 9 over, Runyan ranked just behind Bantam Ben as golf's best little big man, the 5-7, 125-pound product of Hot Springs, Arkansas, owning a Depression-era toughness and deadly short game that earned him the nickname "Little Poison." Runyan's moniker recalled Lloyd Waner, a Pittsburgh Pirates' star of the 1920s and 1930s, who was called "Little Poison" to brother Paul's "Big Poison."

Born in 1908, Runyan was the son of a dairy farmer who believed in keeping his boy busy by assigning him multiple chores. Young Paul eventually found he could make money caddying at a nearby club and working for the pro. He earned a quarter for every lost ball he found while shagging stray shots.

Because he was not naturally gifted on the golf course, Runyan resolved to work harder than his fellow caddies, who were routinely beating him. Like Hogan, Runyan said he dug his success out of the ground, pushing himself constantly to improve his game. "I had to work for it," he said. "I was not a natural. All the kids in the caddy pen beat me, until I just dug it out and became better."

Made an apprentice at his club, Runyan would play four holes of golf on the way to school in the early-morning hours and four more holes on his way home in late afternoon. He turned pro at age 17 and by the following year was the head club pro at a Little Rock club. By 1931, Runyan had moved east to serve as an assistant to Craig Wood at Forest Hills Golf Club in White Plains, New York. Three years later, the student bested his teacher when Runyan edged Wood in extra holes—1 up on the 38th hole—to win the PGA Championship.

His slight size made Runyan realize he would need a strong short game to compete with bigger men who played power golf. "Through necessity, I began my lifelong devotion to the short game," he said, "the searching for shortcuts that would somehow let me compete, and hopefully excel, in a world of stronger players."

At Oakland Hills, the 42-year-old Runyan saw his strategic short game as his prime weapon in defeating The Monster while at the same time demoralizing his opponents. "I've taken some pleasure out of being the little guy who has beaten the big fellows," Runyan remarked.

Runyan was a toy terrier constantly nipping at the heels of power hitters like Slammin' Sam. At the 1938 PGA Championship at Shawnee Country Club in Delaware, Runyan defeated The Slammer in golf's ultimate David versus Goliath story.

Runyan's swing was known for its pronounced sway that produced drives off the tee that barely averaged 230 yards on Shawnee's legendary fairways. Snead routinely outdrove him by an estimated 35–75 yards— The Slammer stated that some of his drives were 100 yards longer—but Runyan retaliated with his reliable fairway-wood approaches. The bigger, stronger Snead figured to have a huge advantage on the par 5s, but it was the tiny Runyan who birdied six of the seven holes played.

Sepia film of the 1938 PGA Championship shows Runyan as a diminutive dandy dressed in a crisp, white, short-sleeved shirt and gray slacks. When he took off his floppy fedora, Runyan's dark hair was wet combed off his high forehead in a devil-may-care style straight out of F. Scott Fitzgerald's *The Great Gatsby*.

In one clip, Runyan used a niblick, the equivalent to a modern 9-iron or wedge, to jump his ball over Snead's and into the cup. "This isn't golf; it's magic," The Slammer drawled during the final, which went to Runyan 8 and 7.

It was a pool-hustler's shot and, as the crowd roared in disbelief, Runyan reached over and flipped Snead's ball back to him, a savage ball toss that reflected Runyan's rugged approach to golf.

Gentleman's game? Yeah, right!

Preening like a peacock, Little Poison proved to be a big problem for Slammin' Sam, shooting 24 under par for the 196 holes played. Runyan went 64 straight holes without going over par.

Runyan brought some of this same magic to his third round at Oakland Hills. A cool, deliberate sharpshooter, his peculiar brand of popgun golf made his performance all the more amazing. The Monster mocked light hitters, but Runyan replied by drilling drives that were deadly straight. His killer instinct on the course saw him attack with amazingly accurate fairway-wood approaches and reliable irons. Runyan's wrist-free stroke was a staple of a short game that found success against the brutal course; the finest chipper in the game gained revenge against Trent Jones's torturous design with a third round 72 following earlier rounds of 73 and 74.

"If you have [mastered] chipping, putting, and short pitching," Runyan stated, "you've got golf 65 to 80 percent whipped."

He looked to whip The Monster by mastering its traps. Runyan used minimal clubhead penetration if his ball was sitting atop the white sand. When his ball sat deeper, he employed a more descending downswing with his sand wedge. If his ball was fully buried, he would pull a pitching wedge or 9-iron to get deeper clubhead penetration.

Snead stated once that Runyan could "get the ball up and down from a manhole." Runyan did that at Oakland Hills, playing himself into contention in a wild third round.

"Little Poison," Snead said. "He didn't hit the ball very far by any means but, oh, what a short game he had, second to none."

Runyan applied a mathematician's approach to his short game. He knew, for instance, if he carried a 3-iron three feet on The Monster's green that was neither uphill nor downhill, it would run about 10 times as far as it carried. On the other hand, Runyan knew that if he were carrying a sand wedge on that same three feet of green, it would run one-and-a-half times as far as it carried.

So why not pitch the sand wedge farther? That, the wily Runyon knew, was comparable to "drawing to inside straights in poker." His goal was to hit the shot that had the least airtime. Throughout the Open at Oakland Hills, the scrappy, self-reliant razorback refused to be rattled by The Monster's taunting, trapping layout.

"Don't let the bad shots get to you," he would say in his Arkansas twang. "Don't let yourself become angry."

Runyan lived his own advice, and it resulted in his claiming 29 Tour victories from 1930–1941. Nine of those wins came in 1933, making him one of just seven golfers to earn nine or more victories in a single PGA season. He followed with six more in 1934, including the first of his two PGA titles. It was enough to earn the money title in the first year such records were kept. It amounted to $6,767, a hefty sum in the Depression years.

In the inaugural Masters in 1934, originally called the Augusta Invitational, Runyan's playing partner for the first two rounds was Bobby Jones. If Runyan was awed to be in the presence of greatness, he didn't show it. He tied for third, two shots behind champion Horton Smith and one behind his mentor, Wood.

Runyan made himself into the best light-hitting golfer ever, a title the Hall of Famer still holds; Scotland's Fred McLeod, nicknamed "The Wasp" for his 5-4, 108-pound frame, was smaller than Runyan and also had a fine record, winning the U.S. Open in 1908.

Few golfers before or since have hit chip shots like Runyan. Byron Nelson bestowed upon him the lofty title of being the best chipper he ever saw. Runyan was a short-game guru, whose techniques around the green were devastating.

On top of that, he was cocky and indomitable, and his fierce competitive fire ensured that few players in history were more feared than Little

Poison. "I don't suppose anyone ever got more out of their golf game than Paul Runyan," Snead stated.

Runyan's tenacity was in full view at Oakland Hills as he ferociously fought The Monster on every hole. "You are in the fight of your life," he said. "It is instinctive that I fight."

Heafner likewise brought a fiercely competitive attitude into his fight with The Monster. At 6-2 and 230 pounds, the hefty North Carolinian's rugged mountain-man physique contrasted sharply with that of the mighty-mite razorback, Runyan. Yet the two shared a similarity in that Heafner, like Runyan, was one of the more feared competitors on the PGA Tour. Two years prior to Oakland Hills, Heafner had finished as runner-up to Middlecoff at Medinah in the U.S. Open.

One of the best strikers of the ball of his era, Heafner won several Tour events and would have won more had it not been for his volcanic temper. "Clayton was the most even-tempered golfer I ever saw," Snead quipped. "He was mad all the time."

Heafner made little effort to spare the feelings of others. Charlie Price, a talented writer, tried to make it on the PGA Tour and sought advice from Heafner. Clayton told Price he would review the younger man's swing—for a fee. Heafner studied Price's swing on the practice range and then played several holes with him.

"Charlie," he finally said, "did you notice that all the guys doing well out here on tour are built like truck drivers but have the touch of hairdressers? Well, you're built like a hairdresser and have the touch of a truck driver."

Heafner's bluntness extended even to golfing legends. He told Demaret in 1947 that Locke would win more tournaments the rest of that summer than Jimmy or Ben Hogan. Demaret quickly accepted Heafner's bet and just as quickly lost a lot of money.

Heafner's skill as a ball striker and ferocious combativeness helped him shoot 73 in the third round and tie Hogan and Douglas for fifth place. As competitive as Locke, Demaret, Boros, Runyan, and Heafner were, none of them saw this tournament as Hogan did—a personal war with The Monster.

The very thing Hogan loved—conquering a great golf course—was killing him. The Monster was proving to be a course even Hogan couldn't master. In his latest attempt to tame the beast, Hogan had missed again. As Lincoln Werden wrote in the *New York Times*, Hogan "blamed himself for overclubbing, for making mistakes."

The tournament-tough Hogan was still hanging on, and, being just two strokes off the lead, still hanging in. "I guess all of the boys are making more [mistakes]," he said.

Thoughts of failure infuriated The Hawk. He couldn't comprehend a course too tough for him to overcome. The Monster was most formidable; courage and pride would push Hogan forward, but to win he would have to dig deep within himself to overcome his limitations—his pain, his frustration. With grim resolve, he returned to the course carrying within him the cold rage of his morning round.

Fueled by his inner fire, the "Iceman" cometh. As he stepped to the first tee of the fourth and final round, resolute was the look of Hogan, indomitable the look of The Monster.

10

FINAL ROUND

Combat at the Country Club

Beneath a clear, blue sky, a U.S. Open–record crowd, which was the largest ever to witness a golf tournament in the state of Michigan, lined the fairways and greens for the final round of Open Saturday.

Writing in the *New York Times*, Lincoln Werden stated that thrill-hungry fans had seen firsthand The Monster's "narrow fairways and strategically placed traps, the greens of rolling contours, and two par-4 holes that many thought should have been rated at 5." It was enough to prevent anyone from recording a round below par. Yet Ben Hogan's 71 in the morning, Werden wrote, "was something in the way of an inspiration" for the crowd.

Fans rushed to the first tee for the afternoon round, surging and pushing forward to get a glimpse of golf's biggest superstar, one of sport's most notable celebrity champions. Peering through periscopes, they fixed their gaze on Hogan.

The habitual white linen cap was pulled low over his dark, hawklike gaze, his tanned face surrounded by cigarette smoke. And there in his gabardine slacks were the outlines of the elastic bandages that encased his damaged legs.

Lined up at Hogan's heels was what writers and USGA officials recalled as the "biggest mob in history ever to follow a golfer." Having finished his lunch, the champion fashioned his strategy for this final round with The Monster.

It was Hogan's practice not to alter his course strategy until the final round. He had formulated his original plans for dealing with The Monster prior to Thursday's opening round. But he broke with his own tradition when he devised a new strategy following the second round. As he would at Carnoustie two years later, Hogan changed tactics for one reason only.

"I'm in a corner," he said later, "and have to fight my way out."

For Hogan, this final round of the 1951 U.S. Open represented the biggest fight of his career, The Monster being his toughest opponent. Yet, despite the demanding and draining physical, mental, and emotional tests that Open Saturday presented with its 36-hole format and championship pressure, it was common for Hogan to feel energized entering the afternoon round. Joseph C. Dey Jr. noticed it immediately. Dey was serving as referee and knew Ben rarely engaged in small talk with anyone.

It was to Dey's surprise then that he found the champ "unusually chatty" as he prepared to tee off. Hogan told Dey he was still "burned up" by the back nine 39 that morning, letting *this* monster get away from him. Herbert Warren Wind thought Hogan had been on the verge of a round "so dazzling that it would have had the effect of taking the heart out of his opposition."

Hogan said once that his degree of sharpness governs his attack and expectations. He was razor sharp in the morning round, and just as Walter Travis had turned the insults directed his way in 1904 to become the first non-Brit to the win British Open, Hogan would use the affronts heaped upon him by The Monster as fuel for his fire in the afternoon. Pulling his patched-up body erect, Hogan drew a deep breath. Confident he could "go low" in the afternoon round, Hogan turned to official Ike Grainger. "I'm going to burn it up, Ike."

Writer Frank Hannigan said Hogan made the statement without a show of swagger. "It was a statement of the determination and faith which marked his life—the determination which kept him alive in 1949 when he was near death."

Despite his discomfort, Hogan felt stronger heading into the final round. He attributed this to his bloodstream getting "an extra shot of adrenaline from his body." Knowing this added strength would enable him to hit the ball farther in the fourth round than he had in the previous three rounds, he would purposely underclub each shot. Where he used a 5-iron in the first three rounds, a 6-iron would be his club of choice in the afternoon round.

Hogan was teeing off directly behind co-leader Jimmy Demaret at a 12-minute interval. Bobby Locke, Demaret's co-leader, was still playing his third round and wouldn't tee off to start his final round for another 90 minutes.

No longer the lush greenery that greeted golfers in Thursday's opening round, Trent Jones's beastie by Saturday afternoon resembled a Revolutionary War battlefield, replete with divots and spike marks. Hogan ignored the battle scars and gripped his driver in his hard hands. Having selected his club, The Hawk fixed The Monster with his cold stare—a glare fellow golfers called "the steelies."

Dan Jenkins saw "the steelies" and was reminded that Hogan never liked any course very much at a major. "Ben thought the course was his enemy," Jenkins said. "He went out and tried to kill it."

Like an ancient harpooner, Hogan had already stuck a couple dozen irons into the great leviathan. Trent Jones's layout offended Hogan like no other course ever. It demanded that the man revered as the best shot maker in golf history use practically every club in his bag to have any shot at success.

The Monster mauled the field the first two rounds, but Herb Graffis noted in *GOLFing* magazine that the last half of this Open would be played under different conditions. The fairways had dried and were playing with more bounce and roll than they had in the first two rounds. The greens were faster, there was no wind, and the markers were forward.

"Oakland Hills," Graffis stated, "was a different course than it had been here Thursday and Friday."

The fact that the final two rounds were played on the same day benefited the field but benefited Hogan the most. Writer Ben Rives remarked that in the afternoon round Hogan had an advantage unintentionally provided by the USGA to golfers astute enough to make the most of it.

"Since 36 holes had to be played in one day," Rives noted, "it was impossible to change the positions of the pins for the afternoon round."

This allowed Hogan to know exactly where the holes were, and while the rest of the field had the same knowledge, it was The Hawk who would use that information to the fullest advantage. He would choose his shots with cool deliberation, boldly firing for the flag on every green.

From the tee that sat 20–25 feet above The Monster's target area, Hogan began a routine recognized by even the most casual sports fans—the address, the waggle, the crack of the clubhead against his Spalding ball, and the follow-through of his swing. Hogan launched his artillery assault by lashing at a hole that was straightaway from tee to green. Playing what appeared to be a downhill shot gave Hogan and the field a psychological lift. Still, this was not an easy hole due to its 440-yard length and Trent Jones's nest of traps lining both sides of the fairway 230–250 yards out. Hogan followed with a 7-iron to the kidney-shaped green and two-putted for par.

The champion recorded his second-straight par on No. 2. To handle the slight dogleg left, Hogan went driver, 3-iron, and wedge, eclipsing much of the 510 yards and reaching the treacherous greens. It took two putts for him to successfully negotiate the extremely fast surface and break even on the par-5 hole.

The gallery groaned when The Monster stirred and trapped Hogan on No. 3. The par 3 turned into a 4 when Hogan overshot with a 2-iron off the tee, wedged out from a diagonal bunker and two-putted for a bogey. Hogan held his own on No. 4, using a driver and his iconic 1-iron to reach the green. He two-putted on a surface whose undulations made putting difficult and parred the hole.

His drives whistling like rockets, Hogan battled the brute on even terms through holes 5, 6, and 7, each a par 4. Hogan gripped his driver on 5 and slashed at the downhill fairway. He pulled a 3-iron to put his approach shot on the sloped putting surface and once again two-putted on treacherous greens. Hogan's strategy was becoming clear. He was using his driver where possible on each par 4 and par 5 and taking dead aim on the pin on his approach shots, rather than trying to place his ball on the wide part of the green.

"I've played Oakland Hills many times," Ben Wright says, "and if you're going to make a score you have to make it early. Oakland Hills gets more and more difficult as the rounds go on. That's what makes it fabulous."

On No. 6, the shortest par 4 in Trent Jones's layout, Hogan again went driver off the tee and used his 9-iron to loft an approach shot to the tricky greens. The putting surface was slick but not as treacherous as the greens on Nos. 2 and 5, and Hogan two-putted for the sixth consecutive hole.

One-third of his way through the final 18, Hogan was determined but sullen. He was holding steady but running out of time to make good on his promise to "burn up" the course.

"Hogan," James R. Hansen wrote, "understood that it was time to attack. . . . If he lost the tournament and failed to defend his Open titles he would at least go down fighting rather than surrender to the bullying schemes of Jones's redesigned golf course."

Standing in the tee box on No. 7, Hogan was facing the same hole that cost him a bogey 5 in the morning round. He studied the dogleg and its cluster of traps on the upper left-hand side of the fairway. Graffis wrote that Hogan's "head was at work" on No. 7. Earlier that day, his tee shot had found the pond that sat to the right of a sloping fairway. "He'd driven into the ditch," Graffis wrote, "and cost himself a 5."

Pulling a brassie from his bag, Hogan hugged the left side of the fairway, avoiding the bothersome brook. He used a 7-iron to pitch to the long, narrow green that was set slightly on a diagonal and had defensive trapping at the front left and flank trapping on the left and right sides. Hogan laid his iron shot two feet from the pin.

"He placed his drive perfectly," Graffis wrote, "and knocked his second shot up for a 2-foot putt."

The same enormous gallery that sighed when Hogan bogeyed No. 3 shook the ground with a roar of approval for his skilled shot making on 7. Turning to the crowd, The Hawk issued a thin smile. "Wait until I make it," he said. Hogan made it, rattling home the short putt for a birdie 3, his first birdie of the afternoon.

Squinting down the fairway, The Hawk returned to his driver for No. 8. The hole was protected against a long hooked shot by a dogleg left and trapping on the left-hand side. The Monster's thick rough snared

Hogan's drive, but the champion slashed his way free with an 8-iron. He stuck with his 8-iron to carry the severe trappings on the left, right, and in back. He placed his approach shot five feet from the flag and saved a strong par 4 with a putt that perfectly negotiated the fast, undulating green. Remarked an observer, "This hole demonstrates the tremendous retaliatory power of Hogan, never daunted in the face of adversity, always completely absorbed by the shot at hand."

One of The Monster's strongest par 3s was No. 9, and The Hawk attacked it off the tee with an audacious 1-iron. Straight shots and draws were demanded from the tee and Hogan obliged. Once on the green, the contouring was extremely severe; keen judgment was needed to line up putts. The kidney-shaped green would be three-putted often in the tournament, but Hogan two-putted and was out in his front nine with a 35. He was at even par, with nine holes left.

The champion was confident but concerned. Hogan was playing power golf at a ferocious pace—he finished the turn in 90 minutes—but Trent Jones's hideous creation was still capable of hard pars and easy bogeys. Danger lurked on every hole, and disaster beckoned from The Monster's fairways, traps, rough, and greens. That much was being proven by the fact that of those in contention only Clayton Heafner and Lloyd Mangrum were playing as well as Hogan.

"Word was drifting back to me that he was going great," Heafner said once. "I had it on my mind all day. Every chance I got I would look at the scoreboards.... I was playing my best; he was just shooting the lights out."

The Monster's fury in the finale produced one of the highest-scoring rounds in U.S. Open history. Douglas followed his second-round 70 with a 75 and 74. Paul Runyan's popgun, pool-hustler game was likewise meat for The Monster, his final round a 75. Burly Julius Boros fought the good fight, but his final-round 74 was a victory for The Monster. Fred Hawkins's harrowing duel with the Ogre of Oakland Hills saw him finish with his best round of the tournament, a 71. Al Besselink was two strokes behind at 73, Ol' Bessie having never fully recovered from being mauled by The Monster in earlier rounds.

Writer Harry Grayson pointed out that Hogan and Runyan demonstrated at Oakland Hills that golf is above all a game of accuracy. Bantam

Ben and Little Poison were the two smallest men in the field, yet they remained very much in the hunt as the final round teed off. Observers watching Hogan and Runyan witnessed two golfers whose games were strikingly dissimilar despite their similar size.

Grayson compared Hogan and his "glorious and powerful swing" to New York Yankees hurler Vic Raschi. Runyan, by contrast, was a softball pitcher, according to Grayson. Eyeing Runyan from a distance, Grayson said, could lead one to mistake him for "a hacking club member on a practice round." Little Poison was called the little man with the big spoon because, as Grayson noted, "he has to use one where the average crack shot employs an iron."

In his duel with the devil of Oakland Hills, Runyan did not card a hole of more than 5, which Grayson found amazing under the circumstances. No other contestant could match that. Because he couldn't get home with an iron, Runyan used wood clubs off the tee and in the fairway 30 times in his opening round alone. Hogan, by contrast, averaged 20 wood shots per round.

As afternoon shadows stretched dramatically across the sunlit stretch of Oakland Hills, Hogan had just nine holes left to instill his will on The Monster, nine holes to prove he could master any course. With the pressure building, Hogan's wide mouth contracted into a thin line, as writer Henry Longhurst noted it did in such situations.

Even Bobby Jones hadn't accomplished the three straight titles Hogan was seeking. Jones's undoing in the 1924 U.S. Open at Oakland Hills had come on No. 10, a hole he never quite figured out. Two of his four attempts to master the troublesome 10th in 1924 had resulted in his recording a gut-wrenching 6 each time. It was the most challenging par 4 on the course and one of the toughest in the world. Through the first three rounds, The Monster had surrendered but three birdies on 10. Locke lost the lead on that hole late on the morning of Open Saturday when he, like Bobby Jones before him, carded a 6.

Hogan dug his spikes into the same patch of short grass that Bobby Jones had three decades earlier. The tee was elevated 20 feet above the distant target area. Hogan sized up an unforgiving 448-yard par 4. The Monster's defensive trappings were everywhere—on the fairway at 230–250 yards out, etched into a hillside at 250–260 yards, deep to the right, and a shallow one to the left of an elevated green. Ironically, one of the distant bunkers on the right had been added after Hogan took Trent Jones up on his pre-tournament dare to carry a sand trap that sat 215–230 yards out on the right fringe of the fairway.

Hogan made par on No. 10 in each of his first three rounds, but he recognized the problems the hole presented. It was a test of accuracy, offering a limited landing area for the tee shot; statistically, it was the toughest target area to reach in regulation. One writer thought it looked "like an obstacle course in the 230–280 yard range." Playing a drive short all but eliminated the chance of getting on the green in two. Trent Jones kept a hole-by-hole chart of the 1951 Open he titled "Location of Tee Shots," and it showed that in the morning round with the wind against them a third of the field missed the fairway on 10 and not one player carried a tee shot over the bunkers on the left or right.

Hogan said the trouble on 10 only started at the tee and that additional problems loomed large. "The landing area was a small target because of a bunker on the left side of the fairway, and since the fairway has quite a sharp slope from left to right, it was most tough to miss the bunker and keep the ball in the fairway.

"Obviously, the key to this hole was first the tee shot. Many good tee shots found their way rolling down the hill into fairly deep rough. Since the second shot required a high long iron to an uphill blind green, it was nearly impossible from this position to get the necessary elevation and length to land the ball on the green and hold it.

"Fortunately my drive stopped short of getting into the rough on the right and from that position I hit a 2-iron (5 feet) from the hole and made a most important birdie."

Hogan lashed violently and drilled his tee shot 265 yards into The Monster's short hairs. "Hogan's drive," said an observer, "sailed down the fairway like an arrow." He followed with a long, high 2-iron to the slope-top green; it covered nearly 200 yards and stopped five feet from the cup, a masterstroke. Hogan called his 2-iron "my best shot of the tournament. . . . it was exactly what I wanted every inch of the way."

Rifling his irons, this was the famous Hogan shot making that fascinated fellow champions. Jack Nicklaus once saw Hogan hit 18 consecutive greens in the second round of the U.S. Open and the first 34 of 36 on Saturday. "That's 52 straight greens in a U.S. Open in regulation," Nicklaus noted. "Unbelievable."

Robert Trent Jones Jr. would walk courses with Hogan in the mid-1950s and be amazed at his shot making. "He could hit the ball right where he wanted—left of the bunker, right of the bunker," Trent Jones Jr. remembers. "His swing adjusted to the aerial game and the kinds of courses he was asked to play."

Associated Press sportswriter Will Grimsley noted in his story that Hogan "rifled the ball within five feet of the cup." *Life* magazine writer Marshall Smith watched Hogan's shot soar 200 yards straight for the pin and pull up within the shadow of the cup. "Undoubtedly the finest shot in all the tournament," wrote Grimsley.

Dave Press felt the electricity in the crowd. The caddie recalled his boss having "dead aim" at this point in the final round. Hogan's five-foot putt on 10 was his second birdie of the round and came on a hole that Press said, "nobody was making birdie on." Decades later, Press still considered it possibly the best birdie he'd ever seen.

Hogan would call it a "career" shot, and his birdie caused the crowd to erupt in another wild celebration. It was at this point, Marshall Smith felt, that Hogan "finally had all the answers to all the problems of Oakland Hills."

Hogan agreed, telling reporters later, "I felt good after that. I knew I had a chance."

Locke knew it as well. The White Rabbit was just finishing his third round when The Hawk was taking wing on 10. Hogan's birdie and the roar of the crowd unsettled Locke. He bogeyed the first hole at the same time Hogan was earning his birdie, and the two were now tied for the lead. Public address announcer Ralph Hutchison, however, believed the momentum was with Hogan.

"After I saw Ben birdie the 10th hole on that last round," he said, "I figured him a good bet to win."

Still, Locke was a match for any golfer, Hogan included. And if Locke could work his customary magic with his ancient blade putter, his contemporaries knew they could be in for a duel in the sun. "He's the greatest putter I've ever seen," Snead said. Remarked Hogan, "Everyone examines greens, but only [Locke] knows what he's looking for."

Four years earlier at the *Philadelphia Inquirer*'s tournament, the roles had been reversed, Locke rallying past a suddenly erratic Hogan. Herbert Warren Wind observed that Hogan's surprisingly unsteady play in Philadelphia seemed to bear out the belief that he needed to temper the "intensity" of his tournament golf.

There would be no tempering the intensity of Hogan's golf at Oakland Hills. Herbert Warren Wind was following Hogan in the final round and thought him extremely purposeful. "I've never seen a man so determined," Wind wrote. An assured, accurate shot maker once again, Hogan kept the pressure on Locke with a par on 11, using a driver off the tee to a valley below. His 1-iron to a long and narrow green set up a two putt. The Hawk followed with a second straight par on 12, the longest par 5 on the course at 566 yards. He drove off the tee into a fairway trapped on the left 260–280 yards out. A 3-iron and 9-iron put Hogan on the contoured green, where he two-putted for par to stay at 1 under heading into his final six holes.

Demaret believed success with the putter the most amazing part of Hogan's game. He had watched Hogan in earlier years struggle with his short game. Believing most good putters are born and not made, Demaret doubted Hogan would ever get the touch. But Hogan's hard work allowed him to succeed. "Ben made himself into a great putter," Demaret said.

Trent Jones watched his creation being attacked by Hogan and knew the champ had finally figured out The Monster. "In order to conquer it," the architect explained, "you had to assault it."

It had taken three rounds, Trent Jones said, but the players had finally realized that they could not play The Monster "safe." Clubbing down off the tee had resulted in longer second shots. The longer the second shot, the higher the probability of error. It was small wonder players were posting high scores.

"During the last round, Hogan attacked," Trent Jones observed. "He used his driver off the tee on every par 4 and par 5. He played his approaches for the pin."

The furious assault confirmed Gene Sarazen's belief that Hogan was the most merciless golfer of his era. "He plays with the frigidity of dry ice," The Squire stated.

Sarazen theorized that Hogan's temperament might have derived from the rough, anguish-filled years of his childhood. Whatever the reason, Hogan was a golfer who Sarazen said was "perpetually hungry." The Squire recalled a time when he and The Hawk were on their way to winning the 1941 Miami Invitation Four-Ball. Sarazen and Hogan went to lunch 8 up in one of their early-round matches. Prior to starting out that afternoon, Sarazen suggested taking it a little easier.

"I should say not," Hogan snapped. "We ought to keep piling it on. If we can beat these guys 14 and 12, I'd like that."

Hogan's intensity propelled him to 2 under with a birdie on Oakland Hills's short 13th, one of the finest holes on the course and one that presented a multitude of intriguing problems. The champion's icy, impeccable shot making tamed The Monster's shortest hole—a 169-yard par 3—with a 6-iron off the tee that carried to a green surrounded on all sides by traps. He then curled in a 14-foot putt for a birdie deuce that brought another tremendous roar from the crowd.

"The little man is moving up!" echoed excitedly across The Monster's massive meadow. A carnival-like gaiety engulfed the crowd, and there came Hogan, the trim Texan, trudging the bright green grounds, his eyes burning with intensity. Sam Snead knew the look; it was the look of Hogan's card-dealing days when he was trying to make ends meet. "That's how he learned that stone face," Snead said.

Hogan was raising his game against The Monster, but still lying in wait were the troublesome 14th and 15th holes. It was at this point in the morning that Hogan's round began to collapse. True to form, The Monster punched back on 14 in the afternoon, delivering a bogey to Hogan for the second time that day. The 14th was deceptive in that, while there were no fairway traps, the angle of the entrance to the green was difficult if the tee shot were hooked or pushed off line. A fallaway green featured a swale in the middle and traps on the left and right fronts. Making the hole more problematic was a stiff wind that blew in and forced adjustments in club selection; 2-irons, 3-irons, and fairway woods became the weapons of choice. No matter what club was used, The Monster had its way on 14, not allowing even one birdie on the demanding hole for the entire tournament.

Even Hogan couldn't solve 14. Graffis noted that The Hawk, no doubt recalling his trouble on 14 in the morning round, initially grabbed a 5-iron on 14 in the afternoon before thinking twice and gripping a 3-iron; others reported it as a 4-iron. Either way, Graffis thought it Hogan's first error in judgment in the final round. Just as he had in the morning, Hogan overshot the green with a daring approach and full-blooded iron shot. Visibly upset, he wedged out of the sand; he acknowledged that the chip shot was the hardest for him to make, and it showed on several holes. His chip was short, and he two-putted for a bogey 5.

Hogan's war with The Monster was growing grim and dangerous. The afternoon was wearing on, shadows continuing their boardinghouse reach. Hogan and The Monster were locked in the universal and eternal struggle of predator and prey, and reversing their roles seemingly from hole to hole. The central conflict—man at odds with nature—was deepening; that Hogan was feeling the nerve-shredding pressure was evident in his drawing ever deeper on his cigarettes.

Knocked back to 1 under by The Monster, Hogan headed to the fateful 15th remembering full well the indignities that same dogleg hole had visited upon him earlier in the day. Hogan's drive had sailed too far left and landed in the deep rough, the result being a double bogey 6. That he learned from his morning round was evident in his club selection. He had used his driver to avoid the central bunker that sat squarely in the middle of the fairway. He failed, landed his ball in the rough and lost two shots.

For the afternoon round, Hogan ignored his driver and waggled a 4-wood on the tee; playing it safe with what one observer described as "gauged caution," Hogan stayed two yards short of the bunker in the middle of the fairway. He took a 6-iron and lofted a tremendous shot that stuck six feet from the stick. Dan Jenkins thought Hogan's 6-iron a "deadly" shot. "Don't tell Ben how to get even with a golf course," Jenkins said.

Hogan had caught fire. The U.S. Open was played on The Monster's turf, but it was now being played on Hogan's terms. His six-foot putt gave him a birdie 3 on 15—half the number of shots Hogan had needed on that hole in the morning round—and sent The Hawk soaring to the top of the leaderboard for the first time in the tournament. He was back to 2 under, and the huge crowd was back to being hysterical. The grand old game had rarely, if ever, been played in the superlative manner in which Hogan was now playing it, and fans wanted to be a part of it. Dey remembered the gallery being "extremely large" and "very difficult" for the tournament's marshals to handle.

Free of his caddie duties, Jack Fowler followed Hogan on his final round. "The crowds got bigger every day," he recalls, "and I was wondering where the heck people were parking their cars. By the final round it was so crowded, I couldn't get close."

Knowing the lay of the land, Fowler hurried to high ground, where he would have a vivid view of Hogan's late charge. "Hogan went wild in that final round," Fowler remembers. "Those were amazing shots he was hitting. At contact the ball would jump off his club and there were a lot of 'Ooohs' and 'Aaahhs' from the crowd."

Fowler heard from Press what it was like caddying for Hogan in that cauldron of heat and noise. "Dave said Hogan was very quiet and barely asked a question," says Fowler. "Hogan wouldn't ask Dave about yardage but he did ask him about the greens and the slope, left or right."

Dave Press said that, since there wasn't any real security, "the crowd was running all over the place." Fans were rooting for Hogan, urging him on. He pressed on to the 16th; accompanying him were marshals carrying ropes, which they stretched in a solid line across the fairways to hold back fans while players hit their shots. Once the ball was hit, fans surged forward. Hogan wasn't seeing any of his fairway shots land. As soon as his ball was struck, the crowd enveloped him, screening his view. It was bothersome to Hogan, who considered the trajectory of his shots crucial to their success.

At one point of the pressure-filled final round, Hogan used the surging crowd to take his mind off The Monster.

"Joe," he said to Dey, "golf fans certainly put up with a lot."

"What do you mean?"

"They park miles away," Hogan stated. "They get pushed around by the other fans. And they really don't see many shots if they're seeing what I see."

"Ben, they do this because they admire your skill."

Holding a 4-wood in his hand, Hogan studied it for a second or two.

"Maybe it does take skill," he mused. "Maybe it does."

Hogan then returned his focus to The Monster.

"He was all business after that," said Dey.

Business resumed on the 16th, Trent Jones's treacherous lake hole. It was the start of the finishing holes that Bruce Devlin calls "plenty of trouble."

"Talk about difficult holes, 16, 17, and 18 at Oakland Hills are extremely difficult," Devlin says. "Pick any three-hole combination on any golf course and you have to pick 16, 17, and 18 at Oakland Hills as tough as any."

The 16th is the most spectacular hole and the most dangerous, largely because of the lake that flanked the right side. Trapping was solid on the left flank and at the back of the green. The safest way to play 16 was to drive to the left and onto the green, and try to get home on two putts. Twenty-one years later, Gary Player would make his miracle shot from the right rough, over the trees, to the peninsula to win the 1972 U.S. Open. It is one of golf's most legendary shots; fittingly, it came on a legendary hole.

When Hogan reached 16, he learned that Locke's game had gone sideways. Bad Boy Bobby was in a bad stretch—three consecutive bogeys. Locke later complained that one of The Monster's bunkers on No. 5 was hidden, causing him to bogey in the morning and double-bogey in the afternoon. Trent Jones dismissed Locke's complaint. "[S]ince this was the final day after a week of practicing and competition, Locke surely knew the bunker was there."

Now in the lead, Hogan delivered a drive off the tee that was far to the right and rolled to a stop 290 yards out and just two yards from the deepest rough on The Monster's layout. Herbert Warren Wind called it "a whale of a drive." Hogan used a 9-iron to wedge his way over the water to within six feet of a pin positioned tantalizingly close to the lake. It was a beautiful shot and put him within four feet of the flag and another birdie.

"The ball came off Hogan's club," Fowler recalls, "and it was precise to the target." Hogan lined up his putt and sent his Spalding spinning toward the hole.

"No dice," wrote Wind. The Hawk fixed a fierce stare at the missed shot, his ball running 20 feet past the hole. Hogan two-putted for par.

The roar of the record-sized gallery echoed through the green canyons like thunder. Hogan, however, held his poise amid the noise. "I've got to restrain myself," he recalled thinking. "I'm not in yet."

Self-control, Grayson knew, is crucial in course management. "The player has to be in command of himself," he wrote, "before he can guide a golf ball." Grayson studied The Hawk's stern face. "The concentration of his emotions," he said, "is Hogan's secret."

Years later, Nicklaus would notice the same quality in Hogan. "He always seemed to play well within himself," he stated.

Two months later, Dick Collis would witness firsthand The Hawk's burning intensity at Tam O'Shanter that Press also saw at Oakland Hills. Hogan was paired with Jimmy Demaret in the third round when Demaret's 3-iron from 200 yards on No. 4 found the bottom of the cup. The crowd roared—"went bananas," Collis recalled—but when Hogan got up to the green he asked Collis where Demaret's ball was. It was then that Collis realized that Hogan was in his own world. Collis was startled; he had never seen such concentration. Hogan's cocoon-like concentration carried over into the final round. Trailing Demaret by five strokes, Hogan hit his worst shot of the tournament on No. 4. Needing a miracle to card a birdie, Hogan engineered a 50-foot chip shot through a bunker, over a mound, and into the hole. Collis stared in disbelief at The Hawk, who issued a wry smile. He had fired a final-round 66 to win; business as usual for Hogan.

Hogan was rallying in the same fashion at Oakland Hills. Locke said later he was shook by the dramatic comeback, so shook his celebrated short game suffered. Locke, who rarely lost leads, lost this one en route to carding a 73. Bobby would leave Oakland Hills believing The Monster's final six holes were the "toughest in the world."

As the White Rabbit sagged, The Hawk soared. Word reached the champion that Locke was locked in combat with The Monster on the front nine, that Demaret and Boros were being roughed up, and that only Heafner was playing at a level that approached Hogan's.

Among those watching Hogan's every move was Trent Jones. The architect studied the champion's skilled shot making and thought it "indicative of Hogan's ability to map out a course and then apply his skill to make the necessary shots."

Hogan was hammering Trent Jones's creation with terrifying accuracy, and The Monster maker knew it. "It is difficult for the architect to defend against that kind of ability, nor should he want to. That's what the game is all about."

Sarazen thought a "throbbing necessity to win" is what drove Hogan on, and Oakland Hills was proving to be another example. Werden wrote that Hogan "seemed determined to 'beat' the course. He looked grim." Herbert Warren Wind said Hogan made playing Oakland Hills "a personal matter."

Hogan would reveal in 1959 that waging war with the golf course was his first priority. "First, I went after the golf course," he stated. "Generally, I figured that if I could beat the course I could stay ahead of the competition. I also played against my own standards. It was a constant struggle of one kind or another—but always a pleasant one."

The afternoon was growing late. The weather was still sublime, sunny and in the 70s, with an occasional cooling breeze, but the air was thick with tension. The par-3 17th remains one of the best short holes in golf, a plateaued green that sat 30 feet above the tee and was flanked on all sides by protective traps that caused Hogan to card a bogey in the morning. In the afternoon, he pulled a 1-iron from his bag and fired at a pin 194 yards away. The Monster's green required careful reading, and its pronounced slope caused Hogan to two-putt.

The beast had bitten back; The Monster was wounded but would still have its moments. It was taking down Hogan's final-round competitors— Demaret shooting a 41 on the front nine and Boros, a 38—and appeared to be still capable of grounding the high-flying Hawk.

Hogan would have none of it. He had become the tee-to-green machine that fans favored and foes feared. He was hammering drives with the awesome authority that caused Colonial Country Club's Frank Holland to state, "That man could hit his irons like nobody."

Watching the champion's charge, Will Grimsley thought Hogan's nerve was matched "only by the cold steel of his deadly irons. Ben played boldly, firing at the pins rather than the fat part of the greens."

Hogan's aching legs carried him to the elongated 18th; his competitive spirit carried him farther. "This was Hogan's second 18 [holes] of the day a little over two years after the accident that nearly killed him and left his legs in a very weakened condition," says Glenn Diegel. Because a typical 18-hole walk on the South Course covers seven miles, Hogan had now walked 14 miles of hilly, rolling ground in heat and humidity. He once described the pain in his left knee as "feeling as if someone were stabbing me with an ice pick." He lived in constant fear his knee would collapse on him, yet refused to give in to pain. "I'll walk as long as I can," he once told Tommy Bolt.

"My mother walked the entire 36 holes with Hogan," Trent Jones Jr. remembers. "Hogan smoked a lot and never said anything except, 'You're away.' He was in pain a great amount of the time, and he was greatly admired because of his courage."

Having played Oakland Hills, Devlin knows the physical and mental toll it takes on those who play it. "That's a long and difficult course," he says. "It wears you out."

There would be no faltering now. Hogan, limping on his left side, approached the heavily bunkered 18th, one of the best finishing holes in golf. The Hawk squinted at the dogleg right and the defensive trapping 280 yards out on the left and right sides that protected the target area. He was by now familiar with the new bunkers put inside the crooked dogleg to discourage cutting the corner. The Monster's bunkers on the left snagged tee shots that failed to fade and went through the fairway. Trent Jones's redesign was made more rugged with its conversion from a par 5 to a par 4, and at 459 yards it was the longest par 4 in The Monster's makeup.

Hogan knew another par would give him a 68 for his final round and the title by one or even two strokes. A soft breeze blew across the course. It was a favorable wind, Trent Jones's detailed charts showing that in the morning round Hogan and at least a dozen other players had carried the bunkers and sent their tee shots soaring some 300 yards out. With the wind at his back in both a literal and figurative sense, The Hawk would look to carry the bunkered ridge in the angle of the dogleg right.

Dropping the last of his half-smoked Chesterfields to the ground, Hogan took hold of his driver. Sensing the weight of the moment, he took a little longer than usual to settle into his stance. He waggled once, twice, and drew back his driver.

The 18th hole at Oakland Hills demands drama and dares golfers to be great. It continues to be ranked as one of the toughest holes in the world. According to *Golfweek* magazine, during the 2008 PGA Championship at Oakland Hills the 18th produced a scoring average of 4.661, one of the highest on any course anywhere. A total of 10 triple bogeys or worse in 2008 led to The Monster's 18th being ranked the second-toughest hole on the Tour.

Bolstered by the breeze at his back and now supremely confident, Hogan believed the risk he was about to take was a worthy one. The fired-up champion gripped and ripped, the sun glinting off his driver. His forceful swing sent his Spalding streaking down the center of the fairway.

"A tremendous drive," Marshall Smith wrote. Decades later, Tiger Woods's swing coach Butch Harmon would analyze The Hawk and conclude that, until Tiger came along, no one Harmon had seen generated as much speed through the ball as Hogan. Al Barkow thought the flight of Hogan's shots made it appear as if he had succeeded in slicing out his own exclusive sliver of sky. As Hogan's shot soared, the crowd roared. With the near cloudless sky serving as a blue backdrop, the white tracer appeared to clear the bunkered ridge, finally settling in the fairway 280 yards from the tee.

Hogan's drive was incredibly daring. The golfer with movie-star celebrity unfurled a cinematic swing that sent another current of electricity through the enormous gallery. Werden said fans hemmed the green, pushing forward in order "to view another phase of his courageous bid to keep the crown."

Among the overflow crowd were media members whom Hogan referred to as the "camera guys." The clicking shutters of their black, box-shaped Speed Graphic cameras, which ruled newspaper photography for the first half of the twentieth century, reminded the Texan of the sounds made by a prairie rattlesnake.

Amid the clicking of the camera shutters there came Hogan, marching across a green meadow speckled with sun and shadow. His face was tanned and taut beneath his bright white cap. Moving up to his approach shot, Hogan's mind mapped out his next shot.

Flashing a 6-iron, he pegged his approach at the pin. Hogan then floated a towering shot that split the middle of The Monster's shallow green, pin high and 15 feet from the flag. Back on the 10th tee, Locke heard the echoes of another huge cheer coming from 18. He stopped and stood composedly to let the noise subside.

"How far away is he?" he asked.

"Less than 20 feet," he was told.

Locke shook his head. "He'll make it."

Cameras continued to click as Hogan headed to the 18th green. Traversing The Monster's length and uneven topography had taken a toll; now trudging on tired legs to his 36th hole of the day, Hogan's limp became more pronounced.

"There's a reason for the *hills* in Oakland Hills," Glenn Diegel states. "It's not a flat course."

Hutchison said if he lived to be a hundred he would still see "Ben come up over that hill." From his pin-high position, Hogan studied The Monster's sunbaked green. Some criticized him for taking too much time with his shots—"The Surveyor" they called him—but Hogan was looking over the green on 18, trying to figure out a contour separated by a shoulder mound through its center. In addition The Hawk was studying the grass on The Monster's green and sizing up the distance to the cup.

"He played meticulously," wrote Grimsley, "measuring every assignment carefully."

"If he took more than a quick look at the hole, it escaped me," Hutchison said. "All I could see him doing was stare at his ball. Honestly, I thought he had frozen, that's how tense he seemed to be. Now I've seen Hogan play many a round of golf, but never have I seen him do this."

The delay heightened the drama. Werden thought the champion stood over his ball for a full 30 seconds; Hutchison, for reasons unknown even to him, put a clock on Hogan and said it was nearly twice that long. "For 57 seconds he did nothing but look at his ball." An observer noted that the green by now was "completely ringed by the gallery, with only the front entrance clear, and fans standing twenty and thirty deep, craning to see the finish."

"Then," Hutchison recalled, "as calmly as if it didn't mean a thing, he putted." The gallery held its collective breath. Hogan watched his Spalding spin across the green toward the white cup. There was a sound of silence as the ball trickled slowly at first before gathering momentum and speed as it tumbled toward the high corner of the hole.

"The ball rolled true to the line," remembered Hutchison.

And fell in for a birdie 3.

The massive gallery exploded in cheers.

Hogan had done it. In conquering a course considered unconquerable, he had brought The Monster of Oakland Hills to its knees.

"The greatest golf round of Ben Hogan's life—a three-under par 67 at 'impossible' Oakland Hills—was complete," Marshall Smith wrote.

Al Besselink had teed off two hours behind Hogan and had just hit a near-perfect 1-iron to the 9th green, the ball stopping a yard behind the hole, when he heard the crowd roaring on the 18th green. Besselink knew what it meant.

"Hogan just finished with a heck of a round," he said. "No doubt about that."

The Monster was felled, and the collapse of the colossus shook the sports world. The leviathan lay inert, brought down by Hogan's skilled shot making in the pressure-filled final day. His ferocious intensity in the final three holes of the afternoon round left observers believing that Hogan seemed to always hit the exact shot needed at a given moment. It's what great champions do, and few, if any, did it better than Hogan.

The final nine holes had seen him card four 3s and one 2. He played the last six holes in 20 strokes. He shot 3 under on a course on which no one had yet broken par. Amid the pressure of Open Saturday, Hogan posted 32s on each nine. His rounds included 39 pars, 14 birdies, 17 bogeys, and two double bogeys. He was in the rough 10 times, in traps 10 times, and missed 16 greens.

Trent Jones's Monster demanded expert reading of the course, and as Graffis noted, Hogan was "the best in the business at reading a course from tee to cup." In a final round that saw the field average 75, Hogan shot 8 under.

Besselink believed Hogan's advantage at Oakland Hills was as much about course strategy as it was ball striking. "Between his left ear and his right ear Hogan was the smartest golfer who ever lived," opined Besselink, who thought Hogan's victory at Oakland Hills was due to his mental strength. Longhurst put it succinctly when he said, "if Hogan means to win, you lose."

Exhausted by the effort required to beat The Monster, Hogan reached into the cup for the final time, retrieved his ball, and handed it to Dave Press. As he reached the center of the green, Hogan was filmed removing his hat and acknowledging the thousands of fans banking the green. The champion draped his arm around the shoulders of his smiling caddie as they strode from the green. Press put the prized ball in his pocket; he was offered as much as $50 for it—at the time a sizable amount for a souvenir.

A cordon of police surrounded the man who would be king and escorted him to the clubhouse amid the cheers of a crowd. It was, wrote Werden, "another stirring chapter in the golfing story of Hogan."

Hogan conquered his tormentor with a tournament-best 67, which was a stunning 3 under par. The Monster had been slain, and even its creator applauded Hogan's effort.

"Magnificent," Trent Jones said.

The Monster was built for dramatic theater and Hogan obliged, finishing with a flourish to furnish the first subpar round of the 1951 Open and posting a score most believed to be impossible. True to his word to Grainger, Hogan did indeed "burn it up" in the final round. He shot 35 on the front nine, 32 on the back. His card showed five birdies against just two bogeys.

"Yes," Hogan said, "I would say this is my greatest round."

Because Locke, Clayton, and three-fourths of the field were still on the course waging their own wars, Hogan would have to wait nearly two hours for his victory to become official. Yet his total of 287—the same score he had shot to win at Merion the previous year—seemed unassailable. Locke admitted as much.

"That took the starch out of the rest of us," he said of the 67 that was posted on the leaderboard next to Hogan's name. Playing nine holes behind Hogan, Locke made the turn at 37 and needed three birdies to tie Hogan's 287. He birdied No. 10 and barely missed a birdie on 12. On 13, Locke tried to edge his shot close to the pin but didn't carry the bunker; the White Rabbit was snared. Losing his main weapon—his famed putting touch—in the final-day grind, Locke bogeyed three consecutive holes and eventually fell from contention. At day's end, he signed off on a 73 after shooting 74 in the morning and placed third at 11 over 291.

Heafner fared better, shooting 69 to produce the only other subpar round of this Open. Clayton created excitement with a birdie on 15 that brought him to within two shots of Hogan. He arrived at the 18th needing an eagle to tie. He drilled a tremendous drive, but it sailed into the rough on the right. Heafner's powerful second shot landed in the rough on the left. He blasted up to 18 inches and sank his putt for par. It was an exceptional round, and it put Heafner second at 9 over 289.

Some 35 reporters crowded around the champion who had made history. Hogan paid homage to The Monster. "It's the toughest course I've ever played and the best round of my life."

He believed The Monster the most challenging test any group of golfers had ever faced. "I haven't played all the courses in the world, but I don't want to, especially if there are any that are tougher than this one."

He admitted there was a time during the tournament when he doubted his chances of shooting such a round. "To be honest, I didn't think I could do it," he said. "My friends said last night that I might win with a pair of 69s. It seemed too much on this course."

Nearly everyone had thought the same, prompting Grimsley to call Hogan's comeback "incredible" in his Associated Press story:

Golf's mighty little "comeback man," Ben Hogan, staged another of his incredible finishes today to win his third National Open Championship.

Werden wrote in the *New York Times* that Hogan's final round made for a "smashing finale." Graffis declared, "The toughest golfer won over the toughest course." Hogan won, Graffis said, because he "played better golf between the ears. The others can play the same fine shots and putt the same as Hogan. Where he beats them is in that critical scoring area called the brain. They fret about controlling the ball. Hogan successfully applies himself to controlling his head. That's the decisive difference in a field of stars, all of whom can hit the ball about equally well."

Graffis thought Hogan's 67 "spectacular" and said the champion made just one error in judgment. That came on the 14th, when Hogan initially pulled a 5-iron from his bag before replacing it with a 4. The result was a bogey 5. Graffis reminded readers that Hogan started the tournament with a 76, made a three-stroke improvement in the second round, knocked another two strokes off in his third round, and finished with a 3 under 67. "Experience taught Hogan how to solve the course." One observer said Hogan passed Trent Jones's test "with uncanny ability."

Hogan's victory was historic on several fronts. He became the first U.S. Open champion to successfully defend his title since Ralph Guldahl in 1938 and was just the third man to claim at least three U.S. Open titles. Hogan's 67 was the lowest round of the week and at the time the second-lowest final round recorded by a U.S. Open champion, one stroke behind Sarazen's 66 at Fresh Meadow in 1932.

Grayson noted that Hogan had actually shot a 64 this day, if one considers his 32 on the front nine that morning and 32 on the back nine in the afternoon. In the process, Grayson wrote, Hogan showed that "rigged-up Oakland Hills was manageable."

Werden thought it "another great comeback" by Hogan. When Heafner walked wearily into the clubhouse, he drew consolation from the fact that he hadn't lost the tournament; Hogan had won it. "I told myself second place wasn't the worst place to wind up," he recalled. "But then came the crusher."

As Heafner prepared to leave the locker room for the trophy presentation, Hogan came walking down the corridor between the lockers, reading a telegram. The two men bumped shoulders and Hogan looked up and said, "Oh hi, Clayt, how'd it go today?"

Hogan's breezy question stunned the second-place finisher. "He was dead serious," Heafner said. "He didn't even know that I had come close to winning the tournament. . . . When he asked that question in the locker room, I knew then that I had some concentration practicing ahead of me or I'd never again stay on the golf course with that little man."

At the trophy celebration, Hogan was handed the silver trophy. He had sipped a cold beer, showered, and was now dressed in a fresh shirt and checkered blazer. As he clutched the cherished chalice, Hogan smiled and issued the most famous quote in golf history.

"I'm glad I brought this course—this Monster—to its knees."

The quote later puzzled Press, who could not recall hearing Hogan say it; neither did a friend of Press who was also a caddie.

Herbert Warren Wind believed Ben derived "colossal satisfaction" from his victory. Hogan's satisfaction no doubt stemmed from his eventual mastery of The Monster, a mastery reflected in the ever-improving scores of his rounds: 76, 73, 71, and 67.

"Hogan's accomplishment," says Diegel, "is more amazing considering his score for the finishing 9 holes."

As he departed the course and headed back to the clubhouse, Hogan passed Ione Jones, the charming wife of the architect whose design had left him drained physically and emotionally. Genuinely thrilled by Hogan's performance, she offered her congratulations.

"My mother was very enthusiastic, very outgoing and Hogan was very intense," Robert Trent Jones Jr. recalls. "She said, 'Oh, Ben, I walked every step with you. What a marvelous round!' He turned toward her and said, 'Mrs. Jones, if your husband had to play the courses he designed, you'd be in the poorhouse.'"

Trent Jones said Hogan's victory at Oakland Hills confirmed that only a great player could win on a great golf course. He suspected that, deep in his heart, Hogan believed the same. Sarazen wrote the USGA to say The Monster was a masterpiece. "It was a challenge to the player," Sarazen wrote. "The best players finished on top."

The Squire was one of five former U.S. Open champions who struggled with The Monster, shooting 74, 76, 76, and 77, for a 303, to finish tied for 35th. Lloyd Mangrum (293, tied for fourth), Lew Worsham (296, tied for 14th), Cary Middlecoff (301, tied for 24th), and Craig Wood (307, tied for 47th) were all roughed up by the rugged course. Following Hogan, Heafner, and Locke were Mangrum and Boros, who tied for fourth at 293. Hawkins, Besselink, Douglas, and Runyan shot 294 to tie for sixth; Snead tied for 10th at 295. Chuck Kocsis carded a 297 to beat Bo Wininger by five strokes for the USGA's Amateur Medal. The high scores were testament to The Monster's toughness; the field averaged 7 over 77 for the tournament.

Marshall Smith wrote that Hogan, in achieving his remarkable feat, should be grateful to Trent Jones, whose redesign stressed brains, experience, and fortitude, attributes that Hogan had in abundance. The Monster brought out the best in Hogan, but he was not inclined to be grateful to its creator. Nor did Hogan's fury fade with final victory. Jenkins said that, while Hogan called the course "this Monster" in public, he called it something very different in private.

As darkness descended on Oakland Hills, Fowler found himself in awe of what he witnessed that afternoon. Decades passed, but Fowler's memory of the final round burns as bright as that long-ago summer sun. "Hogan," he states, "was a rare player."

And The Monster was a rare course. Robert Trent Jones Jr. says that at the trophy presentation the crowd "simultaneously called for my father to take a bow. He did."

EPILOGUE

Greatest 18 Ever Played?

Decades after the sun had set on the 1951 U.S. Open, Bruce Devlin continues to consider the final round at Oakland Hills the greatest 18 holes Ben Hogan ever played.

"Hogan winning at Oakland Hills under those conditions," Devlin says, "was remarkable."

Bobby Locke would have agreed. When he was told Hogan shot a 67 against Trent Jones's Monster, Locke was stunned. "Did he play every hole?" Hogan's performance prompted writer Frank Hannigan to call The Hawk's round "the masterpiece of his career." Where it ranks all-time is open to debate. Hogan carded 67s in other majors, including the 1948 U.S. Open at Riviera and in the 1953 U.S. Open at Oakmont. He shot 66 in the third round of the 1953 Masters, setting a 54-hole scoring record at 205 (-11). None of those scores, however, were recorded amid the pressures of a final round and on a course like The Monster.

Hogan maintained that, under the circumstances, his final round at Oakland Hills was his greatest ever. Many believe it's the greatest in U.S. Open history and in major championship history.

At the time, Hogan's round was considered the best ever shot in the U.S. Open, better even than Gene Sarazen's 66 at Fresh Meadow in Long Island, New York, in 1932 due to the difficulty of the course. In its coverage of Oakland Hills, *Life* magazine titled its story "Greatest Round Ever."

There have been spectacular final rounds since Hogan's at Oakland Hills, and it's open to debate if it exceeds superlative performances at other majors—the 65 carded by Arnold Palmer when he thrilled his Army with a comeback at Cherry Hills in 1960; 46-year-old Jack Nicklaus turning back time at Augusta with a 65 in 1986; Tom Watson's 65 at Turnberry in the celebrated "Duel in the Sun" with Nicklaus in the 1977 British Open; Johnny Miller at Oakmont in 1973, when he carded the first 63 in major championship history; Gary Player at the Masters in 1978, when he overcame a seven-shot deficit in the final round with a string of birdies on the back nine for a 64, proving once more the adage that "the Masters doesn't begin until the back nine on Sunday."

Does The Hawk at Oakland Hills in 1951 surpass The Shark, Greg Norman, in the British Open at Royal St. Georges in 1993, or a Tiger, Eldrick Woods, at Valhalla in the 2000 PGA Championship?

In terms of physical courage, was the sight of Hogan hobbling at Oakland Hills more dramatic than Ken Venturi in a literal life-and-death struggle with the dangerous heat at Congressional in 1964, or more epic than Tiger overcoming a torn ligament and broken tibia in a playoff at Torrey Pines in 2008?

Dan Jenkins believed Hogan's performance at Oakland Hills the most epic. Because many consider The Monster the most rugged course in history, Jenkins said Hogan's 67 remains the "Rembrandt" of U.S. Open final rounds.

"The average score of the field that afternoon at Oakland Hills was 75," Jenkins wrote. "In that sense, you can say that Hogan's 67 was actually 8 under par on what he would call 'the monster'—and it *was* the last round of the Open, right? Case closed."

In his book *The U.S. Open: Golf's Ultimate Challenge*, Robert Sommers wrote that, while there had been other great finishes in the U.S. Open, none compared to Hogan in 1951.

"Hogan," Sommers said, "shot his magnificent round over a brutal golf course knowing he needed just such a score to win."

Devlin is among those who consider Hogan's final round at Oakland Hills the greatest in U.S. Open history. "I think it is. To shoot 67 on that brute you have to put it at the top of the list."

Hogan's round left Trent Jones elated. It proved that his creation, no matter how monstrous, was an honest test of golfing skill.

"Hogan's 67 saved my face," he said. "Hogan proved that if you played great golf, it could be done at Oakland Hills, too."

Two years after Hogan's heroics at Oakland Hills, he followed with a season that ranks as one of the best ever. Hogan won each of the three majors he entered; a scheduling conflict with the British Open prevented him from competing in the PGA Championship. He claimed his second Masters and fourth U.S. Open and won The Open in his only appearance in the British championship.

Hogan's victory at Oakmont in 1953 was his record-tying fourth U.S. Open title. Jacque Hogan says her uncle believed he had won five U.S. Open Championships because of his victory in the 1942 Hale America National Open tournament, the U.S. Open being postponed that year due to World War II.

"He truly thought he won five U.S. Opens," she says. "Only one pro didn't play, and that was Sam Snead."

Held at Chicago's Ridgemoor Country Club, the Hale America tournament was as close to a U.S. Open as the nation would have in 1942. The tournament promoted physical fitness and raised funds for the Navy Relief Society and United Service Organization. There were so few entries initially that Bing Crosby and Bob Hope were, by organizers, asked to play in order to generate interest. Enthusiasm among golfers for the Hale changed when Hogan and Bobby Jones submitted their entries.

As the field swelled to 1,528 and included a Who's Who of golf—Nelson, Sarazen, Jimmy Demaret, and 1941 U.S. Open champion Craig Wood—district and sectional qualifiers similar to those in the U.S. Open were held. The course at Ridgemoor wasn't up to usual U.S. Open standards, and the pros went wild, posting 50 rounds of scores in the 60s. It was said in the *New York Times* that par took such a beating that even contestants could not take the course seriously.

Hogan, upset that he shot 72 in the first round, practiced for two hours prior to the second round and shot a 62 that playing partner Tommy Armour called "the nearest thing to a perfect round."

Hogan climbed to three strokes off the lead, and he was tied for first at the end of the third round. Paired with Jones for the final round,

Hogan finished three shots ahead of Demaret and was rewarded with a golf medal and $1,200 worth of war bonds.

The Associated Press reported that Hogan had finally won that major championship that eluded him. The AP also reported that Hogan's name would not appear in golf's record book as a winner of the National Open title. "Because of the war," the AP stated, "there will be no Open tournament this year."

"What difference does it make?" Hogan told reporters. "If this wasn't an Open Championship, I don't know what could be. Everybody was in it. I'm glad to win, whatever they call it."

Says Jacque, "The USGA should recognize his win in the 1942 Open."

If the Hale America tournament was, in the words of the *New York Times*, "an improvised event, carrying no official championship designation," Hogan's U.S. Open Championship in 1953 was official and an integral part of what he called "the greatest year of my life." Byron Nelson, who saw every great golfer from Bobby Jones to Tiger Woods, ranked Jones's 1930 season No. 1. He rated his own 1945 season second, Hogan's 1953 campaign third, and Tiger's 2000 season fourth.

Hogan's performance at Carnoustie in 1953 ranks with his triumphs at Oakland Hills and Merion as the most dramatic of his major championships. Fighting through a flu and Scottish rain, Hogan won the British Open, his final-round 68 setting a course record. He won 11 tournament titles following his accident, five of them majors. He also endured gut-wrenching defeats—a playoff loss to Sam Snead in a 1954 Masters showdown between the two men who had combined to win the previous three titles at Augusta, and another playoff loss the following year, this to Jack Fleck in the U.S. Open at the Olympic Club.

The loss that lingered longest came five years later to Palmer in the 1960 U.S. Open at Cherry Hills. Three generations of golfing legends converged as an aging Hogan, a prime Arnold Palmer, and amateur Jack Nicklaus battled at Cherry Hills. Hogan was tied for the lead in the final round when he gambled with a wedge shot on 17. The ball spun backward off the green and into the water for a bogey. Now needing a birdie to tie on 18, a deflated Hogan triple-bogeyed and tumbled to ninth place.

Nearly 30 years later, Hogan told Venturi that his wedge to the green on 17 still caused him sleepless nights. "I find myself waking up at night thinking of that shot," Hogan said. "There isn't a month that goes by that doesn't cut my guts out."

The 1960 U.S. Open represented a passing of golf's torch from Hogan to Palmer. Herbert Warren Wind saw Palmer's victory at Cherry Hills as a case of Arnie becoming "Destiny's new favorite." The aging master, however, could still summon on occasion the magic of his glory years. One such performance occurred in May 1964 at the Houston Country Club. It wasn't a tournament but a televised exhibition between Hogan and longtime rival Sam Snead on *Shell's Wonderful World of Golf*. Fred Corcoran, who in the years following World War II proved pivotal in guiding golf into its golden era, arranged the dream match between the Bantam and the Slammer.

It was seen by many as the Match of the Century, two of golf's preeminent players going mano a mano. Hogan and Snead combined to win 16 majors and 146 PGA tournaments in all, and this would be the final duel between the two legends. Snead, as he never failed to point out when comparisons with Hogan were made, had won each of the three playoffs he and Hogan had engaged in—66–68 in a match-play tournament in San Francisco in 1941, 72–76 in Ben's 1950 comeback tournament in the Los Angeles Open at Riviera Country Club, and 70–71 at the 1954 Masters.

According to Nielsen ratings, nearly 3.5 million people tuned in to *Shell's Wonderful World of Golf* for this final confrontation between Hogan and Snead. At the time, it was one of the largest viewing audiences recorded for a golf event. As competitive as they were, Hogan and Snead played the 18 holes as if it were a major. In the process, their dream match produced a dream round from Hogan, his 69 bettering Snead's 72. In his story for *Sports Illustrated*, Alfred Wright wrote, "Someday someone is going to play the perfect round of golf. . . . Until that perfect game of golf is played, the 18 holes that Ben Hogan turned in from tee to green in Houston will have to do."

Three years later at the 1967 Masters, Hogan overcame sweltering heat in the third round and shot a sizzling 66 to climb to within two shots of the lead. Hogan's performance electrified Augusta. His back nine—3,

3, 2, 4, 4, 4, 3, 4, and 3, for a 30—was an extraordinary accomplishment for a 54-year old man wincing from the pain of an aching shoulder and trudging haltingly in near 90-degree heat on aching legs. Even as veteran a writer as Wind was among those who exulted. "How that exhibition of flawless golf lifted everyone! Hogan sent us home as exhilarated as schoolboys."

The 1967 Masters marked the final memorable moment for Hogan; The Monster of Oakland Hills, however, continues to terrorize. Ten years following Hogan's famous win, Oakland Hills hosted the U.S. Open, and The Monster rose up to test a new generation of golfers. The young guns included Palmer, Player, and Nicklaus, the successors to the Nelson, Hogan, and Snead triumvirate of the 1940s. Hogan was one of five U.S. Open champions in a field that would take on a course that, while still formidable—"Toughest course of them all," *Sports Illustrated* called it in its cover story—was not nearly as scary as a decade earlier.

The rough that had been so heavy and thick in 1951 that it bent beneath its own weight had seen its growth inhibited by a late spring. Ten years after cursing The Monster, Hogan sang its praises. "The course is magnificent," he said. "They've widened the fairways and the rough isn't as brutal."

Fleck thought the course too accommodating. "The spray gun artists," he declared, "aren't going to be penalized sufficiently here."

Palmer, the reigning champion, arrived as the favorite. The battle between The Monster and the swaggering Arnie brought record crowds to Oakland Hills. The young master struggled to solve the brute, limping home with a 75 on the first day. Player likewise scored 75, and Hogan surged past the young princes by draining a 90-foot approach shot for an eagle 3 on No. 2 and carding a 1 over 71. "The course is playing easier," Hogan said. "Four 71s won't win this tournament."

He proved right; five players beat or tied 284. Those who predicted that modern players would massacre The Monster proved prescient in the second round when the brute bent beneath the pounding of 10 sub-par scores and six pars. The Ogre of Oakland Hills seemed no more; the Associated Press referred to it as a "docile puppy dog." The Monster recovered, however, and surrendered just seven birdies over the final 36 holes.

Hogan said hello again to The Monster and felt its wrath; finishing tied for 14th with a 9 over 289. Palmer barely made the cut and fought his way to consecutive 70s to tie Hogan. Nicklaus was in the running until the back nine of the final round. Crew-cut Gene Littler, nicknamed "The Machine" and owning a swing that Sarazen said was similar to Snead's, posted a 68 in the final round to finish with a winning 281.

"That is a tough golf course," Littler said. "You had to hit the ball well or you couldn't play it."

Hogan continued to compete before finally bidding farewell to the Tour at the 1971 Houston Championship Invitational. Gray faced with age and pain, the old champion shot a 9 on the par-3 4th in the opening round. Frustrated, he threw his club in despair. "I hate to play and quit—it burns me up," Hogan told reporters. "My left leg started acting up. It was miserable. I couldn't keep up with the boys. I just had to give up."

As a lion in winter, Hogan impressed those who came to know him. Robert Stennett knew Hogan the last 20 years of his life and was intrigued with how well the aging legend could still hit a golf ball. "His swing speed at age 65 was phenomenal and his hands had such great lag and such great release that his shots all went to the same place, and he was way past his prime."

Those in Hogan's inner circle saw a different side of the man. "Mr. Hogan was very considerate of people, especially young kids," says Stennett. "He was approachable and compassionate. He enjoyed being with friends and was a true friend."

Lisa Scott only knew Hogan in his post-playing years. "He was my uncle first and foremost," she says. "The times I was with him he didn't discuss his success and wasn't one to volunteer (information about his career). I didn't truly understand his accomplishments until I was older."

She recalls one conversation in particular with her grand-uncle. "I remember vividly being a sophomore in high school and him asking me about my grades. He said, 'Don't worry about college. I'll pay for it.' He was a lot nicer and warmer than people expected. He loved kids and dogs."

Still, there was something mysterious about Hogan, and the mystery remains to this day.

"It's the mystique—Did Mr. Hogan figure out the secret of golf?" Stennett says. "I don't know if he had a secret but he had a mystique. He was kind of a shy guy and the mystique has built on itself. People are still wondering if he had a secret."

Says Scott, "He had a reputation for being unapproachable and that made him a mystery."

The Monster remains a mystery as well, frustrating generations of golfers from Hogan, Snead, and Locke to Palmer, Player, and Nicklaus; from Trevino, Watson, Chi-Chi, and The Shark to Tiger, Phil, and Big John Daly. "It's deceiving," Tom Watson said. "There's a lot of strategy involved." Players can't just fire the ball at the pin; they have to fit the ball in. On top of that, Watson said in echoing golfer Frank Walsh from 1951, "there is not a let-up hole on the golf course."

Watson believed The Monster the toughest course in the U.S. Open rotation. Jack Nicklaus, when he was still active on the Tour, called The Monster "as demanding and difficult a course as any we play." If the beast's greens were any faster, Nicklaus stated, "They'd be beyond the point of being fair." David Graham, the 1981 U.S. Open champion, said The Monster's greens were the hardest he'd ever played. "Every green on the course is a potential three-putt green."

In 1972 Oakland Hills hosted the PGA Championship for the first time, and the result was a tournament that once again broke attendance records as it paid witness to Palmer glaring at The Monster's wavy greens and Trevino looking like a man whistling his way past a graveyard as he tried to laugh off the menacing layout.

Palmer, as vexed by the PGA Championship as Snead was by the U.S. Open, took out his frustrations in characteristic fashion. Arnie amped his Army with five birdies but brought groans with four bogeys. His 69 tied him for second place at the close of the first day, but The Monster got even with the King the following day, Palmer posting a 75.

Nicklaus, seeking the first "American" slam—Masters, U.S. Open, and PGA Championship—shot 72 in the opening round but endured a second-round 75. The Monster's greens gobbled up Palmer's putts, and the same fate befell Nicklaus, his short game suffering on the swerving surface. Nicklaus brought the big gallery to a fever pitch with a sizzling 31 on Saturday's front nine, and his rally caused crowds to call out, "Get 'em, Jack!" The Monster bit back, and the Golden Bear, growling at his missed shots, tied for 13th.

The Monster, Nicklaus declared, offered golfers "less breathing room" than any course he had ever competed on. Injured physically and still suffering the effects of an emotional loss in the British Open, Nicklaus's erratic play was no match for The Monster. "I just didn't have it in me," he said.

Player called Oakland Hills the toughest course in America. "When Hogan said this was a 'Monster,' he wasn't kidding." Nearly demoralized by the difficulty of the course, the Black Knight birdied the 16th, "the most evil of the 18 evil holes at Oakland Hills," according to Dan Jenkins. Player's blind second shot to within four feet of the pin remains one of the more dramatic moments in major championship history. Player called it "one of the best shots of my career," and it helped him post a 1 over 281 for the win.

The PGA Championship returned in 1979, and Oakland Hills again set attendance records, providing the largest gallery in history to that point. Low rough and soft, slow greens helped nine golfers post subpar rounds, leading a modern-day David, David Green, to defeat the Goliath. So weakened was The Monster by course conditions that Green and Ben Crenshaw tied at 8 under 272; Green's total was achieved by carding a final-round 65, despite a double bogey on 18. Green's great putting on the first and second holes of the playoff paved the way for his clinching birdie on the third.

In the aftermath of Green's win, it wasn't only Oakland Hills's club members who bemoaned the crippling of The Monster, but the pros as well. "We aren't seeing the true character of Oakland Hills," Crenshaw stated. "I can't stand on the 10th tee without thinking about the double bogeys Jones made there and the birdie Hogan made."

In 1981 Oakland Hills welcomed golfing legends for the second U.S. Senior Open, a product of *Shell's Wonderful World of Golf*. Palmer gained his lone victory over The Monster, outlasting Billy Casper and Bob Stone in an 18-hole playoff. Oakland Hills played predictably tough, and Arnie's 9 over 289 is the highest-winning score in tournament history. The 1981 Senior Open is memorable for Palmer's signature charge in the playoff that stirred Arnie's Army one more time. On that manic Monday, the old Palmer magic was too much even for The Monster.

Four years later, Oakland Hills made history again by becoming one of only three venues to host the U.S. Open five times. P. J. Boatwright, the USGA's senior executive director for championships, arrived at Oakland Hills to scout it for the 1985 Open. "You don't have to do anything to Oakland Hills," he said. "Just let Oakland Hills be Oakland Hills."

The pros cringed at the thought of The Monster regaining its swagger. Nicklaus, Trevino, and Tom Watson missed the cut, and Andy North's winning 279 was the lone subpar total of the tournament. North's nine birdies were the lowest by a U.S. Open champion in the post–World War II era. T. C. Chen opened with a course-record 65, but was mashed by The Monster in the final round with a quadruple bogey on No. 5.

A sad fate befell Denis Watson, who tied for second one stroke behind North. Watson received a two-stroke penalty for breaking the 10-second rule and delaying his putt by a few seconds on No. 8 in the opening round. He rallied to tie Chen's 65 the next day, but the penalty proved costly, prompting columnist Jim Murray to write, "Watson lost this tournament to a pencil."

Nicklaus, who had his string of making 21 consecutive cuts at the U.S. Open ended by The Monster in 1985, prevailed in 1991 when the Senior Open returned to Oakland Hills. Nicklaus and Chi Chi Rodriguez dealt with the difficult greens and tied at 282. In the rain-delayed playoff on Monday, Nicklaus outdueled Rodriguez, 65–69. "When you shoot 69 at Oakland Hills, you're playing great golf," Rodriguez said.

A new generation of golfers arrived to try to tame The Monster in the 1996 U.S. Open. Playing alongside John Daly and defending champion Corey Pavin, 20-year-old U.S. Amateur champion Tiger Woods was tied for the first-round lead when The Monster took Tiger by the tail and led him to shoot 9 over on the final five holes. "Unfortunately, my swing kind of left me a little bit," Tiger said. "Out here, you can't do that."

It was left to gutsy underdog Steve Jones who, inspired by Hogan's victory in 1951, shot 278, the lowest total in any of the seven U.S. Opens at Oakland Hills. Among those who struggled was Anthony Rodriguez; he parred the final five holes and still finished 2 over. "It's more than a monster," he said. "The course really did get the best of me." Greg Norman could sympathize. "I hit the ball as well this week as I have all year, and I finished 3 over par," said The Shark, who was puzzled by The Monster's putting greens.

In 2002 Oakland Hills hosted the U.S. Amateur, Ricky Barnes winning what was considered the most successful U.S. Amateur ever. Two years later, the top pros from the U.S. and the U.K. met The Monster in the Ryder Cup. The Woods/Mickelson pairing was expected to provide an early lead for the Americans, but the celebrated duo fell to Colin Montgomerie and Padraig Harrington.

The PGA Championship returned to Oakland Hills in 2008, and fans missed what promised to be an epic encounter between Tiger and The Monster, which had humbled him in their only two prior encounters. While Woods was a notable absentee, his former playing partner at Oakland Hills paid homage to The Monster. "You can hit good shots," Daly said, "and not get rewarded."

Daly found little reward on a course that at 7,395 yards was playing to its longest length for a major. He followed his opening round 74 with a 75 and was one of six champions to miss the cut. Flashing the form he had at Oakland Hills in the 2004 Ryder Cup, Harrington shot a 3 under 277, which was two strokes better than runners-up Sergio Garcia and Ben Curtis. Garcia called the course difficult to an extreme, evidenced by the fact that he and Curtis were the only players to produce subpar totals. Ernie Els battled his way around the South Course, finished with a 71, and said "The Monster" moniker was well deserved. "It was a real beast," he said.

In July 2018, *Golfweek* magazine ranked Oakland Hills among the toughest venues in the world, noting that, in hosting the 2008 PGA Championship, golfers averaged 4.31 shots over par, the 11th-highest mark among major championship courses in the past 25 years. More than half a century later, The Monster remained a menace.

In 2019, Oakland Hills Country Club announced that its South Course would close for 19 months to undergo a dramatic return to its storied past. Gil Hanse and his design team are revitalizing the original Donald Ross design and restoring widened fairways, expanded greens, and bunkers that are staggered and strategic.

Trent Jones's Monster will be no more; its place in history, however, is forever preserved by its war with Hogan. Trent Jones once wrote that the most satisfying thing about Oakland Hills in 1951 was that, at the close of the final round of the U.S. Open, the great players' names were at the top of the leaderboard.

"It has always seemed to me," Trent Jones said, "that if I were a Hogan, or a Locke, the more difficult the course, the better I would like it, knowing that the extensiveness of my repertoire of shots would work to my advantage. Such a course, I would know, was not a scrambler's course—a scrambler could not win. Look at the record and the basic truth stands out: when a championship is played on a great golf course, you rarely get a winner who is not a great golfer."

Oakland Hills's general chairman John O'Hara thought it telling that at the presentation ceremony fans gave Trent Jones a hero's reception. The public had become enamored with the test provided to the pros and, in a letter to the USGA, O'Hara wondered "whether the general rank and file of golfers, as well as spectators, feel that golf is difficult for them and they would like to see some of their obstacles placed in the paths of stars."

Trent Jones Jr. cites famed golf architect Alister MacKenzie, who opined that players derived more pleasure by overcoming a challenging course with a well-crafted shot than playing a bland, uninteresting course and achieving a low score. MacKenzie's successors agreed. Following in Trent Jones's footsteps, architects like Pete Dye incorporate the concepts of target golf into courses like Sawgrass, and officials at other clubs have borrowed the "monster" moniker, notably Doral and the "Blue Monster."

The Monster of Oakland Hills, however, stands alone. Trent Jones considered it the top test of tournament golf in the world. He thought target-area trapping more demanding than on any other course and the contours more severe than those of Augusta. He stated that, if the pins were placed six inches from the edge of the green, like at Augusta, Oakland Hills "would be murder."

In 1996, when Oakland Hills was preparing to host the U.S. Open once again, James Cusick recalled in the London broadsheet *The Independent* the USGA's initial attempt to defend par at a major and the resultant redesign by Trent Jones:

"Bertrand Russell, bright but without a decent golf handicap, thought the infliction of cruelty with a good conscience was a delight to moralists, and that was why they invented hell. The United States Golf Association in 1951 must have thought the eternal inferno was a soft option. Instead, it created Oakland Hills."

Hogan, asked once if Carnoustie was the toughest course he had ever played, shook his head. "No. It was Oakland Hills."

Jacque Hogan says her uncle spoke often of The Monster of Oakland Hills. "He remembered every hole, every shot," she says, "and told me how difficult it was."

Howting says that as Hogan grew gray with age he talked fondly of Oakland Hills, sharing "war stories" of his duel with The Monster. *New York Times* sports columnist Dave Anderson wrote that, if there is one tournament Hogan is remembered for, "it is the 1951 U.S. Open at Oakland Hills." In 1979, as Oakland Hills was preparing to host the PGA Championship, Hogan reminisced with Anderson about that long-ago summer.

"I remember that there was very little room for your tee shots," Hogan told Anderson. "In some cases you could hit a perfect tee shot and not be in the fairway because your ball would bounce off a mound into the rough or into a bunker."

Of his splendid 2-iron on No. 10, Hogan recalled, "There's a bunker on the left side of the fairway. But the fairway sloped so much from left to right that you could roll down into the rough. You had to aim your tee shot at the right corner of the bunker and hope it would stay in the fairway so you could hit a 2-iron or a 3-iron to the green. My drive stayed in the fairway, then I hit a 2-iron a foot from the hole for a birdie 3. I knew then that if I held my game together the rest of the way I would win.

"On that last hole, there were six fairway bunkers, three on each side, with big mounds in between them. The first three rounds, they had to tee back and everybody was bouncing their drives into those bunkers. You were forced to play it as a par 5, and everybody was shooting 5 or 6 on the hole. But the last round, they moved the tee up so you could carry the bunkers. I put my tee shot in the fairway and then hit a good iron into the green, about six feet away."

Hogan never fully explained why Trent Jones's creation vexed him so; perhaps the many stories that the course was unconquerable pushed him to prove otherwise. Hogan would tell Gene Gregston in 1953, one of the "driving forces" of his life was proving wrong those who said he "couldn't do this or that."

West Virginia amateur golfer Bill Campbell, who was at Oakland Hills in 1951, alluded to this when he told Hogan biographer James Dodson, "I got the distinct feeling watching him that week that his battle with Oakland Hills was something very personal, almost a blood feud for Ben. Many people were saying Oakland Hills, with all the Draconian changes, was simply beyond even Hogan's abilities. It became a contest within a contest for Ben—something he had to accomplish because no one thought he could possibly do it."

In 1991 Hogan thought back 40 years as he penned the introduction for a book celebrating the Diamond Jubilee of Oakland Hills Country Club. "I was fortunate to win the tournament with some of the best rounds of golf that I have ever played. It was a tough course, but it was such a pleasure to 'bring that Monster to its knees.' Oh, how I would love to experience, just once more, my days of golf at Oakland Hills during the 1951 U.S. Open."

The echoes from that exciting summer still fill the green cathedral. When Lisa Scott visited Oakland Hills in May 2016 for The Monster "51," a centennial celebration, she sat on the veranda facing the course and thought of her grand-uncle. "I remember sitting there and looking out and thinking, 'This is what he was looking at,'" she says. "It's a majestic course, gorgeous."

In the mind's eye, Hogan stands there still, staring out at Trent Jones's diabolical design and burning his cigarette down to his fingertips. The flat white cap is pulled low on his bronzed brow. Gripping his club, Hogan waggles and then unfurls the most famous of all golf swings. His shot scrapes the sunny skies over Oakland Hills and soars toward The Monster. The combat at the country club continues.

SOURCES

Anderson, Dave. "Hogan to Nicklaus: Work." *New York Times*, August 1, 1979.

——. "The Standards of the Man." *The Hogan Mystique*. Greenwich, CT: The American Golfer, Inc., 1994.

Barkow, Al. "Lord Nelson after Pearl Harbor." *Great Golf Stories*. New York: Galahad Books, 1982.

Bennett, Robert. Interview with the author, May 2020.

Bolt, Tommy with Jimmy Mann. *The Hole Truth*. Philadelphia and New York: J.B. Lippincott Company, 1971.

Brumby, Bob. "The Ben Hogan Story." *Sport*, December 1953.

Canfield, Owen. "His Memory of Hogan Is Striking." *Hartford Courant*, January 27, 1988.

Crenshaw, Ben. "The Hawk." *The Hogan Mystique*. Greenwich, CT: The American Golfer, Inc., 1994.

Dann, Marshall. "Holding Big Tournaments Habit at Oakland Hills." *Detroit Free Press*, June 5, 1951.

D'Antonio, Michael. *Tour '72: Nicklaus, Palmer, Player, Trevino: The Story of One Great Season*. New York: Hyperion, 2002.

Davis, Martin. *Ben Hogan: The Man Behind the Mystique*. Second Edition. Greenwich, CT: The American Golfer, Inc., 2002.

Derr, John. "Eyewitness Accounts." *The Hogan Mystique*. Greenwich, CT: The American Golfer, Inc., 1994.

Devlin, Bruce. Interview with the author, June 2020.

Dey, Joseph C. "A Lesson from Hogan in the Open." *USGA Journal and Turf Management*, July 1951.

Diaz, Jaime. *Golf's Greatest Eighteen*. New York: McGraw-Hill, 2003.

Dickinson, Gardner. *Let 'er Rip! Gardner Dickinson on Golf*. Atlanta, GA: Longstreet Press, 1994.

Diegel, Glenn. Interview with the author, May 2020.

Dodson, James. *Ben Hogan: An American Life*. New York: Doubleday, 2004.

Dulio, Tony. *The United States Open Golf Champions: Their Championship and Story*. Stuart, FL: Woodward Press, 2004.

Dunn, Paul, and B. J. Dunn. *Great Donald Ross Golf Courses You Can Play*. Lanham, MD: The Derrydale Press, 2001.

Fay, Michael J. *Golf, As It Was Meant to Be Played: A Celebration of Donald Ross's Vision of the Game*. New York: Universe Publishing, 2000.

Fowler, Jack. Interview with the author, June 2020.

Fry, Norman C., ed. *U.S. Open 85th Championship*. Bloomfield Hills, MI: Oakland Hills Country Club, 1985.

Garrity, John. "Making the Monster." *Sports Illustrated*, June 10, 1996.

Graffis, Herb. "Hogan Tames Golf's Tuffy." *GOLFing: The National Player's Magazine*, June 1951.

Gregston, Gene. *Hogan: The Man Who Played for Glory*. Grass Valley, CA: The Booklegger, 1978.

Grimsley, Will. "Hogan Cards 3-Under Par." *Associated Press*, June 16, 1951.

Hannigan, Frank. "A Backward Look at Oakland Hills." *USGA Journal and Turf Management*, June 1941.

Hansen, James R. *A Difficult Par: Robert Trent Jones Sr. and the Making of Modern Golf*. New York: Gotham Books, 2014.

Hawkins, Fred. Interview with the author, June 2012.

Hogan, Jacqueline. Interview with the author, June 2020.

Hogan, Valerie with Dave Anderson. "The Ben Hogan I Knew." *The Hogan Mystique*. Greenwich, CT: The American Golfer, Inc., 1994.

Hogan Towery, Jacqueline with Robert Towery and Peter Barbour. *The Brothers Hogan: A Fort Worth History*. Fort Worth, TX: TCU Press, 2014.

Howting, Dick. Interview with the author, July 2020.

Jacobs, Jeff. "Nobody's Perfect? Ever Seen Ben Hogan?" *Hartford Courant*, July 26, 1997.

Jenkins, Dan. *Fairways and Greens: The Best Golf Writing of Dan Jenkins*. New York: Doubleday, 1994.

——. "Hogan His Ownself." *The Hogan Mystique*. Greenwich, CT: The American Golfer, Inc., 1994.

——. "Hogan Lore Strikes Again." *The Hogan Mystique*. Greenwich, CT: The American Golfer, Inc., 1994.

——. *Jenkins at the Majors: Sixty Years of the World's Best Golf Writing, from Hogan to Tiger*. New York: Doubleday, 2009.

——. "No Muzzle for the Monster." *Sports Illustrated*, August 14, 1972.

Johnson, Andy. "The Jones Family Legacy: Bellerive." *thefriedegg.com*, August 7, 2018.

Jones, Robert Trent Jr., ed. *Great Golf Stories*. New York: Galahad Books, 1982.

——. "Tough Test for the Open." *GOLFing: The National Player's Magazine*, June 1951.

Jones, Robert Trent Jr. *Golf by Design: How to Lower Your Score by Reading the Features of a Course*. New York: Little, Brown and Company, 1993.

——. *Golf's Magnificent Challenge*. Sagdos, Italy: Sammis Publishing Corporation, 1988.

——. Interview with the author, February 2020 .

Kirchner, George. "Oakland Hills Unfair." *Lancaster New Era*, June 21, 1951.

Kupelian, Vartan. *Forever Scratch: Chuck Kocsis: An Amateur for the Ages*. Ann Arbor, MI: Ann Arbor Media Group LLC, 2007.

——. "How the Wee Ice Mon Conquered a Monster." *The Monster: 1916–2016, 100 Years of Golf and Glory*. Wellington, FL: Legendary Publishing Group, 2017.

LeBrock, Barry. *The Front Nine: Golf's 9 All-Time Greatest Shots*. Chicago: Triumph Books, 2008.

Life magazine. "Par-buster's Nightmare." March 5, 1951.

McDermott, Barry. "A Blast from the Past." *Sports Illustrated* June 24, 1985.

McGrath, Charles. "Ben Hogan: The Pain in Perfection." *New York Times Magazine*, January 4, 1998.

Middlecoff, Cary. *The Golf Swing: The Classic Study of Golf's Greatest Swings*. Saddle River, NJ: Prentice Hall, 1974.

Murphy, Jack. "Battle of the Crippled Champ." *Collier's*, June 25, 1949.

Perry, Bryon A. *75 Years at Oakland Hills: A Jubilee Celebration*. Bloomfield Hills, MI: Perry and White, Inc., 1991.

——. *The Ryder Cup Meets The Monster: A Collection of Words and Pictures Commemorating Golf's Crown Jewel*. Westland, MI: Premier Publishing LLC, 2004.

Povich, Shirley. "A Master Mind Obsessed with Perfection." *Washington Post*, July 26, 1997.

Price, Charles. "The Birth of Golf's Vintage Era." In *Great Golf Stories*. New York: Galahad Books, 1982.

Robledo, Fred. "A Will to Win: Forty-One Years Ago, Ben Hogan Returned to L.A. Open after Nearly Being Killed in a Car Crash." *Los Angeles Times*, February 17, 1991.

Rosaforte, Tim. "Pros Always Have Hated the Oakland Hills Test." *Sun Sentinel*, June 13, 1985.

Ross, Donald. *Golf Has Never Failed Me: The Lost Commentaries of Legendary Golf Architect Donald J. Ross*. Ann Arbor, MI: Sleeping Bear Press, 1996.

Sampson, Curt. *Hogan*. Nashville, TN: Rutledge Hill Press, 1996.

Sarazen, Gene with Herbert Warren Wind. *Thirty Years of Championship Golf: The Life and Times of Gene Sarazen*. New York: Prentice Hall, 1950.

Scott, Lisa. Interview with the author, June 2020.

Scott, Tim. *Ben Hogan: The Myths Everyone Knows, the Man No One Knew*. Chicago: Triumph Books, 2013.

Smith, Marshall. "Greatest Round Ever: Ben Hogan Shot a 67 That Won the U.S. Open." *Life*, July 2, 1951.

Snead, Sam with George Mendoza. *Slammin' Sam: An Autobiography*. New York: Donald L. Fine, Inc., 1986.

Sommers, Robert. *The U.S. Open: Golf's Ultimate Challenge*. Second Edition. New York: Oxford University Press, 1996.

Stewart, C. F. *The Dapper Adonis*. Palm Desert, CA: Sorrento Publishing, 2011.

Strege, John. *Tiptoeing through Hell: Playing the U.S. Open on Golf's Most Treacherous Courses*. New York: HarperCollins Publishers, 2002.

Talese, Gay. *The Silent Season of a Hero: The Sports Writing of Gay Talese*. New York: Walker & Company, 2010.

Towle, Mike. *I Remember Ben Hogan*. Nashville, TN: Cumberland House, 2000.

Vasquez, Jody. *Afternoons with Mr. Hogan: A Boy, a Golf Legend, and the Lessons of a Lifetime*. New York: Gotham Books, 2004.

Venturi, Ken. "Commentary." *The Hogan Mystique*. Greenwich, CT: The American Golfer, Inc., 1994.

———. *Getting Up & Down: My 60 Years in Golf* Chicago: Triumph Books, 2004.

Wind, Herbert Warren. "The Age of Hogan." *Sports Illustrated*, June 20, 1955.

———, ed. *The Complete Golfer*. New York: Simon & Schuster, Inc., 1991.

Wright, Alfred. "A Real Monster of a Course." *Sports Illustrated*, June 12, 1961.

———. "Two Foreign Blokes Shock the Slammers." *Sports Illustrated*, June 28, 1965.

Wright, Ben. Interview with the author, April 2020.

INDEX

Quick, Lyman, xviii, 129, 131–32

race, and integration of PGA tour, 128, 132
Ramsey, Ray, 17
Ransom, Henry, 120, 142
Raschi, Vic, 173
Ray, Ted, 73, 119, 150
Raynor, Seth, 48
Red Cross, 39, 77
Revolta, Johnny, xviii, xxii
Rice, Grantland, xv, xvii, 7, 130
Ridgemoor Country Club, 195
Riegel, Robert "Skee," xviii, 92
River Oaks Country Club, 159
Rives, Bill, 110, 154, 169
Riviera Country Club, 89
Robert Trent Jones Golf Club, Manassas, Virginia, 42
Robert Trent Jones Golf Course, Cornell University, 49
Robinson, Cabell, 42
Rockefeller, Laurence, 43
Rockefeller family, 43
Rodriguez, Anthony, 202
Rodriguez, Chi Chi, xviii, 202
Roosevelt, Eleanor, 33
Roosevelt, Franklin D., 33, 50
Roosevelt Memorial Golf Course, Warm Springs, Georgia, 33
Rosburg, Bob, 15, 77
Ross, Alec, 26, 29
Ross, Donald: American immigration of, 28; criticisms of golf course designs by, 32; death of, 29, 54, 59; early life in Scotland of, 25–27; golf course designs by, 27–39, 48; golfing career of, 26–27, 29–30; Jones and, 41, 49, 54; Oakland Hills designed by, xvi, 24, 27, 31, 32, 34–39, 59; and Pinehurst, 28–29, 35; return of Oakland Hills to design of, 203; success and popularity of, 33

Rothstein, Arthur, 103
rough: Jones's design of, xvi; of Oakland Hills, xvi, 58, 63, 141; on U.S. Open courses, 75–76
route plans, 69
Royal Dornoch Golf Club, 26–28
Rulewich, Roger, 42
Runyan, Paul, xviii, 101, 103, 129, 142, 157, 161–65, 172–73, 190
Runyon, Damon, *The Idyll of Miss Sarah Brown*, 103
Russell, Bertrand, 205
Ruth, Babe, xix, 32, 33–34, 129, 130
Ryder Cup, 21, 39, 42, 102, 203

Sampson, Curt, 140
Sanders, Doug, xv
sand traps. *See* bunkers
sand wedge, 96
Sarazen, Gene, xiv, xv, xviii, 8, 10, 13, 39, 65, 91, 94–98, 101, 135–36, 142, 143–44, 176–77, 182, 189, 190, 193, 195, 199
Savold, Lee, 150
Sawgrass Country Club, 204
Schmeling, Max, 132
Scotland, 25–26, 54
Scott, Adam, 80
Scott, Lisa (grandniece), xii, 6, 9, 23, 110, 125, 199–200, 206
Seitz, Nick, 13
Seminole Golf Club, 35
Shackelford, Geoff, 55
Shady Oaks Country Club, 24
Shell's Wonderful World of Golf (television show), 197, 201
Shepard, Alan, 42
Shinnecock Hills Golf Club, 83–84
Shor, Toots, xix
Shute, Denny, xviii, 38, 92, 100–101, 129, 132–33
Sifford, Charlie, 128
Sinatra, Frank, xix, xxii

United Service Organization, 195
United States Golf Association (USGA):
criticisms of, 75, 83–86; management
of Open course conditions by, xvi,
38–39, 57–58, 60, 63, 66–67, 75,
83–86, 115, 205; rules and regulations
established by, 35, 36, 38–39, 66, 141
U.S. Amateur Championship, 203
USGA. *See* United States Golf
Association
U.S. Open: amateur champion of,
142, 150; challenges presented by,
71–87; Congressional (1964), 76–80;
consecutive wins at, 38; criticisms of
course conditions at, 83–86; foreign
champions of, 150; greatest-round-
ever debate for, 193–95; Hogan's
appearances in, 8, 124, 137, 157,
193, 196–99; Hogan's victories in,
15, 22–23, 24, 77, 79, 80, 92, 98,
105, 195–96; Irwin's victory at, 72–
75; on Jones courses, 42, 45–46, 51,
53, 60; Manero's victory and record
at, xiii, 38, 93, 142; Mangrum's
victory at, 98; Massacre at Winged
Foot (1974), 71–76; Middlecoff's
victory at, 100; Nelson's victory at,
101; at Oakland Hills, 36–39, 59–60,
92; other mentions of, 27, 47, 77, 93,
94, 102, 122, 128, 129, 130, 136,
138, 142, 143, 147, 159, 164, 165,
173, 180, 202; quadruple winners of,
195; redesign of courses for, 57–58,
60, 63, 75; repeat champions of, 109,
173, 189; reputation of, xii; Ross's
appearances in, 30; Sarazen's victories
at, 95–97; Snead's failure to win, 39,
60, 92–95, 119; Torrey Pines (2008),
79–83; triple winners of, 119, 173,
189; Venturi's victory at, 76–79;
Wood's fortunes at, 101; Woods's
victory at, 79–83; Worsham's victory

at, 93–94, 101–2. *See also* 1951 U.S.
Open; Merion Golf Club and Miracle
at Merion
U.S. Senior Open, 201, 202
U.S. Women's Amateur, 37

Vardon, Harry, 73, 97, 138, 145
Vardon grip, xiv, 138
Vardon Trophy, 92, 99, 130, 159
Vasquez, Jody, 138
Venturi, Ken, xiv, 6, 10, 22, 23, 45,
75–80, 194, 197
Vernon, Jim, 80
Von Elm, George, 142
Von Nida, Norman, ix

Wade, Jake, 32
Wadkins, Lanny, 73
Walker, Cyril, 37, 59, 63
Walker, Mickey, 96
Walsh, Frank, 67–68, 109, 200
Walter Winchell–Damon Runyon Cancer
Fund, 127
Wampler, Freddy, 149
Waner, Lloyd, 161
Ward, William, 78
water hazards, 31
Watrous, Al, 62, 65, 68, 118–19
Watson, Denis, 202
Watson, Thomas J., 50
Watson, Tom, 74–75, 194, 200, 202
Wayne, John, 22
wedges, 128, 161. *See also* pitching
wedge; sand wedge
Weekly, Boo, 85
Werden, Lincoln, xix, 124, 166, 167,
182, 187, 188, 189
Western Open, 36
Westwood, Lee, 81–82
Wey, Ernie, 32
White House, 43
Williams, Andy, 81